Schulhausbau/School Buildings

# Schulhausbau.
# Der Stand der Dinge

Der Schweizer Beitrag im internationalen Kontext

# School Buildings.
# The State of Affairs

The Swiss Contribution in an International Context

herausgegeben von:
Hochbaudepartement der Stadt Zürich
Eidgenössische Technische Hochschule Zürich / ETH Wohnforum
Schul- und Sportdepartement der Stadt Zürich
Pädagogische Hochschule Zürich

edited by:
City of Zurich Building Authority
Swiss Federal Institute of Technology / ETH Wohnforum
City of Zurich School and Sports Authority
Zurich University of Applied Science, School of Education

Birkhäuser – Publishers for Architecture
Basel·Boston·Berlin

Redaktion/Edited by:
Daniel Kurz, Alan Wakefield

Übersetzung/Translations:
Robin Benson, Berlin; James Gussen, Sommerville MA; Steven Lindberg, Berlin

Buchkonzept und Gestaltung/Book Concept and Graphic Design:
Alberto Vieceli, Tania Prill & Kristina Milković, Zürich


Dieses Buch erscheint anlässlich der Ausstellung/This book is published on the occasion of the exhibition:

Schulhausbau. Der Stand der Dinge/School Buildings. The State of Affairs
Zürich, 29. Juni bis 11. Juli 2004/Zurich, 29 June to 11 July 2004

Steuerungsausschuss/Steering Committee:
Prof. Dietmar Eberle, Peter Ess, Cornelia Mächler,
Kurt Portmann, Prof. Dr. Roger Vaissière

Vorbereitung/committee:
Rudolf Detsch, Elisabeth Gaus, Daniel Kurz, Jürg Lenzi, Regina Meister,
Adrian Scheidegger, Martin Schneider, Alan Wakefield

Ausstellungsgestaltung/Exhibition Design
Christine Moser, Barbara Staib
Mit/with Tuan Cao, Peter Eberhard, Alan Wakefield, Barbara Willimann
Produktion: Format Guggenbühl, Zürich


Die Veranstalter danken den beteiligten Architektinnen und Architektinnen
für die freundliche Überlassung von Plänen und Fotos, den porträtierten Schulen,
ihren Lehrpersonen, Schülerinnen und Schülern für die Mitwirkung.

The exhibition organisers wish to thank the architects involved for allowing
them to use plans and photographs. They also wish to thank the schools
presented here, including the teaching staff and pupils, for their kind co-operation.


die Bauengineering.

hat die Veranstaltung finanziell unterstützt/has supported the exhibition.

A CIP catalogue record for this book is available from the
Library of Congress, Washington D.C., USA.

Bibliographic information published by Die Deutsche Bibliothek
Die Deutsche Bibliothek lists this publication in the Deutsche Nationalbibliografie;
detailed bibliographic data is available on the Internet at <http://dnb.ddb.de>.

© 2004 Birkhäuser — Publishers for Architecture,
P.O. Box 133, CH-4010 Basel, Switzerland.
http://www.birkhauser.ch
Part of Springer Science+Business Media Publishing Group.
Printed on acid-free paper produced from chlorine-free pulp. TCF ∞
Printed in Germany.
ISBN 3-7643-7092-0

9 8 7 6 5 4 3 2 1

Inhalt/Contents

Zweite Klasse im Schulhaus Mühlebach, 1960
(3. Reihe, 6. von links: Kathrin Martelli).
Foto: W. Haagmans

Mühlebach Primary School, Zurich, 1960.
The girl in the third row (sixth from the
left) is Mrs Kathrin Martelli.
Photo: W. Haagmans

Kathrin Martelli
Vorsteherin des Hochbaudepartements der Stadt Zürich

# Vorwort

Als mein Vater in den zwanziger Jahren die Schule besuchte, teilte er das Klassenzimmer mit 45 Kindern. Ich selber sass 30 Jahre später im gleichen Schulzimmer mit ungefähr 30 Kameraden, und meine Tochter wurde zusammen mit 24 anderen Schülern in dieser Schule unterrichtet. Je weniger Kinder in unserer Gesellschaft grossgezogen werden, so scheint es, desto aufwändiger wird ihre Erziehung in der Schule. Für viele der heute Schulpflichtigen ist das Schulhaus fast der einzige Ort, an dem sie mit Gleichaltrigen zusammenkommen und die Regeln des Zusammenlebens üben. Sie sind es gewohnt, als Individuen zu gelten, nach ihrer Meinung gefragt zu werden und selbst auszuwählen.

Der Unterricht in der Schule hat sich entsprechend verändert und dieser Entwicklung angepasst. Gruppenarbeit, Projektunterricht und Team-Teaching sind fast selbstverständlich geworden. Zugleich wächst der Bedarf an individuellen Stütz- und Förderprogrammen, an besonderen Unterrichtsstunden für ausgewählte Schülergruppen wie zum Beispiel fremdsprachige Kinder. Schliesslich ist ein Wandel in der Einstellung der Familien festzustellen, die mehr als früher erwarten, dass die öffentliche Schule die Aufsicht für ihr Kind auch ausserhalb der Unterrichtszeit übernimmt. Das Angebot an Hortplätzen wird in der Stadt Zürich laufend gesteigert — und trotzdem sind die Wartelisten lang.

Seit einigen Jahren gehören Erweiterungen und Neubauten von Schulhäusern wieder zu den häufiger anstehenden Aufgaben der Stadt Zürich. Zugleich resultiert aus früheren Zeiten des Sparens ein gewaltiger Nachholbedarf beim Unterhalt der Gebäude. So beanspruchen Schule und Sport gegenwärtig über ein Drittel des gesamten Hochbaubudgets. Mit dieser Entwicklung steht Zürich freilich nicht allein da. Der Bau von Schulhäusern ist in ganz Europa wie auch in den USA wieder zu einem lebhaft diskutierten Thema geworden.

Auf dem Höhepunkt der gegenwärtigen Bauwelle haben sich das Hochbau- und das Schul- und Sportdepartement der Stadt Zürich entschlossen, eine Standortbestimmung vorzunehmen. Die Ausstellung «Schulhausbau. Der Stand der Dinge» und der vorliegende Katalog ermöglichen den Vergleich zwischen zürcherischen, gesamtschweizerischen und ausgewählten europäischen Ansätzen im Schulbau. Dabei interessieren uns nicht nur die Tendenzen der Fachdiskussion, sondern auch die baulichen und finanziellen Standards, die gegenwärtig zur Anwendung kommen.

Wir stellen fest, dass die Frage nach zeitgemässen Schulräumen vielerorts zu ähnlichen Anordnungen geführt hat: Der Cluster, die Klassengruppe, verdrängt als flexible Einheit die traditionelle Aufreihung von Klassenzimmern an einem Korridor. Einzelne skandinavische Schulen gehen noch einen Schritt weiter und experimentieren mit offenen Raumanordnungen. Grosse Schulhäuser sind kein Tabu mehr. Der Wunsch, die Schule mit anderen öffentlichen Nutzungen zu verbinden, führt zum Beispiel in Holland zum Bau von eigentlichen Schulstädten, die dort als «breite Schulen» bezeichnet werden. Aus dem isolierten Schulhaus im Grünen wird ein lebhafter Mittelpunkt von Quartieren und Ortschaften.

Begrenzte öffentliche Budgets zwingen in allen Ländern dazu, die Raumbewirtschaftung immer neu zu überdenken und nach Mehrfachnutzungen der einmal erstellten Räume zu suchen. Eine grundlegende Tatsache darf dabei nicht vergessen werden: Die weitaus meisten Schulhäuser der Zukunft wurden vor Jahrzehnten gebaut. Moderner Unterricht wird also weiterhin zumeist in Räumen stattfinden, die für andere pädagogische Konzepte geplant wurden. Diese Räume lassen sich nicht immer wunschgemäss nach heutigen Bedürfnissen umbauen — vielleicht aber anders nutzen. Dies ist ein deutlicher Hinweis darauf, dass im Schulhausbau nur flexible und anpassungsfähige Lösungen Nachhaltigkeit versprechen. Denn für die Zukunft gibt es nur eine Gewissheit: Der Wandel wird weitergehen.

Kathrin Martelli
Head of the City of Zurich Building Authority

## Foreword

When my father attended school in the 1920s, he shared a classroom with forty-five other children. Thirty years later, I found myself sitting in the same classroom with approximately thirty classmates. My daughter was also taught at this school, and she shared a class with twenty-four other children. The fewer children that are brought up in our society, the more demanding their school education, or so it would seem. For many children of school age, the school is more or less the only place where they can meet others their age and learn the rules of living together in everyday inter- action. They are used to being treated as individuals, to being asked what they think and having the freedom to choose.

School teaching has changed accordingly and adapted itself to the new situation. Group work, project teaching and team teaching are almost taken for granted these days. At the same time, there is a growing demand for programmes that provide individual support and for special lessons for specific groups of pupils, such as for those with a different mother tongue. Last but not least, families are changing their attitudes: many increasingly expect state-run schools to take care of their children outside school hours. Yet even though the number of places at Zurich's care centres is growing continually, there are still long waiting lists.

For several years now, the building of extensions and new schools has been on the City of Zurich's agenda. Unfortunately, economies made in the past mean that con- siderable sums of money are now needed just to maintain existing stock. Consequently, more than a third of the City's entire building budget is now spent on schools and sports facilities. Nor is Zurich alone in this respect. School construction has again become the subject of lively discussion throughout Europe and the USA.

Now, at the peak of the school-building boom, the City of Zurich has decided to evaluate the situation. The exhibition *School Buildings. The State of Affairs,* as well as the catalogue now in your hands compare approaches to school construction in Zurich, in Switzerland as a whole, and in selected European cities. We are interested not only in current debates between experts, but also in the building and financial standards currently being applied.

We have seen that the question of up-to-date school classrooms has produced a similar solution in many places: the cluster, the group of classrooms. As a flexible unit, the cluster is replacing the traditional arrangement of classrooms in rows along a corridor. Some Scandinavian schools have taken this a step further and are now experimenting with open-plan arrangements. Large schools are no longer taboo, either. And in Holland, for example, the desire to network schools with other public facilities has resulted in the construction of veritable school cities, referred to locally as "community-based schools". The isolated school surrounded by lawns and trees is giving way to the lively town- and neighbourhood centre.

Tight public budgets are forcing all countries to reconsider room management and find multiple uses for existing rooms. However, one fundamental fact should not be forgotten here: the vast majority of the schools we shall be using in the future were built decades ago. Modern teaching will generally be done in rooms that were devised for teaching practices inspired by very different conceptions of education. Existing schoolrooms cannot always be converted at will to meet contemporary needs, but they can perhaps be used differently. This clearly shows that in school construction only flexible and adaptable solutions guarantee sustainability. For when it comes to the future only one thing is certain: change will continue.

Elisabeth Gaus
**Schulbesuch/school visit**

**Gesamtschule In der Höh, Volketswil**
Das Schulhaus der Zürcher Vorortsgemeinde ist seit 2003 in Betrieb. Ein partizipativer Planungsprozess führte zum baulichen Konzept (vgl. Katalog). Die Schule wird nach modernen Grundsätzen geführt, die von den Jugendlichen hohe Selbständigkeit verlangen.

**In der Höh Comprehensive School, Volketswil**
The school in a Zurich suburb opened in 2003. The concept for the building was developed in a participatory planning process (see catalogue). The school is run in accordance with modern principles, which expect a great degree of independence from young people.

**Cécile, Claudia, Migena,** 2. KlässlerInnen
Uns gefällt es hier viel besser, da wir mehr machen können: Es gibt Computer und wir haben eigene Pulte, die wir umherschieben können. Der Bau gefällt uns, er könnte eigentlich noch grösser sein, breiter und höher.
Mir fehlt hier die alte Lehrerin. — Am liebsten bin ich im Rechnen und in der Handarbeit. — Ich bin auch gerne im Gang.

**Cécile, Claudia and Migena,** second-year pupils
We like it much more here because we can do a lot more: there are computers and we've got our own desks, which we can move around. We like the building, but it could be bigger — wider and higher.
I miss my old teacher. My favourite subjects are arithmetic and needlework, knitting and so on. I like being in the corridor.

**Ariane,** 5. Klässlerin
Jede Woche wechselt der Wochenplan. Darauf sehen wir, was wir geplant haben. Hier ist der Plan für die Computer, wo wir uns eintragen müssen. Wir können am Computer selber einstellen, in welchem Stock ausgedruckt werden soll. Wir können viel selbständig arbeiten. Wenn es im Zimmer zu laut ist, können wir im Gang arbeiten, müssen jedoch leise sein, da dieser auch eine Art Schulzimmer ist. Ich arbeite gerne da draussen. Wenn es zu laut ist, verziehe ich mich an einen anderen Ort. Uns gehört das ganze Schulhaus.

**Ariane,** fifth-year schoolgirl
Every week we have a new timetable, showing us what we have planned. This is the plan for the computers - we have to enter our names there. When we use the computers, we can choose which floor we want to print out our documents on. We can do a lot of work on our own. If it gets too noisy in the classroom, you can work in the corridor. But you have to be pretty quiet there because it's a kind of classroom. I like working out there. If it gets too noisy, I just go somewhere else. The entire building's ours.

**Cornel, Nadine,** Kindergartenkinder
Mir macht es nichts aus, dass es hier so viele Kinder gibt, auch grosse. Ich bin aber nicht gerne draussen. — Ich war noch nie im Innenhof. — Ich nie im 1. Stock.
Der Kindergarten gefällt uns. Ich wünsche mir hier noch ein Pferd. — Ich wünsche mir hier drinnen ein grosses Kapitänschiff, wo ich einsteigen kann.

**Cornel and Nadine,** kindergarten children
I don't mind that there's so many children here - big ones, too. But I don't really like being outside. — I've never been in the quadrangle. — I've never been on the first floor.
We like the kindergarten. I wish we had a horse here, too. — I wish there was a big ship with a captain in here, which you could go into.

**Manuela,** Sek I, In der Höh
Wenn ich einen Umbaukredit hätte, würde ich einen kleinen Park einrichten, zum Ausruhen und Plaudern. Keine Schaukel, kein Fussball, keine Schneeballschlachten — ein Ort, wo uns niemand stört.

**Manuela,** first year secondary-school pupil, In der Höh
If I had a reconstruction loan I'd put a little park here where you could relax and have a chat. No swings, no football, no snowball fights. A place where nobody could disturb us.

**Fabienne, Yelena, Ariane, Anina, Esra,** 4. Klässlerinnen
Der Innenhof ist schön. Im Sommer kann man am goldenen Brunnen trinken. Uns gefällt das Schulhaus sehr gut. Die Schiebewände finden wir gut; der Hund gefällt uns am besten. — Schlecht sind an diesem Schulhaus nur die Holzgriffe bei der Eingangstüre, die schnell kaputt gehen oder die Lampen, die leicht herunterfallen oder die weiche Decke, die schnell Löcher bekommt.

**Fabienne, Yelena, Ariane, Anina and Esra,** fourth-year pupils
The quadrangle is lovely. In the summer, you can drink from the golden fountain. We really like the building. And the sliding partitions. Our favourite is the dog. The only bad thing about the building are the wooden doorknobs on the entrance doors, because they break so easily, the lamps, which fall out easily, and the soft ceiling, which you can easily make holes in.

**Peter Zweerus,** Schulleiter

Transparenz ist uns wichtig, in der Pädagogik wie auch im Schulbau: Die Türen stehen immer offen. Das Haus ist durchlässig; jede und jeder gehört zum Ganzen, nach dem Grundsatz: «Wir und unsere Schule» und nicht «Ich und mein Klassenzimmer».

Die Architektur macht es uns möglich, auf verschiedene Arten zu unterrichten; sie behindert uns nicht und verhindert nichts. Der Schulbau ist wie ein Dorf: Das Klassenzimmer ist das Haus, der Gang mit seinen Lernnischen, Bistroecken und Kulturräumen bildet das Dorfleben. Das Atrium bietet weitere Möglichkeiten und wird sehr rege genutzt.

Mangelhaft ist leider die Akustik des Baus. Der Schall wird durchs ganze Haus getragen und erschwert die Nutzung von Lernnischen. Auch das Konzept der identischen Universalräume hat nicht nur Vorteile: In der Holzwerkstatt oder im Musikraum wäre ein Holzboden viel vorteilhafter als der vorhandene Beton. Dagegen schätzen wir die Wände aus Holz, die sich zum Aufhängen von Zeichnungen und anderem gut eignen.

**Peter Zweerus,** headmaster

We feel that transparency is important both in education and in a school building. The doors are always open. The building is transparent. Everyone is part of a whole, according to the principle: 'We and our school' and not 'Me and my classroom'.

The architecture allows us to teach in different ways. It doesn't hamper us in any way. The building's like a village, with the classroom as the house; the corridor, with its study niches, lunch corners and cultural rooms, represents village life. The atrium also has a lot of potential and it's always being used by someone or other.

Unfortunately, the acoustics are not too good. Sounds travel right through the building making it difficult to work at the study niches. And the concept of identical universal rooms isn't always an advantage, because in the wood workshop or in the music room, for instance, a wooden floor would have been much better than the concrete we've got there now. But we really do appreciate the wooden walls: they are very good for hanging up pictures and other things.

**Dario, Simon, Gabriel, Fejzi,** Sekundarschüler

Früher hatte jeder sein Klassenzimmer. Nun können wir viel selbstständiger arbeiten, es wird uns nicht dauernd gesagt, was zu tun ist. — Wir sind viel freier als früher. — Auch in der Pause können wir wählen, ob wir draussen oder drinnen sein möchten. — Manchmal kochen einige von uns über Mittag.

**Dario, Simon, Gabriel and Fejzi,** secondary school pupils

Everyone used to have their own classroom. Now we can work far more independently. We're not constantly being told what we're supposed to do. — We have a lot more freedom than we used to. — And in our breaks, it's left up to us to decide whether to stay indoors or go outside. — At times, some of us cook a midday meal now and then.

**Vuki,** 5. Klässler

Uns gefallen die Lehrer und das Holz, aber auch die Computer, wo wir hin dürfen, wann wir wollen. Ich vermisse nichts aus der alten Schule. Hier haben wir kleinere Tische, dafür jeder einen für sich allein. Am liebsten lerne ich in der Bibliothek. Ich finde es gut, dass wir klassendurchmischt sind, da können Ältere den Jüngeren helfen — dumm ist nur, dass ich zu den Älteren gehöre.

**Vuki,** a fifth-year pupil

We like the teachers and the wood, and the computers - plus the fact that we can use them whenever we want. I don't miss our old school in the least. Here the desks are smaller, but that means that we each have our own desk. Of all the places in the school, I like studying in the library best. I'm glad that the different years are put together. That way the older pupils can help the younger ones. The only problem for me is that I'm one of the older ones.

**Michael Raich,** Hauswart

Sehr gut sind die vielen offenen Flächen drinnen und draussen zum Spielen in der Pause. Beim schönen Wetter sind die Kinder am liebsten im Freien, sehr begehrt ist der Innenhof, im Sommer ist er schön schattig. Zum Reinigen ist das Schulhaus einfach, nur die Reinigung der Unterrichtsräume ist zeitaufwändiger, da sie mit Möbeln verstellt sind. Mir gefällt dieses Schulhaus, es ist speziell. Auch zum Reinigen ist es anders, ich muss sehr flexibel sein. Da immer und überall Kinder sind, reinige ich den grössten Teil frühmorgens.

**Michael Raich,** school caretaker

One really good thing about this school are all the open areas inside and outside where the kids can play during their breaks. When the weather's good they all want to go outside. And they love the quadrangle, it's nice and shady in the summer. This school building's easy to clean, although the classrooms do take a bit of time, because there's so much furniture in the way. I like this school. There is something special about it. But cleaning is a different thing altogether. You have to be very flexible. There are always kids everywhere you go. I do most of the cleaning early in the morning.

Photos: Claudia Caprez

Hans-Jürg Keller

# Und sie bewegt sich doch ...
# Der Wandel der Schule in den letzten 15 Jahren

### Segmentierung, Pluralisierung, Individualisierung

Die Volksschule, die schon im Namen den Anspruch formuliert, allen Bevölkerungsschichten zu dienen, sah sich in den letzten Jahren einer fortschreitenden Segmentierung und Pluralisierung der Gesellschaft gegenüber. Sie musste versuchen, verschiedenen Bevölkerungsteilen mit unterschiedlichen Werthaltungen, Lebenszielen und -stilen und mit je abweichenden Vorstellungen von Bildung und Erziehung gerecht zu werden. Die Meinungen darüber, was Schule zu leisten und wie sie das zu leisten habe, gehen immer weiter auseinander. Verschiedene Gesellschaftssegmente stellen heute unterschiedliche Ansprüche an die Schule.

Gleichwohl hat diese an ihren wichtigsten Zielen festgehalten: Schülerinnen und Schüler sollen das Potenzial ihrer Begabungen voll ausschöpfen können und zu einem selbstbestimmten und sinnerfüllten Leben fähig werden. Sie sollen sich friedlich verständigen, die Welt verstehen, sie bewahren und gemeinsam weitergestalten können. Selbst-, Sozial- und Sachkompetenz (Heinrich Roth) sollen gleichmässig gefördert werden. Allgemein wird von der Schule erwartet, dass sie — ergänzend zum Elternhaus — den Grundstein für ein erfolgreiches Leben in Familie, Beruf und Gesellschaft legt. Zu ihren Grundfunktionen gehört auch weiterhin, die Schüler je nach individueller Begabung und Leistung Berufsausbildungen oder weiterführenden Ausbildungen zuzuführen.

Während über die Ziele von Schule also noch Einigkeit besteht, wollen die verschiedenen Gesellschaftssegmente jedoch ganz unterschiedliche Akzente setzen, wenn es darum geht, wie sie erreicht werden. Auf der einen Seite sollen der einzelne Schüler und die einzelne Schülerin individuelle Betreuung erhalten, andererseits werden abfragbare, generalisierte Wissens- und Leistungsstandards eingefordert. Diskussionen darüber, wie viel gemeinsamer Unterricht aller Jugendlichen und wie viel Schulung in nach Schulleistungen zusammengestellten Lerngruppen nötig sei, werden seit Jahrzehnten im ganzen deutschen Sprachraum mit Vehemenz geführt. Der Kanton Zürich löst das Problem, indem er den Gemeinden bei der Ausgestaltung der Sekundarstufe I freie Hand lässt.

### Offene Bildungsinhalte

Bei der Frage nach den Bildungsinhalten, die Schule vermitteln soll, ist ebenfalls kein Konsens zu erzielen, denn ein eigentlicher Bildungskanon ist kaum mehr sichtbar. Die Frage, wie viel Raum für die Förderung von musisch-gestalterischen Fähigkeiten neben der Vorbereitung auf das Erwerbsleben bleiben darf, manifestiert sich im Streit darüber, ob zu Gunsten von Englischunterricht Handarbeitsstunden gestrichen werden dürfen oder nicht. Ein Blick auf die Lehrpläne zeigt, dass auch innerhalb der einzelnen Fächer nicht mehr von einem Bildungskanon gesprochen werden kann. Die vor rund 15 Jahren fertig gestellten Lehrpläne schreiben vermehrt Lernziele vor, die anhand verschiedener Inhalte erreicht werden können. Dies bietet die Chance zu situativem Lernen. Die Lehrpersonen können je nach Alltagserfahrungen, Lebenswelt und Interessen ihrer Schülerinnen und Schüler ein Ziel mit der Behandlung von ganz verschiedenen Inhalten erreichen.

In der ersten bis dritten Klasse der Primarschule lernen die Schülerinnen und Schüler im Kanton Zürich zum Beispiel in «Mensch und Umwelt», Einblicke in Zusammenhänge zu gewinnen. Eines der dabei verfolgten Ziele ist, Veränderungen und Entwicklungen nachzuspüren. Dieses Ziel kann nun — auf den ersten Blick erstaunlicherweise — mit Hilfe der Inhalte «Von der Raupe zum Schmetterling», «Geburt und älter werden» oder «Auch Gegenstände werden älter» erreicht werden. Der Lehrplan stellt in diesem Fall also nur sicher, dass die Schülerinnen und Schüler sich mit «Entwicklung» befasst haben. Es besteht aber keine Garantie, dass sich alle Schülerinnen und Schüler in der Unterstufe mit der Metamorphose von der Raupe zum Schmetterling auseinander gesetzt haben — Kritiker mögen dies als postmodernes «anything

Hans-Jürg Keller

# And Yet It Moves …
# The Transformation of the School over the Past Fifteen Years

### Segmentation, Pluralisation, Individualisation

The *Volksschule* [literally, people's school, which comprises primary and secondary school], whose name alone articulates a claim to serve all classes of the population, has been confronted in recent years with an advancing segmentation and pluralization of society. The schools sought to do justice to various parts of the population with various systems of values, life goals and lifestyles, each with its own conception of education and training. Opinions on what schools should do, and how they should do it, are growing increasingly divergent. Today, various segments of society place different demands on schools.

Nevertheless, the school has stayed true to its most important goals: pupils should be able to realise fully the potential of their talents and be able to have a self-determined and fulfilled life. They should be able to communicate peacefully, understand the world and be able to protect it and work together to shape it for the future. Self-, social and technical competence (Heinrich Roth) should be promoted in equal measure. The expectation of the school in general is that it — complementing the parental home — lays the foundation for a successful life in family, career and society. One of its basic functions is still to direct pupils into career training or further education according to individual talent and performance.

Although unity still exists on the goals of the school, various segments of society want to place very different emphasis when it comes to how these goals should be achieved. On the one hand, the individual pupil should receive individual attention; on the other, there are demands for testable, generalized standards of knowledge and performance. Heated discussions have been underway for decades in the entire German-speaking region on how much common instruction is necessary for all young people and how much schooling should be done in learning groups classified according to school performance. The canton of Zurich has solved the problem by giving local communities free rein in the design of secondary level I *(Sekundarstufe I)* schools.

Likewise, no consensus can be achieved on the question of the content of education that should be conveyed by schools, since an actual educational canon is scarcely identifiable any longer. The question of how much space may remain for the promotion of visual and artistic abilities alongside preparation for professional life has manifested itself in the conflict over whether handicrafts classes may be cancelled in favour of English classes.

A look at teaching plans shows that an educational canon no longer exists within individual subjects, either. The teaching plans drawn up about fifteen years ago prescribe an increased number of learning goals that can be reached for various topics. This offers the opportunity for situative learning. Teaching staff can reach a learning goal according to the experiences, daily life and interests of their pupils by treating widely varying topics.

In the first through third grades of primary school *(Primarschule),* the pupils in the canton of Zurich learn in 'Person and Environment', for example, how to gain insights about environments. One of the goals pursued in this is that of following changes and developments. This goal can be reached — it seems astounding at first — with the help of the topics 'From Caterpillar to Butterfly', 'Birth and Growing Older' and 'Objects Grow Older Too'.

In this case, the teaching plan merely ensures that pupils deal with 'development'. There is no guarantee, however, that all pupils have engaged with the metamorphosis of the caterpillar into the butterfly — critics may condemn this as post-

goes» verurteilen. Wie die Gesellschaft selbst ist auch die Schule unübersichtlicher geworden. Sie orientiert sich stärker am einzelnen Individuum und seinen Interessen. Dabei ist hervorzuheben, dass es ihr bisher recht gut gelungen ist, als Brücke zwischen verschiedenen Gesellschaftssegmenten zu fungieren und Kinder und Jugendliche unterschiedlichster kultureller, weltanschaulicher und sozialer Herkunft in Kulturtechniken einzuführen, ihnen Orientierungswissen (wie physikalische Gesetze oder historische Zusammenhänge) zu vermitteln und ihnen in einigen Bereichen das Zusammenarbeiten, das gemeinsame Ringen um das Verstehen der Welt und das gemeinsame Erarbeiten eines gegebenen Themas zu ermöglichen.

Aus didaktischer Perspektive gesehen, ist die Vielfalt der Unterrichtsformen gross geworden. In der Multioptionsgesellschaft hat sich das Auswählen auch in der Schule zu einer wichtigen Grösse entwickelt. Schülerinnen und Schüler bearbeiten im so genannten «Werkstattunterricht» verschiedene Aufgaben, und sie teilen sich ihre Arbeit im «Wochenplanunterricht» selbst ein. Häufig ist auch der «projektorientierte Unterricht» anzutreffen: In einer ganzen Klasse oder in einzelnen Gruppen wird eine bestimmte Fragestellung verfolgt, Informationen müssen bei ganz verschiedenen Quellen besorgt, und schliesslich muss das Erarbeitete auch noch präsentiert werden. Die Informatisierung der Schule wirkt sich dabei positiv aus. Internet und Mediotheken werden rege genutzt. Wichtig sind aber auch die Erfahrungen aus erster Hand, das Experimentieren, das Befragen von Fachleuten und die Präsentation, bei der neben Plakaten und Folien auch Hypertext und Powerpoint zum Einsatz kommen. Solche Projekte sind meist interdisziplinär angelegt. Ziele aus Sach- und Umweltkunde, Deutsch und Fremdsprachen werden gleichermassen verfolgt.

Neben dem Lernen von Inhalten wird der Verfolgung eigener Lernprozesse mehr Gewicht zugemessen. «Lernjournale» oder «Reisetagebücher» werden geführt, in denen Schülerinnen und Schüler ihren eigenen Lernweg dokumentieren, aus Sackgassen und Umwegen lernen und von der Lehrperson mit Kommentaren, beispielhaften Lösungswegen und Anregungen zur weiteren Arbeit ermuntert werden. Dabei hat der Austausch mit einer Lernpartnerin oder einem Lernpartner einen hohen Stellenwert. Problemlösefähigkeiten, das gemeinsame dialogische Lernen und Teamarbeit werden bewusst gefördert. Die Schule muss sich damit abfinden, dass sie Kindern und Jugendlichen nur noch wenig Wissen mitgibt, das sich während ihres Lebens nicht verändert. Deshalb wird die Bereitschaft der Schülerinnen und Schüler gefördert, permanent weiter zu lernen. Solche Lehr- und Lernformen wechseln sich mit traditionellen Unterrichtsformen wie Frage und Antwort ab. So attraktiv diese Unterrichtsformen auch sein können, die Frage nach Effizienz und Effektivität muss gestellt werden. Nach den PISA-Untersuchungen wurde darauf hingewiesen, dass die zur Verfügung stehende Zeit nicht immer ergiebig genutzt wird und dass Unwesentliches und Wesentliches nicht immer genügend unterschieden wird.

## Regeln aufstellen und durchsetzen

Während die Schule in ihren Bildungsinhalten und Methoden die gesellschaftlichen Entwicklungen aufgenommen hat, konnte sie auf dem Feld der Regeln und Normen einen Kontrapunkt setzen.

Weil es nicht möglich ist, all die unterschiedlichen Erziehungsstile, Wert- und Normvorstellungen der Eltern zu integrieren, geben sich Schulen eigene Regeln. Ob zu Hause bei einer Meinungsverschiedenheit endlos diskutiert wird, ob die Kinder sich durchsetzen oder ob der Vater immer Recht hat — in der Schule gelten andere, von der Lehrerschaft aufgestellte oder mit den Schülerinnen und Schülern gemeinsam erarbeitete Regeln.

Hier hat in den letzten 15 Jahren ein gravierender Wandel stattgefunden. Wusste man in den sechziger Jahren spätestens beim Einatmen von Bohnerwachsgeruch auf den Korridoren genau, welche Regeln galten, so wurden in den siebziger und achtziger Jahren die Klassenregeln eher von der Lehrperson durchgesetzt. In den neunziger Jahren haben sich vermehrt Schulregeln etabliert, die (zum Beispiel in Schulkonferenzen) mit allen Beteiligten diskutiert und anschliessend auch durchgesetzt werden. Gemeinschaftserlebnisse wie Schulprojekte, Erzählnächte oder Schulfeste tragen dazu bei, dass sich alle Beteiligten einer Schule und nicht einer Klasse zugehörig fühlen.

modern 'anything goes'. The school, like society itself, has become more difficult to see in overview. It is increasingly orienting itself around the individual and individual interests. It should be emphasised that hitherto the school has succeeded admirably in functioning as a bridge between different segments of society, introducing children and young people from the most disparate backgrounds in terms of culture, worldview and social origin to cultural techniques, conveying to them orientation knowledge (like physical laws or historical connections) and making possible for them, in some areas, working together on, that is, grappling with the tasks of understanding the world and applying themselves to a given theme.

From a didactic perspective, the multiplicity of forms of teaching has grown large indeed. In a society of many choices, selection has acquired significance in the school as well. Pupils develop various tasks in their so-called 'workshop lessons', and they divide up their work themselves in 'weekly planning lessons'. 'Project-oriented lessons' are also frequently encountered: A specific question is pursued by an entire class or by individual groups, information must be found in widely varying sources and finally the completed work must be presented. This is a positive consequence of the 'computerising' of the school. Active use is made of the Internet and media libraries. Also important, however, are first-hand experience, experimentation, asking specialists and making presentations, in which not only signs and overhead transparencies but also hypertext and PowerPoint are used. Such projects are usually interdisciplinary in their conception. They pursue in equal measure goals in general and environmental knowledge, German and foreign languages.

Alongside learning content, more weight is now given to the tracking of the individual's own learning processes. Pupils keep 'learning journals' or 'travel diaries', in which they document their own learning path, learn from back alleys and detours, and are encouraged by teaching staff with comments, example solutions and suggestions for further work. This attaches much importance to exchange with a learning partner. Problem-solving abilities, learning in common dialogue and teamwork are consciously promoted. The school must come to terms with the fact that today the amount of knowledge that it can give children and young people that will not change during the course of their lives is small. The pupils are therefore trained to be ready to learn permanently. Such forms of teaching and learning alternate with traditional forms of instruction like question and answer.

As attractive as these new forms of teaching may be, the question of efficiency and effectiveness must also be raised. The PISA studies gave multiple indications that the time available for teaching is not always used productively, and that the essential and the non-essential are not always sufficiently distinguished.

### The Schoolhouse as Community, Establishing and Implementing Rules

While the school has incorporated developments in society in its methods and topics of education, it has been able to establish a counterpoint in the area of rules and norms.

Since it is not possible to integrate all of the parents' varying styles of education and systems of values and norms, the schools make their own rules. Whether or not differences of opinion are discussed endlessly at home or the father is always right — at school other rules apply, set by the teachers or worked out in cooperation with the pupils.

A momentous change has taken place in this area in the last fifteen years. In the 1960s, school rules were clear at the first whiff of floor polish in the corridors. In the 1970s and 1980s, however, class rules were mostly implemented by teaching staff. In the 1990s, new school rules were established that were discussed (at school conferences, for example) by all involved, and then implemented by all as well. Community experiences such as school projects, storytelling nights and school festivals

Solche Regeln sind umso wichtiger, als Schulen auch mit den Schattenseiten des Wandels konfrontiert sind. Gewalt, Erpressung und Vandalismus machen vor den Schultüren nicht Halt. Solchen Auswüchsen ist durch einzelne Lehrpersonen nicht mehr beizukommen. Die Zusammenarbeit in der Schule, unter der Lehrerschaft, im Team mit Fachleuten wie Schulsozialarbeitern, Schulpsychologen und schulischen Heilpädagogen führt dagegen zu guten Ergebnissen. Standen am Anfang der Entwicklung das Verständnis für die schwierigen Umstände, in denen viele Kinder und Jugendliche leben, sowie allgemeine Verhaltensappelle, so ist man inzwischen zu der Einsicht gelangt, dass die Jugendlichen sich der Verantwortung für ihre Handlungen nicht entziehen können. Dieser Erkenntnis entsprechen erzieherische Massnahmen, die bis zu einer Auszeit von der Schule reichen, in welcher zum Beispiel ein begleiteter Arbeitseinsatz geleistet werden kann.

Multikulturalität gehört heute zur Schule wie der Pausengong. Während sie häufig gar nicht mehr auffällt oder als bereichernde Gegebenheit wahrgenommen wird, hat sie manchmal auch zu rassistischen Tendenzen oder zur Bildung von nach Nationen zusammengesetzten Schülerbanden geführt. Individuelle Förderung und Zusammenarbeit im Schulteam haben sich in beiden Fällen bewährt. Wichtig ist hier die Mitarbeit der Lehrpersonen für heimatliche Sprache und Kultur sowie der Migrantinnen- und Migrantenverbände.

### Ökonomisierung, Teilautonomisierung

In den letzten 15 Jahren wurde die Schule unbestritten auch durch vorherrschende ökonomische Paradigma geprägt. Sie sah sich vor allem der internationalen Konkurrenz und dem Leistungsvergleich stärker ausgesetzt als früher. Gute Schulen sind im internationalen Wettbewerb ein Standortvorteil. Der Druck, Schule nach den Vorstellungen der Wirtschaft zu gestalten, ist gewachsen. Begriffe wie «Benchmark», «Outcome» oder «Standards» haben auch im Klassenzimmer Fuss gefasst. Die Schulen werden an dem gemessen, was sie effektiv erreichen. Klassen- und schulübergreifende Leistungsmessungen sind im Vormarsch, und die aus den Vergleichen resultierenden Publikationen von «best practice» im Schulbereich werden stark beachtet und berücksichtigt, sogar ein gesamtschweizerisches «Bildungscontrolling» ist im Aufbau. Die Forderungen nach früherem und flexiblerem Schuleintritt und zeitlicher Straffung der Unterrichtsjahre sind unüberhörbar geworden und haben — zum Beispiel in Bezug auf die Mittelschuldauer — bereits Auswirkungen gehabt. Die Diskussion um einen flexibleren Übergang zwischen Vorschul- und Primarstufe (Basisstufe, Grundstufe) hat nicht nur ökonomische Gründe, sie ist vor allem eine pädagogische Antwort auf die sehr unterschiedlichen Vorerfahrungen, die Kinder heute beim Schuleintritt mitbringen. Viele von ihnen können bereits lesen und rechnen, während anderen elementare Grunderfahrungen abgehen.

Die Teilautonomisierung der Volksschule («geleitete Schulen», «Teilautonome Volksschulen»), die in den letzten Jahren an vielen Orten eingeführt wurde, hat sich bewährt. Sie geht zumindest teilweise ebenfalls auf die Ökonomisierung zurück, die mit dem «New Public Management» auch starke Auswirkungen auf den gesamten öffentlichen Bereich hatte. Schulen sollen schneller reagieren können; sie sollen durch Schulleitungen professionell geführt werden, und sie sollen sich ein Leitbild mit schuleigenen Schwerpunkten und einem prägnanten Aussenauftritt verschaffen. Die anfänglich skeptische Lehrerschaft liess sich an den meisten Orten, in denen das neue Modell eingeführt wurde, von seinen Vorteilen überzeugen. Die vom Volk gewählten Schulbehörden können so die operativen Aufgaben weitgehend abgeben und entlasten sich von vielen im Milizsystem kaum mehr leistbaren Aufgaben.

### Schule und Eltern

Wie die Bevölkerung nicht mehr bereit ist, grosse Eingriffe durch den Staat in ihr Leben zuzulassen, so sind die Eltern auch nicht mehr bereit, Entscheidungen der Schule einfach zu akzeptieren. Die Mitsprache der Eltern bei Übertrittsentscheidungen von der Primarstufe in die Sekundarstufe I ist unterdessen festgeschrieben. Zeugnisgespräche, bei denen die Lehrpersonen den Eltern die schulischen Fortschritte erläutern, sind institutionalisiert. Die Elternorganisationen sprechen in der Schulpolitik ein wichtiges Wort mit.

helped all involved to feel they belonged to a school and not just a particular class. Such rules are all the more important when schools are also confronted with the dark sides of change. Violence, extortion and vandalism do not stop at the schoolhouse door. Such behavioural excesses can no longer be handled by individual teaching staff alone. However, collaboration in schools between teachers and specialists such as school social workers, school psychologists and school-based remedial educators has produced good results. Although the first reaction to this development was understanding for the difficult circumstances in which many children and young people live, as well as general appeals for good behaviour, it has been recognised since that young people cannot escape responsibility for their own actions. This recognition has corresponded to educational correctional measures that can be as severe as a suspension from school, during which a supervised employment commitment, for example, can be carried out.

Today, multiculturalism is as much a part of school as the break-time bell. Although multiculturalism often attracts no attention or is perceived as an enrichment and a settled fact, it has also led in some cases to racist tendencies and to the formation of school gangs organised along national lines. Individual intervention and collaborative work in the school team have proven effective in both cases. Important in this connection is the work of teaching staff for homeland language and culture *(heimatliche Sprache und Kultur)*, as well as that of the migrant associations *(Migrantinnen- und Migrantenverbände)*.

## Economisation, Semi-Autonomisation

Over the past fifteen years, the school has been marked indisputably by the dominant economic paradigm. Above all, schools were more exposed to international competition and performance comparisons than they had been before. Good schools are an advantage for a community in international competition. Pressure has grown to design schools according to the ideas of business. Terms like 'benchmark', 'outcome' and 'standards' have gained a foothold in the classroom. The schools are measured by what they achieve effectively. Performance assessments of classes and entire schools are on the rise, and the publications resulting from these comparisons of the 'best practices' in the educational sector are closely watched and studied. One may even speak of an emerging Switzerland-wide 'education review'.

The calls for earlier and more flexible entry into schools and for the tightening of the duration of instruction have grown impossible to ignore and have — in regard to the length of middle school *(Mittelschule)* study, for example — already had consequences. The discussion of a more flexible transition between preschool and primary school level *(Vorschul- und Primarstufe)* (base level *[Basisstufe]*, ground level *[Grundstufe]*) is not just about economics, but is above all a pedagogical response to the highly various prior knowledge that children today have when they begin their schooling. Many of them can already read and do arithmetic, while others lack elementary basic experience.

The semi-autonomisation of the *Volksschule* ('directed schools', 'semi-autonomous *Volksschulen*') that has been introduced in many areas in recent years has proven itself. This process goes back at least in part to economisation, which, with the program of 'New Public Management', also had major consequences for the entire public sector. Schools must be able to react faster; they must be professionally managed by school directors, and they should create a model for themselves with school-specific specialisations and a pithy external profile. In most areas where the new model was introduced, the teachers, sceptical at first, grew convinced of its strengths. The popularly-elected school authorities can thus in large degree hand over the operative tasks to others and unburden themselves of many of the tasks that had become scarcely affordable in the militia system *(Milizsystem)*.

Die ausserschulischen Betreuungsaufgaben der Schule haben sich dagegen bis jetzt nicht flächendeckend durchgesetzt. Tagesschulen, Schülerclubs und Mittagstische existieren zwar als besondere Angebote, sind aber noch nicht Standard. Die Schule geht in ihrer Organisationsform im Grossen und Ganzen nach wie vor von Familien mit zwei Elternteilen aus, von denen sich eines ganz der Familienarbeit widmen kann — eine Auffassung von Familie, die zwar politisch gestützt wird, die aber angesichts der tatsächlich existierenden Familienstrukturen eher anachronistisch wirkt.

Mit den Blockzeiten kommen die Schulen immerhin dem Bedürfnis vieler Eltern entgegen, nicht ständig «Rangierbahnhof» spielen zu müssen: das eine Kind in die Schule zu schicken, während das andere eine Stunde später schon wieder in Empfang zu nehmen ist.

### Die Lehrpersonen

Das Berufsbild der Lehrpersonen hat sich stark verändert. Durch die Informatisierung der Gesellschaft hat die Schule das Wissensmonopol in allen Altersstufen vollständig verloren. Lehrpersonen führen die Schülerinnen und Schüler nur noch selten in vollständig neue Welten ein. Es gibt nichts, was sie nicht schon durch Fernsehen, Internet oder CD-ROM kennen gelernt hätten. Lehrerinnen und Lehrer sind in diesem Umfeld von Wissensvermittlern zu Lernbegleitern geworden — zu Personen, die Zusammenhänge aufzeigen, beim Verknüpfen von Wissensinseln helfen, die Halbwissen zu fundiertem Wissen erweitern und dazu anleiten, Informationen kritisch zu beurteilen.

Lehrerin oder Lehrer ist zwar immer noch ein Beruf mit einem hohen Mass an Selbständigkeit, doch alle Lehrpersonen sind unterdessen stark zu Teamarbeitenden geworden. Arbeitsteilung setzt sich auch im schulischen Feld durch. Zudem besteht mit der neuen Schulstruktur und der Neukonzeption der Lehrerinnen- und Lehrerbildung auch für Lehrpersonen vermehrt die Möglichkeit zu vertikaler und horizontaler Mobilität. Lehrpersonen können sich zu Schulleitungsmitgliedern weiterbilden; sie können Zusatzausbildungen machen, um sich für eine andere Schulstufe, weitere Fächer oder einen anderen Beruf im schulischen Umfeld zu qualifizieren.

Die Schule hat sich — entgegen ihrem Image — in den letzten Jahren stark verändert, und sie wird sich in Zukunft noch stärker verändern. Wenn es ihr gelingt, mit den gesellschaftlichen Entwicklungen Schritt zu halten, gleichzeitig aber auch ein Ort zu sein, an dem bei aller Beschleunigung nicht nur Flüchtiges Platz hat und an dem man sich Zeit nimmt, die Welt zu erklären und zu verstehen, wird sie bei der weiteren Gestaltung dieser Welt eine wichtige Rolle spielen.

## Schools and Parents

Just as the population is no longer willing to allow major interventions by the state into their lives, parents are no longer willing to simply accept decisions made by the school. Consultation with parents on conversion decisions from the primary level to the secondary level I *(Sekundarstufe I)* is meanwhile guaranteed by law. Discussions of marks, in which teaching staff explain school progress to parents, have been institutionalised. Parent organisations play an important role in school politics.

By contrast, the tasks of looking after pupils outside of school have not been implemented comprehensively to date. Day schools, pupil clubs and luncheons do exist as special offers, but are not yet standard. In its organisational form, the school continues to work largely from the assumption of families with two parents, of whom one can devote him- or herself wholly to family work — a view of the family that is indeed supported politically, but which is rather anachronistic in light of actually existing family structures.

School block times nonetheless help to comply with many parents' needs not to play 'shunting yard' all the time: sending one child to school, then picking up another an hour later.

## Teaching Staff

The professional profile of teaching staff has changed dramatically. In an information society, the school has altogether lost its monopoly on knowledge at all age levels. It is seldom that teaching staff introduce pupils to entirely new worlds. There is nothing that pupils have not already encountered through television, the Internet or CD-ROMs. In this area, teachers have changed from conveyors of knowledge into learning companions — into persons who point out connections, help to bridge together islands of knowledge, expand half-knowledge into well-founded knowledge and in so doing show how to evaluate information critically.

Teaching remains a career with a high measure of independence, yet all teaching staff have become over the years very much members of a team. The division of labour is also being implemented in the area of the schools. With the new school structure and the new conception of teaching education, there arise multiplied possibilities for vertical and horizontal mobility for teaching staff. Teaching staff can continue their education and become members of the school administration; they can also pursue additional education to qualify for another school level *(Schulstufe)*, other fields, or another school-oriented career.

Contrary to its image, the school has changed dramatically in recent years, and it will change still more dramatically in the future. When schools succeed in keeping pace with social developments, yet at the same time remain a place where, amidst the world's acceleration, there is space for more than fleeting things, and where time is taken to explain the world and to understand it, then the school will play an important role in the future form of this world.

Schule in Bewegung. Zwei Klassenzimmer sind durch eine Faltwand verbunden. Gesamtschule In der Höh, Volketswil. Foto: Christoph Ruckstuhl

School in motion: Two classrooms are connected by a folding wall. Concentrated group work using moveable furniture. In der Höh Comprehensive School, Volketswil. Photo: Christoph Ruckstuhl.

Alan Wakefield, Daniel Kurz

# Der Stand der Dinge
# Neues vom Schulhausbau

In diesem Band sind 31 Schulhäuser und Schulbauprojekte der Volksschulstufe versammelt. Die Auswahl konzentrierte sich auf Bauten, die vor allem in schulischer Hinsicht neue Wege suchen und beschreiten. Sie zeigt, dass sich die Schule in der Schweiz und in Europa, ähnlich wie in den dreissiger und siebziger Jahren des 20. Jahrhunderts, in einer Zeit des Wandels befindet. Neue Unterrichtsmodelle, der Ausbau der Betreuungsangebote und der PISA-Schock haben die Diskussion über das zeitgemässe Schulhaus neu lanciert.

Die Frage, wie die Schule funktionieren soll und welche Gebäudetypologie dazu am besten geeignet ist, wird heute je nach Situation sehr unterschiedlich und teilweise auch mit Rückgriff auf bewährte Konzepte beantwortet. Das verschiedentlich proklamierte «Neue Schulhaus» oder das «Schulhaus von morgen» lässt sich angesichts der Vielfalt der — teilweise auch widersprüchlichen — Anforderungen nicht eindeutig fassen. Bei näherer Betrachtung der Projekte schälen sich dennoch einige Tendenzen heraus, die den momentanen Stand der Dinge reflektieren.

### Die Schule bewegt sich

Die Erinnerung an schrille Pausenglocken und lange, glänzend gewichste Korridore mit Reihen gleichförmiger Türen — sie hilft im aktuellen Schulhausbau nicht weiter, denn die klaren Zeit- und Raumaufteilungen haben sich relativiert: Die heutige Schule ist in Bewegung. Nutzungen überlagern sich zeitlich und räumlich. Die multifunktionale zentrale Halle, ein Thema der skandinavischen Moderne der dreissiger Jahre, das Herman Hertzberger in den niederländischen Montessori-Schulen seit 30 Jahren weiterentwickelt, hat in vielen Schulen die eindeutig definierten Erschliessungszonen abgelöst.

Das traditionelle Klassenzimmer öffnet sich. Der quadratische, abgeschlossene Raum, den die Lehrperson einst autonom beherrschte, ist Teil grösserer Raumfluchten geworden. Mehrere Klassenzimmer, Gruppenräume und gemeinsame Arbeitsbereiche für klassenübergreifenden Unterricht bilden Cluster: offene, aber überschaubare Einheiten. Schülerinnen und Schüler arbeiten in Gruppen wechselnder Grösse oder auch still für sich. Für längerfristige Projekte wie Theateraufführungen bieten die gemeinsamen Arbeitsbereiche neue Möglichkeiten. Angefangene Arbeiten können hier, auch über längere Zeit, einfach liegen bleiben. Entscheidend ist, dass die gemeinsame Zone genügend Tageslicht erhält und möblierbar ist. [fig. 1/2]

Je weniger abgeschlossene Räume und je mehr multifunktionale Zonen eine Schule umfasst, desto wichtiger

Alan Wakefield, Daniel Kurz

# The State of Affairs
# What's New in School Construction

This volume brings together 31 school buildings and school construction projects for the primary and secondary school levels. The selection concentrates on buildings which are seeking and following new avenues, particularly with regard to schooling, and it shows that, just as in the 1930s and 1970s, schools in Switzerland and in Europe are finding themselves in changing times. New models of teaching, the expansion of day-care offerings and the PISA shock have once again set in motion a discussion about the modern school building.

How the school should function and which building typology is most suited to it are questions answered very differently today depending on the situation and sometimes also with recourse to tried-and-tested ideas. The occasionally proclaimed 'new school building' or the 'school building of tomorrow' cannot be clearly conceptualised given the variety of demands — which can sometimes also be conflicting. A closer examination of the projects nevertheless reveals some trends which reflect the current state of affairs.

### The School Is in Motion

Memories of shrill school bells and long, brightly polished corridors with rows of uniform doors — these recollections are no longer helpful in current school construction, for the clear division of time and space has become relative: today's school is in motion. Uses overlap one another temporally and spatially. The multi-purpose central hall, a theme of Scandinavian modernism in the 1930s which has been further developed for over 30 years by Herman Hertzberger in the Dutch Montessori schools, has superseded the clearly defined access zones in many schools.

The traditional classroom is opening up. The self-contained square space once autonomously dominated by the teacher has become a part of a larger series of spaces. Several classrooms, group spaces, and common work areas for instructing several grade levels simultaneously are joined to form clusters: open but manageable units. Pupils work in groups of changing size or quietly by themselves. The common work areas offer new possibilities for longer-term projects such as theatrical performances. Materials needed and work already begun can simply be left in these areas, and over a long period of time as well. [fig.1/2]

What is crucial is that the common zone get sufficient daylight and can be furnished. The fewer self-contained spaces and the more multi-purpose

fig.1 Klassencluster: Vier Klassen teilen sich einen zentral gelegenen, gemeinsamen Arbeitsbereich. **Kindercluster Voorn,** Utrecht.

Foto: Arjan Schmitz

Class cluster: Four classes share a centrally located common workspace. **Kindercluster Voorn,** Utrecht.

Photo: Arjan Schmitz

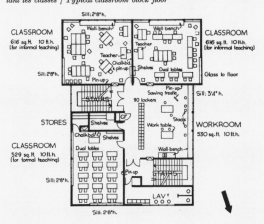

*Typisches Klassengeschoß, zirka 1:350 | Etage type du bâtiment abritant les classes | Typical classroom block floor*

fig.2 Frühes Beispiel: In der Zeitschrift «Werk» zeigte Alfred Roth schon 1952 einen Cluster-Grundriss. **Sekundarschule Wokingham,** England.

Plan: Werk 3 (1952)

Early example: As early as 1952 Alfred Roth showed, in the magazine *Werk*, a cluster ground plan. **Wokingham Secondary School,** England.

Werk 3 (1952)

wird auch die Frage der Raumakustik. Eine lärmige Hallenerschliessung kann dazu zwingen, die Klassenzimmertüre geschlossen zu halten.

Längst hat man sich an den Anblick von Sofas und Teppichen aus dem Brockenhaus oder ausrangierten privaten PCs neben dem offiziellen Schulmobiliar in den Klassenzimmern gewöhnt. Der Klassenraum löst sich durch solche «Fremdkörper» in unterschiedlich gestimmte Teilzonen auf. Die Schulmöbel werden, da die Kinder nicht mehr stundenlang am gleichen Platz verharren müssen, leichter und transportabler, zulasten der maximalen ergonomischen Anpassungsfähigkeit. Während die Mobiliarhersteller mit neuen Möbelprogrammen auf diesen Trend reagieren, zögern die Behörden mancherorts noch. Anders in den Schulen In der Höh (Volketswil) und Heimdalsgade (Kopenhagen): Dort sind Materialboxen und Tische mit Rollen versehen. So können die Flächen jederzeit kurzfristig ummöbliert und unterschiedlich genutzt werden.

zones a school contains, the more important the question of acoustics becomes. A noisy open hall area can mean that classroom doors have to be kept closed.

One has long become used to seeing sofas and carpets from second-hand shops or discarded private PCs in classrooms alongside official school furnishings. Such 'foreign elements' cause the classroom space to dissolve into sub-zones of varying character. As children no longer have to remain in the same seat for hours, school furniture is becoming lighter and more portable, at the expense of ergonomic adaptability. While furniture manufacturers are reacting to this trend with a range of new furnishings, the school authorities in many places are still hesitating. Not so in the In der Höh (Volketswil) and Heimdalsgade (Copenhagen) schools: there, boxes for materials and tables are equipped with small wheels. Thus the furniture can be moved and changed at any time and at short notice and the space used in a variety of ways.

## Grossraum oder Schulstube?

«Die Schulräume sind in kleine Einheiten gruppiert. Es gibt Türen zwischen den Klassenzimmern, Glaswände für den Austausch. Jede Einheit verfügt über Nischen für Gruppenarbeit und ein Arbeitszimmer für die Lehrer. Das traditionelle Lehrerzimmer wurde durch die Cafeteria für alle Angestellten ersetzt.» So beschreibt Kaisa Nuikkinen, leitende Architektin im Helsinki City Education Department, das finnische Konzept im Schulhausbau. Durch Transparenz und Offenheit entsteht eine kommunikative Atmosphäre, die den Austausch zwischen Lernenden und Lehrenden, aber auch innerhalb der beide Gruppen fördern soll. [fig. 4]

Die Auflösung der Klassenzimmersituation kann noch wesentlich konsequenter verfolgt werden, wie die Beispiele Bakkeløkka in Norwegen von NAV Architekten und Hellerup in Dänemark von Arkitema zeigen. Beide Schulen verzichten ganz auf Klassenverbände und stellen offene Lernlandschaften zur Verfügung. Unter der Führung von Mentorinnen und Mentoren stellen sich die Schüler ihr persönliches Lernprogramm zusammen. Mit offenen Raumstrukturen dieser Art wurde in Skandinavien und Deutschland schon um 1970 experimentiert. In der 1974 gegründeten Bielefelder Laborschule zeigen nachträgliche Baumassnahmen, dass die gegenseitigen Störungen in der offenen Raumsituation für gewisse Unterrichtsfächer zu belastend sind. Von den Pädagoginnen und Pädagogen wurden vor allem fehlende Rückzugsmöglichkeiten und Vorbereitungsräume beklagt. In Hellerup sind diese geschützten Bereiche vorhanden. Die Schule in Bakkeløkka gliedert sich zudem in klar begrenzte Untereinheiten von rund 90 Schülerinnen und Schülern, denen neben offenen auch abschliessbare Räume zur Verfügung stehen. [fig. 3/5]

Dass ablenkungsfreie Räume für konzentrierten Unterricht den Lernerfolg wesentlich unterstützen können, belegt eine jüngere Studie zu erfolgreichem Schulunterricht.[1] Viele Pädagoginnen und Pädagogen betonen die Bedeutung des konzentrierten und zum Teil auch des frontalen Unterrichts im Klassenverband.[2]

Also doch eher Schulstube als Grossraumbüro? Das reizvolle architektonische Wechselspiel zwischen intimen Lernräumen und öffentlicher Erschliessungszone, wie es exemplarisch beim Schulhaus in Paspels von Valerio Olgiati umgesetzt wurde und als Bild bei vielen Schweizer Architektinnen und Architekten nachhaltig verankert ist, findet sich auch im Primarschulhaus Linden in Niederhasli von Bünzli & Courvoisier. In der Mehrzahl der Projekte kommt jedoch das Bedürfnis nach vermehrter Offenheit und Transparenz zum Ausdruck; die Schule will als grosse Einheit und nicht als Ansammlung von Einzelklassen verstanden werden.

Wie eine solche Community-Schule funktioniert, lässt sich am Beispiel der Privatschule in Wädenswil von Galli und Rudolf eindrücklich erleben. Unabhängig von irgendwelchen Pausenglocken strömen die Kinder durch das Haus, gruppieren sich zu den verschiedensten Aktivitäten oder ziehen sich zum Lesen in eine Nische

1 Das Klassenzimmer-Video von Christine Paul und Kurt Reusser in: NZZ am Sonntag vom 11.5.2003, S.72

2 Miklos Gimes: Alte Schule, in: Das Magazin, 29.11.2003

## Open Plan or Schoolroom?

'The school rooms are grouped into small units. There are doors between the classrooms, but glass walls allow for visual exchanges. Each unit has niches for group work and a workroom for teachers. The traditional teachers' room was replaced by a cafeteria for all employees.' This is how Kaisa Nuikkinen, the head architect in the Helsinki City Education Department, describes the Finnish concept of school construction. Transparency and openness create a communicative atmosphere which should promote an exchange both between and among those learning and those teaching. [fig.4]

The dissolving of the classroom condition can be even more rigorously pursued, as shown by the examples of Bakkeløkka in Norway by NAV architects and Hellerup in Denmark by Arkitema. Both schools completely renounce class units and provide open learning landscapes. Under the guidance of mentors, pupils put together their own personal program of learning. Germany and Scandinavia were already experimenting with open spatial structures of this type around 1970. Subsequent construction measures in the Laborschule [laboratory school] Bielefeld, founded in 1974, show that the back-and-forth disruption arising from an open spatial situation is too high for certain subjects. Educators particularly bemoaned the lack of places to retreat to and preparation rooms. Such protected areas are available in Hellerup. The school in Bakkeløkka has been, moreover, divided into clearly defined sub-units of around 90 pupils. These units have at their disposal open spaces as well as spaces which can be closed off. [fig.3/5]

That distraction-free spaces for concentrated lessons can substantially boost school performance is verified by a recent study on successful school instruction.[1] Many educators emphasise the significance of concentrated, and some of them of frontal, instruction in the class unit.[2]

So, then, schoolroom rather than open plan? The interesting architectural interplay between intimate learning spaces and public-access zones, as exemplarily implemented at the school in Paspels by Valerio Olgiati and permanently embedded as an image in the minds of many Swiss architects, is also found in the Linden Primary School in Niederhasli by Bünzli & Courvoisier. In the majority of projects, however, the need for increased openness and transparency is finding expression; the school wants to be understood as a large unit and not as an aggregation of individual classes.

How such a community school functions can be seen in a striking example: the privately run International School in Wädenswil by Galli and Rudolf. Independent of any bells sounding the beginning and ending of classes, the children stream through the building, arrange themselves in groups for all

1 See Christine Paul and Kurt Reusser, 'Das Klassenzimmer-Video', NZZ am Sonntag, 11 May 2003, p.72.

2 Miklos Gimes, 'Alte Schule', Das Magazin, 29 November 2003.

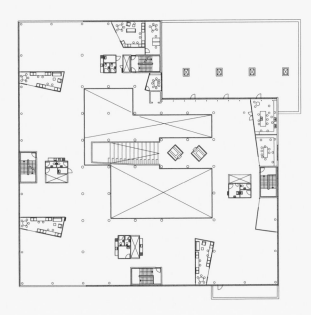

fig.3 Open Space: Die Teambüros der Lehrenden und
die Sanitärkerne bilden Inseln in der
offenen Lernlandschaft und definieren vier
«home areas» von 330 bis 400 Quadratmetern.
**Gesamtschule Hellerup,** Kopenhagen.

Plan: Arkitema

Open Space: The team offices for teachers
and sanitary facilities form islands in
the open learning landscape and loosely define four 'home areas' of 330 to 440 square
meters. **Hellerup Comprehensive School,**
Copenhagen.

Plan: Arkitema

fig.4 Die Halle ist das Identifikationszentrum
der **Aurinkolahti-Schule** in Helsinki.
Sie dient gleichzeitig als Mensa, Theatersaal,
Erschliessung, Begegnungs- und Arbeitsort.

Foto: Mikko Auerniitty

The hall is the identifying centre of the
**Aurinkolahti School** in Helsinki. It serves
simultaneously as a canteen, auditorium,
access area, meeting and work place.

Photo: Mikko Auerniitty

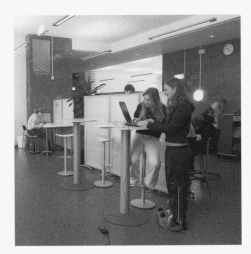

fig.5 Lernen in Arbeitsatmosphäre.
**Bakkeløkka-Sekundarschule,** Nesodden-Oslo.

Foto: Kim Müller

Learning in a work atmosphere: **Bakkeløkka
Secondary School,** Nesodden-Oslo.

Photo: Kim Müller

zurück. Schüler und Eltern informieren sich am Empfangsschalter über das Schulangebot und Veranstaltungen. Durch die internen Fenster kann in jedes Unterrichtszimmer geblickt werden — meist stehen aber ohnehin alle Türen offen. Konsequenterweise werden Unterrichtszimmer und Korridorbereich hinsichtlich Beleuchtung und Akustik gleich behandelt. [fig.6/10]

Um die richtige Balance zwischen Intimität und Austausch zu finden, hat Peter Märkli beim Schulhausprojekt Im Birch die Erschliessungswege getrennt und bedient sich darüber hinaus verschiedener anderer Mittel: Glasbausteine, Vorhänge und halböffentliche Vorzonen. Die Transparenz wird dosiert und kann individuell reguliert werden. Das Leben im Schulhaus soll spürbar sein, gleichzeitig muss aber konzentrierter Unterricht stattfinden können. Der steuerbare Austausch in überschaubaren Einheiten mit zwei bis sechs Klassen findet sich immer wieder als Thema bei den von uns zusammengestellten Projekten.

### Die Nutzbarkeit der öffentlichen Bereiche

Hohe Sicherheitsstandards erschweren in der Schweiz das Bemühen, die «brachliegenden» Korridorflächen als Aktionsräume für den Unterricht zu aktivieren. Die feuerpolizeilichen Vorschriften lassen eine Bespielung der Erschliessungsbereiche nur zu, wenn die Klassenzimmer über zusätzliche Fluchtwege verfügen. Dies lässt sich bei Neubauten durchaus mit vertretbarem Aufwand realisieren, wie das Projekt Leutschenbach (Zürich) von Christian Kerez beweist. Dort besitzen die Klassenzimmer je eigene, rückwärtige Fluchtwege über umlaufende Balkone und separate Nottreppen. Dem zusätzlichen Aufwand steht ein Gewinn an Flächen für neue, klassenübergreifende Lernformen gegenüber. Andere Lösungen zu diesem Thema fanden sich in der Zürcher Schulanlage Im Birch wie auch in den Wettbewerbsprojekten Herti (Zug) und Les Ouches (Genf). Die genaue Kenntnis der feuerpolizeilichen Bestimmungen und eine enge Zusammenarbeit mit den zuständigen Stellen sind erforderlich, damit die öffentlichen Zonen später tatsächlich auch nutzbar sind. Der Blick auf die skandinavischen Beispiele zeigt, dass gewisse Bestimmungen dort weniger restriktiv gehandhabt werden. Insbesondere in Helsinki werden die öffentlichen Erschliessungsflächen sehr vielseitig genutzt, ohne dass für alle anschliessenden Räume separate Fluchtwege bestehen. [fig. 7]

### Flexibilität, Identität und Robustheit

Die Forderung nach Flexibilität der Raumstruktur wird sehr unterschiedlich behandelt. Veränderungen in der Raumeinteilung können je nach Konzept innerhalb weniger Wochen, weniger Tage oder sogar ohne Aufwand spontan vorgenommen werden. Während bei der Schulanlage Kügeliloo oder der Ökoschule Mäder die Flexibilität durch Verschieben und Einsetzen von Trennwänden erreicht wird, fehlen in Hellerup die Wände fast ganz. Die Anordnung der Möblierung bestimmt dort die Flächeneinteilung. Durch Öffnen und Schliessen von Trennelementen

sorts of activities, or retreat to a niche in order to read. Pupils and parents find out about the school's offerings and events at the reception window. Glimpses into each instruction room can be taken through the internal windows — though for the most part, all the doors remain open anyway. Instruction rooms and corridor areas are consistently treated in the same way with regard to lighting and acoustics. [fig.6/10]

In order to find the right balance between intimacy and interchange, Peter Märkli separated the access ways at his school building project Im Birch and made use of a variety of other means as well: glass blocks, curtains and semi-public entry zones. The transparency is dispensed in doses and can be individually regulated. Signs of life should be perceptible in school buildings, but at the same time concentrated instruction needs to be able to take place. Controllable interchange in manageable units with two to six classes is a constant theme in the projects we assembled.

### The Usability of the Public Areas

High security standards are hindering efforts in Switzerland to activate 'unexploited' corridor areas as activity spaces for lessons. Fire regulations allow use of the access areas for activities only if the classrooms have additional escape routes. This can feasibly be carried out in new buildings and with justifiable expenditure, as proven by the Leutschenbach Project (Zurich) by Christian Kerez. In this school the classrooms each have their own rear escape routes over balconies encircling the building and separate fire escapes. Offsetting this extra expenditure is the addition of space for new forms of learning that involve more than one class. Other solutions with regard to this issue were found in the school facility Im Birch in Zurich as well as in the competition projects, Herti (Zug) and Les Ouches (Geneva). An exact knowledge of the fire regulations and close cooperation with the appropriate authorities are necessary so that the public zones are indeed usable later. A glance at the Scandinavian examples shows that certain regulations are less restrictively implemented there. In Helsinki in particular, the public access areas are used in such a wide variety of ways without the existence of separate escape routes for all contiguous rooms. [fig.7]

### Flexibility, Identity and Robustness

The demand for flexibility of room structure is dealt with in a wide variety of ways. Changes in the organization of space can be carried out, depending on the concept, within a few weeks, days, or even spontaneously without expenditure. While long-term flexibility is achieved at the Kügeliloo school facility and at the *Ökoschule* [eco-school]

fig.6 Überlagerung und Vernetzung. Eingangshalle und Bibliothek der **Zurich International School,** Wädenswil.

Foto: Hannes Henz

Overlapping and interconnecting: Entrance hall and library of the **Zurich International School,** Wädenswil.

Photo: Hannes Henz

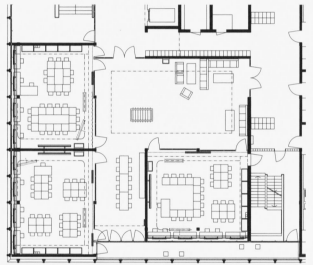

fig.7 Komplexe Lösung. Im **Schulhaus Im Birch** sorgen zusätzliche Fluchtwege über den Balkon oder ins Treppenhaus für die tatsächliche Nutzbarkeit des zentralen Arbeitsbereichs im Cluster. Die Glaswände der Klassenzimmer bringen Licht. Sie lassen sich durch Vorhänge schliessen.

Plan: Peter Märkli

Complex solution: At the **Im Birch School** additional escape routes via the balcony and into the stairwell ensure the actual usability of the central work area in the cluster. The glass walls of the classroom supply light. They can be closed off with curtains.

Plan: Peter Märkli

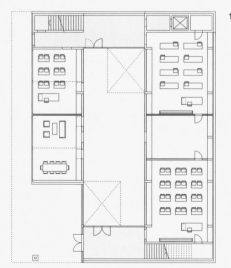

fig.8 Die Jahrgangseinheit: Im Projekt für die Gemeinde Oetwil schlagen Enzmann + Fischer eine flexible Struktur vor: Die Klassenzimmer eines Clusters können über den Jahrgangsraum zusammengeschlossen werden.

Plan: Enzmann + Fischer

The 'year unit': In the project for the municipality of Oetwil Enzmann + Fischer propose a flexible structure: The classrooms of a cluster can be combined via a 'year group space' located in the middle.

Plan: Enzmann + Fischer

können im Schulhaus In der Höh Klassenzimmer miteinander verbunden werden. Beim Wettbewerbsprojekt Herti von Enzmann + Fischer Architekten können Gruppenbereiche zu einem «Jahrgangsraum» kombiniert werden. Zur weiterentwickelten Grundrisslösung für ein neues Schulhaus in Oetwil am See (Wettbewerb, 1. Preis) schreiben die Architekten: «Je nach Ausstattung der Klassengeschosse resultiert ein zellenartiger Cluster mit vier Klassenzimmern um den Jahrgangsraum oder eine über Schiebewände veränderbare und hoch flexible Lernlandschaft.» Eine andere Spielart von Flexibilität weist die Gesamtschule Flims von Werknetz Architektur auf. Die Anordnung der Erschliessung und die räumliche Nähe erlauben eine wechselnde Verbindung von funktionalen Einheiten. Betriebliche Flexibilität bedeutet also nicht unbedingt Stützenrastergrundrisse und undifferenzierte Räumlichkeiten. [fig. 8]

Jedes der von uns besuchten Schulhäuser zeichnet sich durch eine eigene, typische Schulatmosphäre aus, die sich auch in der jeweiligen Materialisierung und Farbigkeit manifestiert. Dominiert im Schulhaus Scherr in Zürich die Lichtstimmung und die gewagte Farbigkeit der gemeinsamen Erschliessungszone, so ist im Schulhaus Linden in Niederhasli der Kontrast zwischen den Baustoffen Holz und Beton der vorherrschende Eindruck. Die Reduktion auf Materialfarben und wenige Farbtöne führt zu einer gedämpften, aber heiteren Stimmung in den Schulhäusern von Flims und Volketswil. Noch zurückhaltender sind Materialisierung und Farbigkeit im Projekt Im Birch (Zürich), das erst durch die Benutzer seine Farbtupfer erhalten wird. [fig. 9]

Beim Besuch von Schulhäusern fällt stets die von den Kindern, ihren Zeichnungen und Arbeiten, erzeugte Buntheit ins Auge. Einblicksmöglichkeiten in die Klassenzimmer oder bespielbare Korridorbereiche erhöhen diese Präsenz des Schullebens. Farbigkeit und Materialisierung sind in diesem Sinn vom Ort, der erwünschten Lernumgebung (Wohnatmosphäre, Ateliercharakter, Erlebnisraum, Schulstube etc.) und der zu erwartenden Inbesitznahme abhängig. Der zuweilen raue Schulalltag erfordert eine robuste Farb- und Materialwahl. Dennoch eignet sich eine rohe Werkstattatmosphäre zum Beispiel für eine heilpädagogische Schule oder eine Grundstufenanlage weniger. Sinnlichkeit und haptische Erfahrbarkeit durch die Verwendung von natürlichen Materialien sind ein wichtiger Aspekt für Projekte wie zum Beispiel die Lern-Förderschule Alzenau von Stephan und Stefanie Eberding. [fig. 10]

### Ganztägige Betreuungsangebote

Das Bedürfnis nach ganztägiger Betreuung der Kinder in der Schule wächst, vor allem in den Städten, als Folge veränderter Realitäten in der Familie wie am Arbeitsplatz. Die Stadt Wien, die in den neunziger Jahren eine grosse Zahl neuer Schulen baute, sieht in ihren Neubauten stets Küche und Speisesaal sowie Freizeitbereiche vor.[3] Auch in München gilt der Grundsatz: «Keine neue Grundschule ohne Tagesheim. Auf diese Weise

in Mäder by means of the shifting and inserting of partition walls, walls in Hellerup are almost completely lacking. There the arrangement of the furnishings determines the organisation of floor space. By opening and closing partition elements, classrooms at the In der Höh School can be connected with each other. In the competition project Herti by Enzmann + Fischer Architects, group areas are able to be combined to create a 'year unit' space. Regarding a solution for a more advanced ground plan for a new school in Oetwil am See (first prize in the competition) the architects write: 'Depending on the make-up of the floor where the classes are, the result will be a cubicle-like cluster with four classrooms around the 'year unit' space or a highly flexible learning landscape which is modifiable with sliding partition walls.' Another variant of flexibility is seen in the comprehensive school in Flims by Werknetzarchitektur. The arrangement of access and the spatial proximity allow for a changing connection of functional units. Operational flexibility does not then necessarily mean a ground plan with bearing elements arranged in a grid and undifferentiated rooms. [fig.8]

Each of the schools we visited distinguishes itself through a typical school atmosphere which also manifests itself in the respective use of material and colour. If the feel of the light and the bold colouring of the common access space is predominant in the Scherr School in Zurich, then the contrast between wood and concrete building materials establishes the prevailing impression in the Linden School in Niederhasli. The reduction to the natural colours of the materials and just few shades of colour results in a muted but cheerful mood in the schools at Flims and Volketswil. Even more restrained is the use of material and colour in the Im Birch (Zurich) project where the only dash of colour is provided by the users of the space themselves.

When visiting schools, one is always struck by the colourfulness generated by the children, through their drawings and projects. Opportunities to glance into classrooms and corridor areas which allow for pinning up drawings and so on enhance this visible presence of school life. In this respect, the use of material and colour is dependent on place, the desired learning environment (a home-like atmosphere, the feel of an atelier, a space for practical experiences, a schoolroom, etc.) and the expected occupants. The occasionally harsh everyday life of the school calls for a robust choice of colours and materials. Nevertheless a rough workshop atmosphere is not particularly suitable, for example, at a remedial school or an elementary level facility. Sensory and tactile experiences through the use of natural materials are an important aspect of projects such as the Alzenau Special Learning School by Stephan and Stefanie Eberding. [fig.10]

fig.9 Auch bei geschlossenen Unterrichtsräumen sind die Schülerinnen und Schüler im öffentlichen Bereich präsent. **Schulhaus Niederhasli.**

Foto: Alan Wakefield

Even with closed instruction rooms the pupils leave their mark on the public space. **Niederhasli School.**

Photo: Alan Wakefield

fig.10 Durchblick. **Zurich International School,** Wädenswil.

Foto: Alan Wakefield

Transparency: **Zurich International School,** Wädenswil.

Photo: Alan Wakefield

will man dem grossen Bedarf an ganztägiger Betreuung in einem freundlichen und anregenden Lern- und Lebensraum Rechnung tragen. Für Mittagessen, Übungszeiten, Ruhepausen und freizeit- und sozialpädagogische Betreuung soll ebenso Platz sein wie für den Unterricht.»[4]

Anders als in den Nachbarländern sind solche Grundsätze in der Schweiz — selbst in den Städten — noch immer die Ausnahme. Mensen, Mittagstische und Freizeitangebote in der Schule sind wenig verbreitet. In neuster Zeit wurden solche Angebote indessen als Standortfaktor von Wohngemeinden entdeckt und etwa für den Kanton Zürich durch Ratings klassifiziert (www.betreuungsangebote.zh.ch). [fig.12]

### Überlagerung und Vernetzung

Die wachsenden Ansprüche an die Schulen können in Anbetracht beschränkter finanzieller Mittel immer weniger durch spezialisierte Zusatzräume befriedigt werden. Mehrfachnutzungen sind daher ein wichtiges Thema. Die neue finnische Schule in Aurinkolahti ver-

### All-Day Day-Care Offerings

The need for all-day day-care for children in school is growing, above all in cities, as a result of changed realities both in family life and the workplace. The city of Vienna, which in the 1990s built a large number of new schools, always provides kitchens, dining halls as well as leisure areas in its new buildings.[3] In Munich as well, the basic principle holds: 'No new primary schools without all-day facilities. In this way the great need for all-day day-care can be accommodated in a friendly and stimulating learning and living space. There should be space for eating lunch, exercises, taking breaks, and recreational and socio-pedagogical socialization, just as there is for class instruction.'[4]

Such basic principles are still found only in exceptional cases in Switzerland — even in the cities. Canteens, meals and recreational offerings in school are not widespread. Meanwhile, very

---

3  Nikolaus Hellmayr: Wien, Schulbau. Der Stand der Dinge, Wien 2003

4  Landeshauptstadt München: München baut Schulen für die Zukunft, München 2001

3  Nikolaus Hellmayr, Wien, Schulbau: Der Stand der Dinge (Vienna, 2003).

4  Landeshauptstadt München, München baut Schulen für die Zukunft (Munich 2001).

fügt über eine zentrale Erschliessungshalle, die viele Nutzungen zulässt: Mensa für die Mittagsverpflegung, Fest- und Versammlungssaal, Gruppen-Arbeitsbereich etc. Die Privatschule in Wädenswil zeigt, dass die Verpflegung von 400 Kindern ohne Zusatzraum in der zentralen Halle erfolgen kann, wenn die Esstische nach Gebrauch zusammengeklappt und weggeräumt werden können. Die gleiche Halle dient bei den zahlreichen Grossanlässen dieser Schule als Erweiterung der Aula; die Bibliothek ist zugleich Lese- und Ruheraum für Schüler und Lehrer. Gerade diese Nutzungsdichte in den öffentlichen Bereichen führt zur erwünschten Belebung des Schulhauses und unterstützt die Idee der Schulgemeinschaft. [fig.4/11]

Auch Unterrichts-, Gruppen- und Mehrzweckräume können unterschiedlich benutzt werden, wenn die spezifischen Anforderungen der verschiedenen Nutzungsarten (Essen, Singen, Lesen, Spielen, Theater etc.) klein gehalten werden. So wird zum Beispiel im Schulhaus Riedmatt in Zug der Singsaal auch für den Mittagstisch und Versammlungen genutzt, und das Office kann bei kulturellen und sportlichen Anlässen auch in Verbindung mit der Turnhalle eingesetzt werden. Der Blick auf die in den Schweizer Schulhäusern meist ordentlich aufgehängten Belegungspläne verrät vielerorts ein erhebliches Optimierungspotenzial.

Ein Projekt mit breitem Nutzungsmix ist in Genf geplant: Primarschule, Kindergarten, Krippe, Mehrzweckhalle, Vereinslokalitäten und Räume für städtische Dienste werden im Schul- und Quartierszentrum Les Ouches von Andrea Bassi unter einem Dach zusammengefasst. Die Schule erhält auf diese Weise eine zusätzliche Bedeutung als Mittelpunkt ihres Stadtquartiers.

Die aktuelle niederländische Bewegung der «breiten Schulen» geht noch einen Schritt weiter: Verschiedene Institutionen teilen sich dort das gleiche Areal. Der «Kindercluster Voorn» (Utrecht) kombiniert zwei Schulen, eine Freizeitanlage mit Abenteuerspielplatz sowie die Kindertagesstätte. Im zentralen Bereich der Anlage liegen die gemeinsam genutzten Räume. Andere «breite Schulen» in Holland haben Institutionen wie die Jugendberatung oder die Volkshochschule integriert. Von den Überlagerungen erwartet man sich nicht nur Synergien und finanzielle Einsparungen durch bauliche Dichte, sondern auch eine markantere Präsenz der Schulen als öffentliche Institution.

Doch damit nicht genug: Die «breite Schule» wird ihrerseits Teil noch grösserer Komplexe. In Meerwijk (Haarlem, Holland) integriert Herman Hertzberger eine sehr grosse Schulanlage zusammen mit Freizeitzentrum, Kindertagesstätte und Sporthallen in eine Gesamtüberbauung, die zusätzlich Wohnungen, einen Supermarkt und einen öffentlichen Platz mit einschliesst. Die Schule belegt in der Gesamtanlage das Erdgeschoss. [fig.13/14]

Die Niederländer beschäftigen sich schon in der Phase der Neubauplanung mit späteren Umnutzungsmöglichkeiten: Denn die für Neubauquartiere typische Spitze der Kinderzahl flacht nach 15 bis 20 Jahren ab, so dass

recently such offerings were discovered as being factors in the competition between residential communities and for the canton of Zurich, for example, they were classified by means of ratings (www.betreuungsangebote.zh.ch). [fig.12]

### Overlapping and Interconnecting

Increasingly, as a result of the limited financial means available, the demands on schools cannot be satisfied through specialised supplementary spaces. Multiple uses are, for this reason, an important issue. The school in Aurinkolahti has a central access hall which allows for many different uses: a canteen for midday meals, a reception and assembly hall, an area for group work, etc. The International School in Wädenswil shows that the feeding of 400 children can take place — without a supplementary space — in the central hall as long as the dining tables can be folded up and cleared away after use. The same hall serves as an extension of the assembly hall during the numerous big events that take place at this school; the library is at the same time both a reading and rest area for pupils and teachers. It is exactly this concentration of uses in public areas that leads to the desired enlivening of the school building and supports the idea of the school community. [fig.4/11]

Instruction spaces, group spaces and multi-purpose spaces can also be used in a variety of ways when the specific demands of the different types of uses are kept at a minimum. For example, the singing room at Riedmatt school in Zug is also used for lunch and assemblies, and the office can also be used in conjunction with the gymnasium during cultural and sporting occasions. A glance at the building plans, more often than not found neatly hung on the walls of Swiss schools, reveals in many places a considerable potential for optimizing space.

One project with a broad mixture of uses is planned in Geneva: primary school, kindergarten, nursery school, multi-purpose hall, facilities for clubs, and spaces for municipal services will all be united under one roof at the school and neighbourhood centre Les Ouches by Andrea Bassi. Thus this school will attain additional significance as the centre of its municipal district.

The current Dutch movement 'community schools' (brede scholen), goes even one step further: different institutions share the same premises. The Kindercluster Voorn (Utrecht) combines two schools, a recreational facility with an adventure playground, as well as a day-care centre. The common-use rooms are in the central area of the facility.

Other 'community schools' in Holland have integrated institutions such as youth consultation or adult education centres. From this overlapping of

fig.11 Multifunktionaler Raum. Das «pädagogische Servicecenter» ist Arbeits- und Gruppenraum, Mediathek und Treffpunkt. **Heimdalsgade-Sekundarschule,** Kopenhagen.

Foto: Dorthe Krog

Multi-purpose space: The 'pedagogical service centre' is a work and group space as well as a media library and meeting spot. **Heimdalsgade Secondary School,** Copenhagen.

Photo: Dorthe Krog

fig.12 Mittagessen im **Schulhaus Lachenzelg.**

Foto: Theodor Stalder

Lunchtime at **Lachenzelg School.**

Photo: Theodor Stalder

weniger Schulraum gebraucht wird. Der Kindercluster Voorn ist aus separat erschlossenen, zweigeschossigen Einheiten zusammengesetzt, die im Bedarfsfall einzeln umgenutzt werden können. Dagegen ist die Schule von Herman Hertzberger in Haarlem, die ein Geschoss eines grösseren Gebäudes belegt, auf einer Schottenstruktur aufgebaut: Die Seitenwände der Schulzimmer sind tragende Schotten. Die gleichen Schotten bilden in den oberen Geschossen die Seitenwände von Maisonnette-Wohnungen. Während die innere Struktur der Schule damit festgelegt ist, lässt sich relativ leicht Schulraum zum Wohnen oder Wohnraum für die Schule umnutzen.

## M, L, XL oder XXL?

Günstige Schulhäuser sind kompakt und gross. Diese Erkenntnis ist nicht neu und wird durch die Kostenkennzahlen der «Schulwürfel» in Flims von Werknetz Architektur und in Mäder von Baumschlager Eberle bestätigt. Zugleich lässt sich durch kompakte Gebäudekörper

spaces one expects not only synergies and financial savings thanks to the structural concentration, but also a more striking presence of the school as public institution.

That's not all: the 'community school' may itself become part of an even bigger complex. In Meerwijk (Haarlem, Holland) Herman Hertzberger integrates a very large school facility with recreational centre, day-care centre and gymnasium into a comprehensive superstructure that also includes apartments, a supermarket and a central public area. The school occupies the ground floor of the overall facility. [fig.13/14]

The Dutch already begin to consider later, possible changes of use at the planning stage of new buildings: as the peak number of children typically found in districts consisting of new construction levels off after 15 to 20 years, less school space will be needed. The Kindercluster Voorn is made

Energie sparen. Doch stellt sich vermehrt auch die
Frage nach der Flächenökonomie. Wie könnte bei gleichem
«Nutzwert» eines Schulhauses der Flächenbedarf verrin-
gert werden? Die Architekten Gmür und Steib konnten
das enge Budget für ein Schulhaus der Gemeinde Hittnau
einhalten, indem sie die Erschliessungsbereiche auf
das absolut notwendige Minimum reduzierten. Die Schule
besteht primär aus Unterrichtszimmern und Treppen-
häusern. Genau das Gegenteil lässt sich bei den finnischen und holländischen Projekten beobachten. Dort
werden die Erschliessungsbereiche zugunsten der Nutzbarkeit vergrössert, und so entstehen bespielbare
Galerien und zentrale Hallen für soziale Anlässe — eine
Cafeteria, Aufenthaltsräume etc. Bei der International
School in Wädenswil wurden dagegen Turnhalle und
Unterrichtszimmer zu Gunsten des Gemeinschaftsbereiches
knapp gehalten. Wo die Ressourcen limitiert sind,
wird je nach Schulverständnis unterschiedlich gespart.

Unbestritten ist der Trend zur Zusammenfassung von
Schulstufen, was die Realisierung von jahrgangsüber-
greifenden Modellen wie der Grundstufe erlaubt. Tagesbetreuung, Schulleitungen, Spezialräume, Schulveran-
staltungen etc. erfordern Infrastrukturen, die in grossen Schulanlagen weitaus ökonomischer erstellt und
betrieben werden können als in Kleinschulhäusern. Die
Zusammenfassung verschiedenster Altersstufen auf einem Schulareal bedeutet eine grosse Herausforderung an
die Gestaltung von Gebäude und Umgebung. Während die
amorphen Gesamtschulen der siebziger Jahre vielfach als
unübersichtlich und lärmig galten, scheinen die neuen
Grossschulen durch die verbesserte räumliche Gliederung
und differenzierte Erschliessungsbereiche zu funktionieren. Der äusserlich grosse Massstab bei Schulanlagen
wie Flims, Oberbüren oder Im Birch wird beim Durch-
schreiten der Schulhäuser nicht unangenehm spürbar.
Letztlich sind aber auch die Schülerzahlen meist
bescheidener als bei den Grossanlagen früherer Prägung
und die Platzverhältnisse daher wesentlich grosszügiger. [fig. 15/16]

Von dem so genannten «kindergerechten Massstab»,
wie er von den Vertretern der Pavillonschule postuliert
wurde, hat sich der Schulhausbau im Sporthallenbe-
reich am weitesten entfernt. Durch die oftmals vesenkte
Lage nach aussen wenig präsent, eröffnen sich mit
den Dreifachhallen inklusive Zuschauerinfrastruktur im
Gebäudeinneren eindrückliche Raumdimensionen. Dabei
ist mit dem Wechsel der Spannweiten zwischen kleinteili-
gem Unterrichtsbereich und Sportbereich meist ein
statischer Kraftakt zu bewältigen. Eine interessante
Variante schlägt das Projekt Leutschenbach von Christian
Kerez vor: die Turnhalle als Gebäudekrone. Die Stapelung von Turnhalle und Unterrichtsbereichen verlangt in
jedem Fall eine erhebliche Gebäudetiefe. Da die Richtlinien in Bezug auf die Besonnung und die maximalen
Raumtiefen nur die Klassenzimmer betreffen und da die
moderne mechanische Lüftung keine schmalen Gebäudekörper
aus Gründen der Querlüftung mehr erfordern, werden
Grundrisse mit beträchtlicher Gebäudetiefe erprobt. Die

up of separately developed, two-storey units, the
uses of which can be changed individually and as necessary. In contrast, the school built by Herman
Hertzberger in Haarlem, which occupies a storey of a
larger building, is constructed using a partition
system: the side walls of the school rooms are
weight-bearing partitions. The same partitions form
the side walls of maisonettes on the top floors.
While the inner structure of the school is thus determined, it is relatively easy to shift the use
of space: school space can be used for living space
and vice versa.

## M, L, XL or XXL?

Low-cost schools are compact and large. This
insight is not new and is corroborated by the cost
of the 'cube schools' in Flims by Werknetz Architektur and in Mäder by Baumschlager Eberle. At the
same time, compact building structures can be
energy-savers. Of course, one is also faced, more
often than not, with the question of economy of
space. How might the spatial needs be reduced without changing the 'use value' of a school building?
The architects Gmür and Steib were able to keep
to the limited funds budgeted for a school building
in the municipality of Hittnau by reducing the
internal access routes to an absolute minimum. The
school consists primarily of instruction rooms
and stairways. The exact opposite can be observed in
the Finnish and Dutch projects. There the open
spaces are enlarged in favour of usability, thus
giving rise to galleries available for teaching and
learning and central halls for social occasions — a
cafeteria, recreation rooms, etc. The International
School in Wädenswil, on the other hand, skimped
on the gymnasium and instruction rooms in favour of
common areas. When resources are limited, schools
have different ways of saving, depending on their
understanding of educational priorities.

Without a doubt, the trend is towards combining educational levels, made possible by the
realization of designs that span age-groups, like
the Grundstufe (basic level, i.e., kindergarten
with the first two years of primary school). Day-
care programs, school administration, special
teaching rooms, school functions, and so on require
infra-structure that can be far more economically
constructed and operated in large school facilities
than in small ones. Combining many different age
levels in one school area means a major challenge
for the layout of buildings and their surroundings.
While the amorphous comprehensive schools of the
seventies were frequently regarded as confused and
noisy, the new large schools seem to function
thanks to the improved organization of space and
differentiated access areas. The large scale of
school facilities such as those in Flims, Oberbüren
or Im Birch when perceived from the outside is

fig.13 Breite Schule: Im Projekt **Meerwijk** in Haarlem (NL) belegen zwei Primarschulen das Erdgeschoss in einem Gebäudekomplex mit Kindertagesstätte, Freizeitzentrum, Sportanlage, Wohnungen und Supermarkt. Das Dach der Schule ist ein öffentlicher Platz.

Modellfoto: Herman Hertzberger

Community school: In the **Meerwijk** project in Haarlem, The Netherlands, two primary schools occupy the ground floor of a building complex with day-care centre, recreational centre, sport facilities, apartments and a supermarket. The roof of the school is a public square.

Photo of model: Herman Hertzberger

fig.14 Die zentrale Halle verbindet beide Schulen und erhält Licht von oben. **Meerwijk,** Haarlem.

Skizze: Herman Hertzberger

The central hall connects both schools and is lit from above. **Meerwijk,** Haarlem.

Sketch: Herman Hertzberger

Lichthöfe im Projekt Herti von Enzmann + Fischer erlauben die Belichtung der innen liegenden Gemeinschaftsbereiche und der Turnhalle. Durch solche Gebäudeeinschnitte entstehen spannende innere Blickbezüge in andere Geschosse und Nutzungen. Die damit einhergehende Orientierung nach innen ist beim Volta-Schulhaus von Miller und Maranta auch eine Reaktion auf die fehlende Schulhausumgebung.

### Innovation durch Architekturwettbewerb und Partizipation

Einige junge Schweizer Architekturbüros haben in den letzten Jahren ihre Existenz auf einem gewonnenen Schulhauswettbewerb aufbauen können. Dies ist einerseits eine Folge der vermehrten Schulbautätigkeit und andererseits ein Verdienst des in diesem Bereich funktionierenden Wettbewerbswesens, das auch unbekanntteren Büros oftmals eine Chance zur Teilnahme gibt. Dass junge Architektinnen und Architekten mit besonders lebhaftem Interesse auf die geänderten Bedürfnisse der Schule reagieren, zeigte sich deutlich bei den 2002 durchgeführten Schulhauswettbewerben der Stadt Zürich. Doch nicht nur durch die Selektion von innovativen

not perceived as unpleasant when walking through the school buildings. In the end, however, the number of pupils is also for the most part smaller than in the large facilities of past styles and the spatial ratio is more generous. [fig.15/16]

It is in the realm of the gymnasium that school construction has most widely deviated from the so-called 'child-oriented scale' as postulated by the advocates of the Pavilion School. A minor presence on the outside — because they are often sunken — impressive spatial dimensions open up in building interiors with halls triple in size, spectator infrastructure included. The change in span width between the teaching facilities, which are divided into small sections, and the sports area means one must more often than not cope with structural heavy lifting. Christian Kerez's Leutschenbach Project proposes and interesting variant: the gymnasium as crowning structure. The stacking of gymnasium and teaching facilities always calls for a considerable building depth. As the guidelines with regard to sunshine and maximum spatial depth only concern classrooms, and as modern mechanical ventilation

Teams und Projekten konnten architektonische Umsetzungen zu verschiedenen Aspekten der Schulreform gefunden werden: Die Preisverleihungen waren auch Anlass vertiefter Diskussionen zwischen Architekten und Pädagogen über zeitgemässen Schulhausbau. So erstaunt es nicht, dass einige der hier ausgewählten Projekte von Architektinnen und Architekten stammen, die selber bei Schulhauswettbewerben als Fachpreisrichter wirkten. Ausserdem fällt auf, dass momentan viele Projekte abseits der Städte realisiert werden, die Architekturbüros jedoch mehrheitlich in den urbanen Zentren, insbesondere in Zürich, heimisch sind. Eine häufige Forderung ist der stärkere und frühere Einbezug der Pädagoginnen und Pädagogen im Projektentwicklungsprozess. Diesem Bedürfnis wurde im zweistufigen, moderierten Verfahren der «teilautonomen Volksschule In der Höh» entsprochen. Als Resultat des Wunsches nach vielfach nutzbarem Begegnungsraum ist eine interessante, kleine «Schulstadt» mit internen Wegen und Plätzen entstanden. Das Bild des Schuldorfs findet sich im Projekt der Gesamtschule in Gelsenkirchen von Peter Hübner sehr direkt umgesetzt. Dort wurden mit Hilfe von Projektwochen auch Kinder in die Planung einbezogen. Die Annäherung von Schulanlage und Freizeitpark kann zwar aussenräumlich nicht überzeugen, gibt der Schule jedoch eine interessante Bedeutung im Agglomerationskontext. Durch frühe Zusammenarbeit zwischen Lehrerschaft und Planern ist die Open-Space-Schule in Hellerup entstanden. Dort hat die frühzeitige intensive Auseinandersetzung mit der Aufgabe die Radikalität des pädagogischen Konzeptes erst ermöglicht.

### Die grüne Wiese ist Vergangenheit

Schon 1953 beklagte Alfred Roth in seinem Buch «Die Neue Schule», wie wenig sich die Verkehrsplanung in unmittelbarer Nähe der Schulhäuser um die Qualität der Schulareale kümmert, die durch private Spekulation noch zusätzlich leidet. Seine Forderung nach einer prospektiven Stadtplanung mit ausreichenden Grünflächen für kindergerechte Pavillonschulbauten lässt sich heute nicht mehr erfüllen. Die meisten der aktuellen Projekte müssen bei beschränkter Arealfläche und in teilweise wenig attraktiven Lagen realisiert werden. Die von Roth ermittelte Arealfläche von ungefähr 35 Quadratmetern pro Schüler und die eingeschossige Pavillonschule lassen sich nur noch selten realisieren. Im Gegenteil: Gerade die neuen Raumbedürfnisse der Schule verkleinern oftmals die bestehenden Areale. Der weite Atem mancher bestehender Schulanlage wird durch Pavillons oder Erweiterungsvorhaben bedroht. Mit viel architektonischer Sorgfalt sind dennoch überzeugende Lösungen möglich. In der Schulanlage Bachtobel (Zürich) integrierten Graber + Pulver ein beträchtliches Neubauvolumen in die sensible Kleinschulanlage, ohne die Umgebungsqualität zu schmälern. Die Schulhausumgebungen kommen aber auch durch stetig wachsende Ansprüche an die Freiflächen immer mehr unter Druck: Feuerstelle,

has reduced the importance of cross ventilation and narrow building sections, ground plans with greater depth are being tested. The air wells in the Herti Project by Enzmann + Fischer allow the interior communal areas and the gymnasium to be exposed to light. Such incisions into the building result in exciting inner views into other floors and uses. The inward orientation that results from this at the Volta School by Miller and Maranta is also a reaction to the lack of outdoor space.

### Innovation through Architectural Competitions and Participation

Several emerging Swiss architectural firms have been able to establish themselves in the last few years by building upon a school-design competition they have won. On the one hand, this is the result of increased school construction; on the other hand, it is thanks to the fact that competitions truly do work in this sphere that often lesser-known firms are also given a chance to participate. That young architects are reacting with particularly lively interest to the changing needs of the school is clearly seen by the school construction competitions held by the city of Zurich in 2002. However, it was not simply through the selection of innovative teams and projects that architectural equivalents to different aspects of school reform were found: the award presentations were also occasions for deeper discussions between architects and educators about modern school construction. So it comes as no surprise that some of the projects selected here come from architects who themselves acted as expert jury members for school building competitions. In addition, it is also striking that at the moment many projects are being realised outside of cities while the majority of architectural firms continue to feel at home in urban centres, especially in Zurich.

A stronger involvement and earlier inclusion of educators in the project development process is frequently demanded. This need was met in the moderated, two-stage proceedings of the In der Höh Semi-Autonomous Comprehensive School. As a result of the desire for multiple usable spaces for meeting, an interesting, small 'school city' emerged, with internal paths and open areas. The image of the school village is translated directly into reality by Peter Hübner in his project for the comprehensive school in Gelsenkirchen. With the aid of project weeks, children were also included in the planning process of this school. The convergence of school facility and amusement park cannot, it is true, be spatially convincing from the outside, but it provides the school with an interesting significance in the context of the agglomeration. The Open-Space-School in Hellerup came into being as a result of the cooperation, early in the process, between

fig.15  Die Turnhalle im Dialog mit dem Quartier-
        massstab. **Projekt Leutschenbach,** Zürich.
        Modellfoto: Christian Kerez

        Gymnasium in dialogue with the large scale
        of the district. **Leutschenbach Project,**
        Zurich.

        Photo of model: Christian Kerez

fig.16  Der äusserlich grosse Massstab wird im Inneren
        nicht unangenehm spürbar. **Gesamtschule Flims.**
        Foto: Philipp Wieting

        The large scale as perceived from the
        outside is not unpleasant from inside.
        **Flims Comprehensive School.**

        Photo: Philipp Wieting

Finnenbahn, ökologische Ausgleichsflächen oder neue Spielgeräte sind nur eine kleine Auswahl möglicher Anliegen.

Die Zeit der locker bebauten und raumgreifenden Schulhausanlagen ist zumindest in städtischen Lagen vorüber. Die Umgebungsfläche muss sich heute sehr stark an den Gegebenheiten orientieren. Wohlweislich verzichten die meisten Richtlinien im Schulhausbau auf verbindliche Vorgaben. Um 1900 erstellte die Stadt Zürich im bereits dicht bebauten Arbeiterquartier Aussersihl Schulbauten mit knapper Umgebungsfläche, aber in Verbindung zum öffentlichen Grünraum der Bäckeranlage. Ganz ähnlich werden heute die Neubauprojekte in Zürich-Nord und am Albisriederplatz in Kombination mit öffentlichen Parkanlagen geplant. Wie weit sich Park- und Schulnutzung überlagern lassen, wird sich weisen müssen. Beim Projekt Albisriederplatz stehen als Ausweichmöglichkeit auf allen Geschossen gedeckte Aussenterrassen zur Verfügung, die sich an Duikers Freiluftschule in Amsterdam orientieren. [fig.17/18]

teaching staff and planners. There it was the early, intensive examination of the task that actually made the radical nature of the pedagogical concept possible.

### The Open Countryside is History

As early as 1953, in his book *Die Neue Schule,* Alfred Roth lamented how little traffic planning in the immediate vicinity of school buildings is concerned with the quality of the area around the school, an area that suffers even more as a result of private speculation. His call for a prospective city planning with sufficient green spaces for child-oriented pavilion school structures can no longer be achieved today. Most of the current projects have to be built in areas where space is limited and some in locations that are not particularly attractive. The amount of space determined by Roth, approximately 35 square metres per pupil, and the pavilion school can be realised only in

Im Zuge von gesellschaftlichen Entwicklungen findet
Schule jedoch immer mehr auch an peripherer und
unerwarteter Lage statt. Die am Rande der Industriezone
in Wädenswil eingemietete Privatschule ohne jegliche
Anbindung an ein lokales Wohnquartier steht hier stell-
vertretend für viele andere nicht staatliche Schulen.
Mietlösungen in der Dienstleistungszone werden nicht nur
von privater Seite in Betracht gezogen, wenn es darum
geht, der wachsenden Dynamik des Schulraumbedarfs
Herr zu werden. Beim Projekt Heimdalsgade in Dänemark
wurde eine ehemalige Gewerbeliegenschaft zum Schulhaus
umgenutzt. Dem kleinen Pausenhof stehen der Fabrik-
charme und die Offenheit der Räume entgegen, welche eine
anregende Atelieratmosphäre vermitteln. Die Idee der
Verbindung von Lernen und realem Leben wird im Projekt
City School in New Jersey in grösserem Massstab
verfolgt.[5] Verkommene Gebäude in einem verwahrlosten
Stadtzentrum sollen zu Schulzwecken umgenutzt und
aufgewertet werden. Die Schule dient dabei als Motor
für die Stadtteilreparatur. Der Ort des Lernens verlässt
das geschützte Geviert der Schulanlage. [fig.19]

rare instances. On the contrary: it is actually the
new increased spatial requirements of the school
that often reduce the existing surrounding areas.
The expansiveness of many existing school facilities
is threatened by the construction of pavilions or
added buildings on the site. Nevertheless, great
architectural diligence makes convincing solutions
possible. At the Bachtobel School (Zurich) Graber +
Pulver integrated a large new building structure
into the sensitive small school facility without
diminishing the quality of the surrounding area.
School surroundings are also, however, coming under
more and more pressure as a result of steadily growing demands on open spaces: grill pits, running
paths or new playground equipment are just a small
selection of possible concerns.

The time is past, at least in urban locations,
for uncongested, expansive school building facilities. Today the surrounding areas are forced to
adapt very strongly to existing circumstances.
Most school construction guidelines very prudently
abstain from binding specifications. Around 1900
the city of Zurich erected schools in the already
densely developed working-class district of
Aussersihl. These schools had confined surrounding
areas but were connected to the Bäckeranlage public
park. In a very similar way the projects in Zurich-
North and on Albisriederplatz are being planned
in combination with public parks. Just how far park-
and school uses can overlap remains to be seen.
In the Albisriederplatz Project, covered outside
terraces on each storey provide a place to escape,
following the model of Johannes Duiker's Openlucht-
school [Open-Air School] in Amsterdam. [fig.17/18]

In the wake of social change, schools, however,
are also occurring more and more in peripheral
and undesirable locations. Having taken up residence
on the edge of the industrial zone, the International School in Wädenswil is without any link to a
local residential district — it is for our purposes
representative of many other non-state-run schools.
Renting in the services sector zone is an option not
only considered by the private realm. In the Heimdalsgade Project in Denmark, a once commercial
property was converted for use as a school building.
Countering the small recess courtyard is the charm
of the factory and the openness of the spaces, which
impart a stimulating atelier-like atmosphere. The
conjunction between learning and real life is pursued on a large scale in the New Jersey City School
Project.[5] Dilapidated empty buildings in a run-down
city centre are to be reutilised and upgraded for
school use. The school will then serve as an impetus
for the revitalization of the entire district.
The site of learning is venturing outside the protective walls of the school facility. [fig.19]

5  Roy Strickland: Designing a City of Learning,
   Paterson, NJ, 2001

5  Roy Strickland, Designing a City of Learning,
   (Paterson, NJ, 2001).

fig.17 Schulstadt. Die dichte Bebauung des Schulareals wird durch öffentliche Parks
kompensiert. Die Grösse der Anlage erlaubt
Angebote wie Mensa, Saal und Sporthalle.
**Schulanlage im Birch,** Zürich.

Foto: Georg Gisel

School town: The dense development area
around the school is offset by public parks.
The size of the facility allows offerings
such as canteen, auditorium and gymnasium.
**Im Birch School,** Zurich.

Photo: Georg Gisel

fig.18 Aussenraum: Im dicht bebauten Quartier
Hardau teilt die Schule ihr Areal mit einem
öffentlichen Park. Analog zum Wohnungsbau
besitzt die Schule auf allen Geschossen
den Klassen zugeordnete Aussenräume. **Projekt
Albisriederplatz,** Zürich.

Bild: bbesw Architekten

Outside space: In the dense development district of Aussersihl the school shares its
space with a public park. Analogous to housing construction, the school has outside
spaces associated with the classrooms on all
stories. **Albisriederplatz Project,** Zurich.

Image: bbesw architects

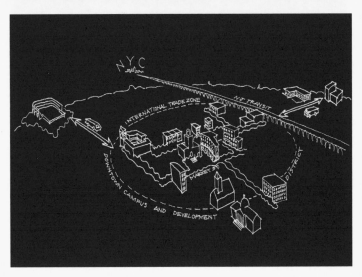

fig.19 Die Anfangsinvestition der Schule ermöglicht
die Instandsetzung von Altbauten auch
für private Nutzungen (Geschäfte, Wohnungen).
**Paterson,** New Jersey (USA).

Bild: Roy Strickland

The school's initial investment makes
possible the restoration of old buildings
for private use as well (businesses,
apartments). **Paterson,** New Jersey (USA).

Sketch: Roy Strickland

Schulhäuser auf dem Bühl in Zürich-Wiedikon,
von Stadtbaumeister Arnold Geiser 1899—1901,
Postkarte um 1920. Bild: Photoglob

Group of schoolhouses, Bühl,
Zurich-Wiedikon (Arnold Geiser 1899—1901),
Postcard (1920): Photoglob

Adrian Scheidegger

# Wie viel Raum braucht die Schule?

## Veränderte Raumverhältnisse

Die Schulanlage Bühl in Zürich-Wiedikon mit zwei Schulhäusern und Turnhalle liegt neben der gleichzeitig erbauten Kirche in beherrschender Lage auf einem Hügel westlich des Stadtzentrums von Zürich. Sie demonstriert mit ihrer eindrücklichen Erscheinung, welch hohen Stellenwert Bildung in der Entstehungszeit dieser Schule besass.

Das Schulhaus Bühl A wurde im Jahr 1901 für 23 Primarklassen mit ungefähr 1'400 Schülerinnen und Schülern gebaut. Die Schule umfasste damals 23 Klassenzimmer, drei Handarbeits- und Werkräume, einen Musik- und zwei Zeichensäle, einen Ausstellungssaal, ein (kleines) Lehrerzimmer mit Sammlung, eine Schulküche und eine Hauswartwohnung. Zusätzlich standen grosszügige Materialräume im Untergeschoss und eine Turnhalle im benachbarten Schulhaus Bühl C zur Verfügung. Die Regelklassen besuchten damals 60 bis 70 Schülerinnen und Schüler, in den «Kleinklassen» wurden rund 30 Kinder unterrichtet.[1]

Und heute? Im Jahr 2004 sind im gleichen Schulhaus rund 350 Kinder in 21 Klassen eingeteilt. Im Verlauf der vergangenen 100 Jahre wurden eine Bibliothek und verschiedene Werkräume eingerichtet, zudem wurde der Bereich für die Lehrpersonen vergrössert. Die Schulküche, die Zeichen- und Ausstellungssäle sowie verschiedene Materialräume wurden dagegen aufgehoben. Doch im Wesentlichen findet der Unterricht in denselben Räumen wie damals statt, in Räumen, die in dieser langen Zeit die verschiedensten pädagogischen und betrieblichen Konzepte «erlebt» haben. Sie bilden den Rahmen für einen immer wieder aufs Neue innovativen und modernen Unterricht.

Die für den Unterricht zur Verfügung stehende Raumfläche ist in den letzten 100 Jahren im Schulhaus Bühl pro Klasse nur leicht angestiegen; hingegen hat sich der Raumbedarf pro Schüler in der gleichen Zeitspanne aufgrund der gesunkenen Klassengrössen etwa verdreifacht.

## Neue Anforderungen an den Schulraum und ihre Umsetzung

Es ist unbestritten: Gesellschaft und Schule haben sich im Laufe des 20. Jahrhunderts grundlegend verändert. Zu Beginn des Jahrhunderts ging es der Schule im Wesentlichen um die Vermittlung grundlegender Kulturtechniken (Lesen, Schreiben, Rechnen) und um die Erziehung zu Disziplin und Gehorsam. Heute sollen und wollen Schülerinnen und Schüler befähigt werden, mit den Herausforderungen der Gegenwart und der Zukunft angemessen umzugehen. Mit den Lehrzielen haben sich auch die Rahmenbedingungen und Methoden des Lehrens und Lernens grundlegend verändert. Dies hat

1 Henry Baudin: Les Constructions Scolaires en Suisse, Genf 1907

Adrian Scheidegger

# How Much Space Do Schools Need?

## Changed Relationships to Space

The Bühl School in Zurich-Wiedikon, with two school buildings and a gym, occupies a commanding position on a hilltop west of the Zurich city centre, next to the church that was built at the same time. With its impressive appearance, it shows the high value placed on education at the time it was built.

The school building Bühl A was built in 1901 to house twenty-three primary classes with approximately 1,400 pupils of both sexes. At that time the school consisted of twenty-three classrooms, three handicrafts and home economics rooms, one music and two drawing rooms, an exhibition hall, a (small) teachers' room with a collection, a school kitchen and a caretaker's flat. There were also spacious storage rooms in the basement and a gym in the neighbouring school building Bühl C. At that time, sixty to seventy pupils of both sexes attended the regular classes, while approximately thirty children were taught in special needs classes.[1]

And today? In 2004 the same school building houses about 350 children, organised into twenty-one classes. In the course of the last hundred years, a library and various work rooms were established, and the teachers' area was expanded. By contrast, the school kitchen, the drawing room and the exhibition halls as well as various storage rooms were abolished. At bottom, however, instruction continues today in the same rooms where it took place then, rooms that throughout their long history have 'lived through' a variety of pedagogical and operational models. They represent the constant frame for a process of instruction that is updated time and again and hence perpetually innovative and modern.

The floor area per class that is available for instruction at the Bühl School has risen only slightly in the last hundred years. By contrast, the available space per pupil has effectively tripled during the same period due to falling class sizes.

## New Demands on School Space and their Implementation

It is an undisputed fact that in the course of the twentieth century society and school changed in fundamental ways. At the century's beginning the school was essentially concerned with the transmission of basic cultural techniques (reading, writing, arithmetic) and the inculcation of discipline and obedience. Today, pupils are supposed to be — and want to be — enabled to relate appropriately to the challenges of the present and the future. Along

1 Henry Baudin, Les constructions scolaires en Suisse (Geneva, 1907).

Auswirkungen auf den benötigten Raum. Fünf Trends charakterisieren die neuen Anforderungen:

1. Die Schülerinnen und Schüler verbringen mehr Zeit auf dem Schulareal. Die Gesellschaft hat heute andere Erwartungen an die Schule: Die Vereinbarkeit von Familie und Beruf beispielsweise ist zu einem wichtigen Anliegen geworden. Die Schule versucht, mit der Einführung von Blockzeiten, dem Angebot von Mittagstischen oder mit ganztägigen schulergänzenden Betreuungsangeboten den neuen Anforderungen gerecht zu werden.

2. Schülerinnen und Schüler werden individueller wahrgenommen. Erfahrungshintergrund, Voraussetzungen und Kenntnisse der Kinder sind bereits beim Eintritt in die Schule stark differenziert. Dem Gebot der Chancengleichheit folgend, reagiert die Schule mit einer verstärkten Wahrnehmung von Stärken und Schwächen jedes einzelnen Kindes, mit individuellen Lernprogrammen und gegebenenfalls mit Fördermassnahmen.

3. Schülerinnen und Schüler beginnen früher zu lernen. Die schweizerischen Kinder werden im interntionalen Vergleich spät eingeschult. In verschiedenen Kantonen werden neue Modelle getestet, die einen früheren und sanfteren Schuleinstieg ermöglichen sollen.

4. Schülerinnen und Schüler sind stärker in Bewegung. Die Vielfalt der heute praktizierten Lehr- und Lernformen ist gross. Werkstattunterricht, Projektlernen oder Gruppenarbeiten lösen Bewegung im Klassenzimmer aus und beanspruchen mehr Platz. Zum Lernen gehören Bewegung und Innehalten, Austausch und Konzentration.[2] Die Vermittlung von Wissen in abgeschlossenen Fachlektionen nach festem Stundenplan wird zunehmend von fächer- und lektionenübergreifenden, selbstbestimmteren Lernformen abgelöst.

5. Schülerinnen und Schüler sind Teil einer Schule, und diese ist Bestandteil eines Quartiers. Die Klasse ist keine abgeschlossene Welt mehr, sie versteht sich als Teil einer Schule. Die Zusammenarbeit über die Klassengrenzen hinaus hat einen grossen — und steigenden — Stellenwert. Innerhalb einer Schuleinheit sollen sämtliche schulischen Angebote erbracht und möglichst alle im Einzugsgebiet wohnhaften Kinder unterrichtet werden können, auch diejenigen mit besonderen Bedürfnissen. Die Schule wiederum versteht sich verstärkt als Teil der Gemeinde, sucht die Zusammenarbeit und öffnet sich für deren Bedürfnisse.

Insgesamt wird der Schulraum aufgrund dieser Trends heute intensiver genutzt als in der Vergangenheit. Gleichzeitig werden die einzelnen Schulen und ihre Leitungen mit den neuen Formen der Schulorganisation stärker in die Verantwortung für die optimale Nutzung der Raumressourcen und für die Öffnung der Räume für schulhausübergreifende Angebote eingebunden. Art und Intensität der Raumnutzung haben sich also in den letzten 100 Jahren deutlich verändert. Die grosse Bedeutung des Raumes für die Entwicklung der Kinder aber ist geblieben.[3]

with their pedagogical goals, the framework conditions and the methods of teaching and learning have also changed fundamentally. This has repercussions for the space that schools require. The new demands are characterised by five trends:

1. Pupils spend more time on the school grounds. Society has changed expectations of schools today. For example, the compatibility of family and career has become an important concern. Schools are seeking to meet these new demands by introducing school beginning and ending times that are the same for all students and offering midday meals or all-day supplementary child care programs.

2. Pupils are considered as individuals to a greater extent. Children's experiential background, qualifications and knowledge are already highly differentiated when they begin school. Following the dictate of equality of opportunity, schools are reacting with a heightened appreciation of each individual child's strengths and weaknesses, with individual learning programs and if necessary special assistance.

3. Pupils begin to learn earlier. Swiss children start school late compared to those of other countries. In various cantons, new models are being tested which should make it possible for children to start school earlier and more gently.

4. Pupils move more than they once did. Workshop instruction, project-based learning, or group work introduce movement into the classroom and require more space. Learning involves both motion and rest, interaction and concentration.[2] The communication of knowledge in self-contained lessons on different subjects and according to a fixed schedule is increasingly giving way to more autonomous forms of learning that cross disciplinary and lesson boundaries.

5. Pupils form part of a school, and the school forms part of a neighbourhood. The class is no longer a world unto itself but regards itself as part of a school. A high and increasing value is placed on collaboration across class boundaries. It is supposed to be possible to provide all school-related offerings and to educate as many as possible of the children who live in the area served, including those with special needs. The school in turn increasingly regards itself as a part of the community. It seeks out possibilities for collaboration and opens itself to the community's needs.

Because of these trends, schools make more intensive use of space today than they did in the past. At the same time, with the new forms of school organization, individual schools and their administrations exercise increased responsibility for the optimal

2 Peter Gasser: Neue Lernkultur. Eine integrative Didaktik, 2. Auflage, Aarau 2002

3 Vgl. Thomas Odinga: Schulbau wohin? Architektur und Pädagogik — ein schwieriges Miteinander, in: werk, bauen und wohnen 1/2 (2003)

2 Peter Gasser, Neue Lernkultur: Eine integrative Didaktik, 2nd ed. (Aarau, 2002).

Ein Kind entwickelt Vertrauen in seine Umgebung, wenn es sich in ihr gut zurechtfindet und wohlfühlt. Die «Orientierungseignung» des Raumes spielt für die Entwicklung des Selbstvertrauens eine wichtige Rolle. Da Kinder ihre Umgebung mit Vorliebe von geschützten Orten aus beobachten und sie schrittweise in Besitz nehmen, sind sie auf Rückzugsnischen einerseits und offene Zonen andererseits angewiesen. Nicht nur der Ausblick in die freie Natur, sondern auch bestimmte Farben und Formen beeinflussen das Wohlbefinden positiv. Die Integration der Schülerinnen und Schüler in die Schulgemeinschaft wird zudem durch eine geschickte Anordnung der Räume und der Begegnungszonen unterstützt. Umgekehrt begünstigen eine abwechslungsarme und wenig stimulierende Architektur, schlechte Ausstattung und zu kleine Räume das Störverhalten von Schülerinnen und Schülern. Doch wie viel Raum benötigt die heutige Schule wirklich?

### Die kantonalen Richtlinien

In den meisten schweizerischen Kantonen sind auf der Stufe der Volksschule die Gemeinden für den Schulbau zuständig. Die Kantone sind vielerorts die Bewilligungsinstanz, zudem beteiligen sie sich an den Baukosten. Im Allgemeinen sind Bewilligung oder Subventionierung an die Einhaltung von bestimmten Anforderungen gebunden, welche in entsprechenden Richtlinien festgehalten sind.

Ende 2003 hat die Stadt Zürich eine Studie zum Vergleich von Richtlinien und Kostenvorgaben im Schulbau in den Schweizer Kantonen in Auftrag gegeben.[4] Ein wichtiges Element in dieser Untersuchung sind die Erhebung und der Vergleich von Richtlinien zu Schulraumflächen in den Schweizer Kantonen. Erste Ergebnisse werden nachfolgend zusammengefasst:

In den meisten Kantonen bestehen «Anforderungsrichtlinien»: Diese legen die Anforderungen bezüglich der Grösse und Ausstattung der Schulräume fest, welche aufgrund der ausgewiesenen Bedürfnisse in ein Raumprogramm aufgenommen werden können. Sie enthalten aber keine Vorgaben zur Anzahl der bereitzustellenden Räume. Aus diesen Richtlinien lassen sich daher keine Kennwerte zum Raumbedarf ableiten.

Einige Kantone verfügen über weitergehende «Planungsrichtlinien». Diese legen Anforderungen, Flächen und Anzahl der Räume fest, welche für eine Schulanlage bestimmter Grösse bereitzustellen sind. Zwischen den Kantonen bestehen deutliche Unterschiede im Detaillierungsgrad und in den enthaltenen Raumgruppen. Die meisten Richtlinien enthalten aber Angaben zu den Klassenzimmern, Spezial-Unterrichtsräumen (Handarbeit, Werkstätten, Schulküche etc.) und zum Lehrerbereich. Andere Raumgruppen (beispielsweise für Infrastrukturen oder für schulergänzende Betreuung) sind nur teilweise abgedeckt. Die nachfolgende Tabelle enthält eine zusammenfassende Übersicht über den Flächenbedarf für einige zentrale Raumgruppen. Es wird zwischen Primarstufe (in der Regel die ersten sechs

use of space and for the opening of that space to programs that transcend the school walls. The way that space is used and the intensity with which it is used have thus changed significantly in the last hundred years. The great and fundamental significance of space for children's development, however, has remained unchanged.[3]

Children develop a sense of trust in their environment when they feel good in it and find it easy to get oriented. The degree to which a spatial environment lends itself to this process of orientation plays an important role in the development of self-confidence. Because children prefer to observe their environment from protected locations and like to take possession of it gradually, they rely on niches to retreat to on the one hand and open areas on the other. Not only a view of the outdoors but also particular colours and shapes have a positive influence on their sense of wellbeing. A skilful arrangement of rooms and meeting areas also helps to promote the children's integration into the school community.

Conversely, a type of architecture that provides little variety and stimulation, poor furnishings and rooms that are too small encourage dysfunctional behaviour on the part of the pupils. But how much space do today's schools really need?

### The Cantonal Guidelines

In most Swiss cantons the municipalities are responsible for the construction of schools at the primary and secondary school level. In many places, the cantons are the allocating authority and also contribute to construction costs. In general, authorization or subsidization are contingent upon adherence to certain requirements, which are embodied in sets of corresponding guidelines.

At the end of 2003, the city of Zurich commissioned a study to compare school construction guidelines and cost estimates among the Swiss cantons.[4] One important element in this study is the gathering and comparison of floor area guidelines for schools in the Swiss cantons. Initial results are summarised below:

In most cantons there are 'requirements guidelines'. These define requirements concerning the size and interior furnishings of schoolrooms, which can then be incorporated into a space allocation program on the basis of demonstrated needs. However, they do not contain any specifications concerning the number of rooms there should be. It is therefore impossible to use these guidelines to derive characteristic figures for the amounts of available space.

Some cantons have 'planning guidelines' that go further. They define the required features, floor areas and number of rooms that must be available for a school of a particular size. There are significant

---

4  Schul- und Sportdepartement und Hochbaudepartement der Stadt Zürich: Vergleich von Richtlinien und Planungsvorgaben im Schulbau – Zwischenergebnisse. Bearbeitung: Metron, Zürich 2004

3  See Thomas Odinga, Schulbau wohin? Architektur und Pädagogik – ein schwieriges Miteinander, in: werk, bauen und wohnen 1/2 (2003).

4  Schul- und Sportdepartement und Hochbaudepartement der Stadt Zürich, Vergleich von Richtlinien und Planungsvorgaben im Schulbau: Zwischenergebnisse, treatment by Metron (Zurich, 2004).

| | Primarstufe / Primary Level | | | | | | | Framework Conditions |
|---|---|---|---|---|---|---|---|---|
| | FR | GE | JU | TG | VD | VS | ZH | |
| **Rahmenbedingungen** | | | | | | | | **Framework Conditions** |
| Jahr der Inkraftsetzung | 1997 | 1989 | 2002 | 1992 | 1984 | 1975 | 1999 | Implementation Year |
| Durchschnittliche Klassengrösse* | 19.8 | 20 | 17.4 | 20.5 | 20.1 | 19.7 | 20.1 | Average Class Size* |
| Anlagengrösse (Klassen) | 12 | 16 | 12 | 6 | 12 | 12 | 12 | School Size (Classes) |
| **Raumflächen pro Klasse (m$^2$)** | | | | | | | | **Floor area per class (m$^2$)** |
| Unterrichtsbereich | | | | | | | | Teaching Facilities |
| Klassenzimmer | 81 | 80 | 64 | 75 | 80 | 64 | 68 | Classrooms |
| Gruppen- / Therapieräume ** | 3.5 | 16.3 | n.B. | 12.5 | 13.4 | 0 | 8.5 | Group and Therapy Rooms** |
| Spezialräume | 27 | 11.3 | 26.7 | 33.7 | k.A. | 18 | 21.9 | Special Teaching Classrooms |
| Unterrichtsbereich total | 112 | 108 | 90.7 | 121 | 93.4 | 82 | 98.4 | Teaching Facilities, Total |
| Gemeinschaftsbereich | | | | | | | | Common Areas |
| Mehrzwecksaal | 11.9 | n.B. | 10.7 | k.A. | n.B. | k.A. | 8.5 | Multi-Purpose Hall, Aula |
| Bibliothek | 6 | 5 | n.B. | 12.5 | 6.7 | k.A. | 5.7 | Library |
| Lehrkraftbereich | 5 | 7.9 | n.B. | 17.5 | 6.7 | 9 | 16.5 | Teachers' Rooms |

| | Sekundarstufe I / Secondary Level I | | | | | | | Framework Conditions |
|---|---|---|---|---|---|---|---|---|
| | BL | FR | JU | TG | VD | VS | ZH | |
| **Rahmenbedingungen** | | | | | | | | **Framework Conditions** |
| Jahr der Inkraftsetzung | 1993 | 1997 | 2002 | 1992 | 1984 | 1975 | 1999 | Implementation Year |
| Durchschnittliche Klassengrösse* | 19.4 | 19.9 | 19 | 19.2 | 19.3 | 20.3 | 18 | Average Class Size* |
| Anlagengrösse (Klassen) | 24 | 18 | 18 | 12 | 18 | 18 | 18 | School Size (Classes) |
| **Raumflächen pro Klasse (m$^2$)** | | | | | | | | **Floor area per class (m$^2$)** |
| Unterrichtsbereich | | | | | | | | Teaching Facilities |
| Klassenzimmer | 66 | 72 | 64 | 80 | 80 | 64 | 68 | Classrooms |
| Gruppen- / Therapieräume ** | 5.5 | 0 | 7.1 | 15.8 | 15.6 | n.B. | 17 | Group and Therapy Rooms** |
| Spezialräume | 52.4 | 68 | 64 | 86.3 | 80 | 42.5 | 67.4 | Special Teaching Classrooms |
| Unterrichtsbereich total | 124 | 140 | 135 | 182 | 176 | 107 | 152 | Teaching Facilities, Total |
| Gemeinschaftsbereich | | | | | | | | Common Areas |
| Mehrzwecksaal | n.B. | 11.9 | 10.7 | 12.5 | n.B. | 4.7 | 5.7 | Multi-Purpose Hall, Aula |
| Bibliothek | 5.5 | 5 | n.B. | 6.9 | 6 | n.B. | 5.7 | Library |
| Lehrkraftbereich | 8.1 | 4.4 | n.B. | 12.5 | 9 | n.B. | 15.6 | Teachers' Rooms |

fig. 1 Schulraumbedarf pro Klasse in Quadratmetern für einige wichtige Raumgruppen nach den Planungsvorgaben verschiedener Schweizer Kantone. Quelle: Vgl. Fussnote 4

Required space per class in square metres for several important groups of rooms according to the planning guidelines of various Swiss cantons. Source: see footnote 4

n.B. Nach Bedarf
k.A. Keine Angabe
* Kantonale Durchschnittswerte für Regelklassen 2001
** Inkl. Reserveklassenzimmer und disponible Klassenzimmer, da diese zumeist als Gruppenräume genutzt werden

a/n: As needed
* Average cantonal figures for regular classes in 2001
** Including reserve and extra classrooms, since these are usually used as group rooms

n.B. > a/n

Primary Level: FR: Freiburg, GE: Geneva, JU: Jura, TG: Thurgau, VD: Vaud, VS: Valais, ZH: Zurich
Secondary Level I: BL: Basel-Landschaft, FR: Freiburg, JU; Jura, TG: Thurgau, VD: Vaud, VS: Valais, ZH: Zurich

Schuljahre) und Sekundarstufe I (Schuljahre 7 bis 9) unterschieden. Die Werte sind jeweils auf den Bedarf pro Klasse in Quadratmetern umgerechnet. [fig.1]

Die Richtlinien sind geprägt von Lehrplan, Schulorganisation und Schulpraxis zur Zeit ihrer Entstehung. Die Flächenangaben sind daher nur beschränkt vergleichbar. In allen Kantonen sind begründete Abweichungen zugelassen und vielerorts auch gängige Praxis. Ebenso werden verschiedene Richtlinien zur Zeit aktualisiert. Zu beachten ist weiter, dass der Flächenbedarf insbesondere bei den Spezialzimmern und den Gemeinschaftsräumen stark von der Gesamtkapazität der Anlage abhängt.

In allen Richtlinien steht pro Klasse ein Klassenzimmer zur Verfügung; in verschiedenen Kantonen wird zusätzlich ein disponibles Klassenzimmer verlangt. Insgesamt dürfte der Raumbedarf für eine Primarklasse für Unterrichtsräume, Gemeinschaftsräume und Lehrerbereich bei etwa 100 bis 150 Quadratmetern liegen, jener für eine Oberstufenklasse bei 130 bis 210 Quadratmetern.

Die bestehenden Richtlinien geben nur über die minimalen Anforderungen Auskunft. Der folgende Abschnitt untersucht den aktuellen tatsächlichen Raumbestand in schweizerischen Schulhäusern.

differences among the cantons in terms of the degree of detail these guidelines go into and the groups of rooms they discuss. Most of the guidelines, however, contain indications concerning the classrooms, the special teaching classrooms (handicrafts, workshops, school kitchen, etc.) and the teachers' area. Other groups of rooms (for example spaces for infrastructure or supplementary child care) are only partially covered. The table above contains a summary overview of the floor area requirements for several essential room groups. The table distinguishes between the primary level (usually the first six school years) and secondary level I (school years seven to nine). The figures are expressed in terms of square metres of floor area required per class. [fig.1]

The guidelines bear the stamp of the curriculum, school organization and school praxis that existed when they were written. The floor area requirements are therefore only comparable to a limited extent. Justified deviations are permitted in all cantons, and in many places they are common practice. Similarly, various guidelines are currently being updated. It should also be noted that the floor area requirements — especially for the special teaching classrooms and the common rooms — are heavily dependent on the school's total capacity.

## Das Raumangebot in bestehenden Schulhäusern

Wie viel Raum steht in den bestehenden Schulhäusern zur Verfügung? Zur Beantwortung dieser Frage hat die Stadt Zürich im Jahr 2000 eine Studie initiiert. Sie sollte den Flächenbedarf an Schulraum in verschiedenen Schweizer Städten vergleichen.[5] Dabei wurden Raumprogramme und Rahmenbedingungen von insgesamt 106 Schulhäusern in neun Schweizer Städten erhoben; es handelt sich um 69 Anlagen der Primarstufe, 21 Anlagen der Sekundarschule I und 16 gemischte Anlagen. Nachfolgend werden wesentliche Resultate und einige weitergehende Auswertungen der Studie zusammengefasst:

Das durchschnittliche Flächenangebot pro Klasse beträgt auf der Stufe der Primarschule rund 220 Quadratmeter; auf der Sekundarstufe I rund 300 Quadratmeter. Diese Flächen enthalten neben Unterrichts-, Gemeinschafts- und Lehrkräftebereich zusätzlich auch die Zirkulationsflächen. Weitergehende schulische Angebote wie Mittagstische oder Ganztagesangebote sind in diesen Zahlen jedoch nicht enthalten. Die Flächen für die Turnhallen wurden zwar erfasst, sind aber in den obigen Kennzahlen und in den weiteren Ausführungen nicht enthalten, da die Vergleichbarkeit in vielen Fällen nicht gegeben ist. Subtrahiert man die Zirkulationsflächen, so entspricht das durchschnittliche Raumangebot pro Klasse etwa dem Bedarf nach den Richtlinien des Kantons Zürich. Auf die eigentlichen Klassenzimmer entfällt in Primarschulen ein Drittel der Gesamtflächen, in der Sekundarstufe I ist es weniger als ein Viertel. Die Gemeinschaftsräume wie Mehrzwecksaal und Bibliothek machen weniger als 10 Prozent der Gesamtfläche aus. Beachtlich ist, dass mehr als 40 Prozent der total zur Verfügung stehenden Flächen als Zirkulationsflächen genutzt werden. [fig.2]

Insgesamt besteht im Vergleich zu den kantonalen Richtlinien ein Defizit an Gruppenräumen; dafür steht etwas mehr Raum in den Klassenzimmern selber zur Verfügung. Dies hängt unter anderem damit zusammen, dass nicht alle untersuchten Schulhäuser vollständig ausgelastet sind. Das Raumangebot der untersuchten Schulhäuser der Primarstufe schwankt stark, es liegt zwischen 140 und 300 Quadratmetern pro Klasse. Bei der Oberstufe bewegt sich das Angebot zwischen 210 und 500 Quadratmetern. Fig. 3 zeigt den erhobenen Raumbedarf pro Klasse in Abhängigkeit von der Gesamtkapazität der Anlage. [fig.3]

Im Rahmen der Studie wurden verschiedene Einflussgrössen erfasst, beispielsweise das Alter des Schulhauses oder der Anteil der fremdsprachigen Schülerinnen und Schüler. Es konnte zwar keine Einflussgrösse gefunden werden, die allein einen wesentlichen Teil der Schwankungen erklären würde. Schulhäuser mit geringem Raumangebot pro Klasse haben aber in der Regel eine hohe Auslastung und wenig Zirkulationsfläche. Zudem sind sie oft «pädagogisch unterversorgt». Es fehlen beispielsweise Gruppen- oder wichtige Spezialräume. Das gewählte Belegungssystem hingegen beeinflusst den Raumbedarf in den untersuchten Schulhäusern nicht: Sämt-

5  Amt für Hochbauten der Stadt Zürich und der Städte Burgdorf, Langenthal, St. Gallen und Thun: Benchmarking Schulraumnutzung. Schlussbericht. Bearbeitung: INFRAS, Zürich 2001

In all the sets of guidelines, there is one classroom for each class. In various cantons an extra classroom is required as well. On the whole, the space requirements for classrooms, common rooms and teachers' area would appear to be approximately 100 to 150 square metres for a primary class and 130 to 210 square metres for an upper school class. The existing guidelines only provide information about the minimal requirements. The following section examines the amount of space that is actually available in Swiss schools today.

## The Space on Offer in Existing Schools

How much space is available in existing schools? The city of Zurich began a study to answer this question in the year 2000. The study was intended to compare the floor area in schools in various Swiss cities.[5] Data concerning space allocation programs and framework conditions were collected for a total of 106 schools in nine Swiss cities. The study involved sixty-nine facilities at the primary level, twenty-one at secondary level I and sixteen mixed facilities. Core results and a number of further-reaching analyses are summarised below:

The average floor area per class stands at approximately 220 square metres at the primary school level and about 300 square metres for secondary school I. In addition to classrooms, common rooms and the teachers' area, these floor areas also include the circulation zones. However, they do not reflect school offerings such as midday meals or all-day programs. The study recorded the floor areas of gyms, but these are not contained in the figures shown above, because in many cases the data are not commensurable. Leaving out the circulation areas, the space on offer per class roughly corresponds, in terms of quantity, to the guidelines of the canton of Zurich. In primary schools, a third of the total area is used by the actual classrooms. At secondary level I, the figure is less than a fourth. Common rooms such as multi-purpose space and library constitute less than ten per cent of the total area. It is striking that more than forty per cent of the total available area is used for circulation zones. [fig.2]

On the whole, there is a shortage of group rooms as compared to the cantonal guidelines. On the other hand, there is somewhat more space available in the classrooms themselves. Among other things, this is because not all of the schools included in the study are being used to their full capacity. The space on offer at the primary schools included in the study varies widely. It ranges between 140 and 300 square metres per class. For the upper school classes, the space on offer ranges between 210 and 500 square metres. Figure 3 shows the floor area per class versus the total capacity of the facility. [fig.3]

5  Amt für Hochbauten der Stadt Zürich und Städte Burgdorf, Langenthal, St. Gallen und Thun, Benchmarking Schulraumnutzung. Schlussbericht, revised by INFRAS (Zurich, 2001).

**Flächenangebot nach Raumkategorie / Space on Offer by Room Type**

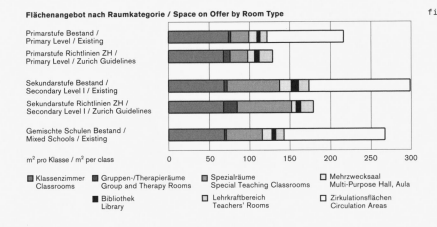

Primarstufe Bestand /
Primary Level / Existing

Primarstufe Richtlinien ZH /
Primary Level / Zurich Guidelines

Sekundarstufe Bestand /
Secondary Level I / Existing

Sekundarstufe Richtlinien ZH /
Secondary Level I / Zurich Guidelines

Gemischte Schulen Bestand /
Mixed Schools / Existing

m² pro Klasse / m² per class

| | | | |
|---|---|---|---|
| ▨ Klassenzimmer<br>Classrooms | ▨ Gruppen-/Therapieräume<br>Group and Therapy Rooms | ▨ Spezialräume<br>Special Teaching Classrooms | ☐ Mehrzwecksaal<br>Multi-Purpose Hall, Aula |
| ■ Bibliothek<br>Library | ☐ Lehrkraftbereich<br>Teachers' Rooms | ☐ Zirkulationsflächen<br>Circulation Areas | |

**Raumangebot pro Klasse / m² – Space on Offer per Class**

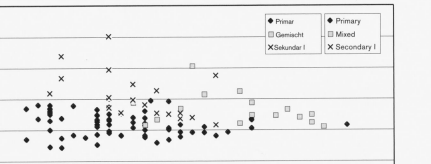

Anzahl Klassen / Number of Classes

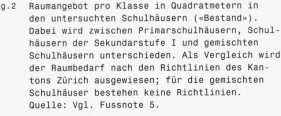

fig.2  Raumangebot pro Klasse in Quadratmetern in
den untersuchten Schulhäusern («Bestand»).
Dabei wird zwischen Primarschulhäusern, Schulhäusern der Sekundarstufe I und gemischten
Schulhäusern unterschieden. Als Vergleich wird
der Raumbedarf nach den Richtlinien des Kantons Zürich ausgewiesen; für die gemischten
Schulhäuser bestehen keine Richtlinien.
Quelle: Vgl. Fussnote 5.

Space on offer per class in square metres in
the schools studied ('existing'). The chart
distinguishes among primary schools, secondary level I schools and mixed schools. For
purposes of comparison, space requirements
according to the guidelines of the canton of
Zurich are also shown (no guidelines exist
for mixed schools). Source: see footnote 5.

fig.3  Raumangebot (Unterrichts- und Spezialräume,
Lehrerbereich, Mehrzwecksaal, Bibliothek und
Zirkulationsflächen) pro Klasse in Quadrat-
metern in den untersuchten Schulhäusern
in Abhängigkeit von der Gesamtkapazität der
Anlage. Quelle: Vgl. Fussnote 5.

Space on offer per class (classrooms and
special teaching classrooms, teachers' area,
multi-purpose space, library and circulation
areas) in square metres in the schools
studied, versus the total capacity of the
school. Source: see footnote 5.

liche Schulhäuser praktizieren eine feste Zuteilung der
Zimmer entweder zu den Klassen oder zu den Lehrpersonen.

### Die Raumprogramme neuer Schulbauten

Unterscheiden sich nun die Raumprogramme neuer
Schulen, welche in den letzten Jahren in grosser Zahl
geplant und gebaut wurden, von denjenigen der bestehenden Schulhäuser? Gibt es Anzeichen dafür, dass
baulich auf die erwähnten Entwicklungen reagiert wird?
Für die Beantwortung dieser Frage stehen zwei Quellen
zur Verfügung. Zum einen hat die Fachstelle für
Schulraumplanung der Stadt Zürich die Raumprogramme von
29 geplanten oder gebauten Schulhausneubauten oder
-erweiterungen aus dem Kanton Zürich untersucht.[6] Zum
anderen wurden für die im zweiten Teil des vorliegenden
Buches präsentierten Schulbauten die Raumprogramme
erfasst und ausgewertet: Die Daten lagen bei Fertig-
stellung des vorliegenden Textes für acht Projekte aus
der Schweiz vor, unter ihnen auch eine Privatschule.
Die aktuelle Datenlage erlaubt keine repräsentativen
Aussagen über den gesamten Raumbedarf pro Klasse;
hingegen können erste Folgerungen zur Grösse verschiedener Raumtypen gezogen werden.

Eine Analyse der durchschnittlichen Raumgrössen in
den neu gebauten oder projektierten Schulhäusern zeigt,
dass der pro Klasse zur Verfügung stehende Klassen-

Various influencing quantities were captured
by the study, including for example the age of the
school or the number of foreign-language pupils.
While it was impossible to find an influencing quantity that would account for a substantial portion
of the variations discovered by the study, schools
with a small amount of space on offer per class tend
to have a high level of utilization and little
circulation area. In addition they are often 'pedagogically undersupplied'. For example, they may
be missing group rooms or important special teaching
classrooms. By contrast, the system employed for
allocating rooms does not influence the amount of
available space at the schools that were studied.
All of the schools practice the fixed allocation of
classrooms by class or by teacher.

### The Space Allocation Programs of
### Newly Constructed Schools

Do the space allocation programs of new schools,
which have been planned and constructed in great
numbers in recent years, differ from those of existing schools? Are there indications that school
designs are reacting to the developments discussed
above? Two sources are available that help to answer
this question.

6  Fachstelle für Schulraumplanung der Stadt
Zürich: Neue Schulbauten im Kanton Zürich: Vergleich von Raumtypen, Zürich 2004

zimmer- und Gruppenraumanteil für die Primarstufe (22 Anlagen) im Durchschnitt bei 88 Quadratmetern liegt, für die Sekundarstufe I (14 Anlagen) bei 95 Quadratmetern. Die durchschnittliche Grösse eines neuen Mehrzwecksaals liegt bei rund 170, diejenige einer Bibliothek bei etwa 120 Quadratmetern. Es wird deutlich, dass die untersuchten Räume in den neu gebauten oder geplanten Schulhäusern durchschnittlich grösser sind als die entsprechenden Räumlichkeiten in den bestehenden Schulhäusern. Zudem sind sie grösser, als von den Richtlinien verlangt. [fig. 4]

Die «neuen» Klassenzimmer (inkl. Gruppenraumanteil) sind im Durchschnitt pro Klasse um mehr als 15 Quadratmeter grösser als die bestehenden, wobei die Differenz bei der Sekundarstufe I grösser ist als bei der Primarstufe. Ein ähnliches Bild zeigt sich bei Mehrzwecksaal und Bibliothek: Hier ist allerdings zu beachten, dass deren Grösse von der Grösse der Schulanlage und von den vorgesehenen externen Nutzungen abhängt. Dies erklärt die grossen Schwankungen.

Es lässt sich vermuten, dass die gewachsenen Raumflächen eine Reaktion auf die veränderten Rahmenbedingungen sind. Grössere Klassenzimmer ermöglichen und unterstützen eine Vielfalt von Lehr- und Lernformen. Bibliotheken und Mehrzwecksäle lassen viele unterschiedliche Nutzungen zu und sind zentrale Elemente im Konzept vieler moderner Schulen. Sie werden häufig für Schule und Quartier gemeinsam bereitgestellt und in ihrer Dimensionierung entsprechend angepasst. Auch für Kindergärten und Betreuungsräume ergeben sich neue Anforderungen. Diese sind an den neuen Schulbauten erst teilweise ablesbar, da die entsprechenden Diskussionen noch am Anfang stehen.[7]

### Fazit und offene Fragen

Die bestehenden Schulbauten sind zu einem grossen Teil innerhalb der letzten 150 Jahre entstanden. Auch wenn sie im Rahmen von Sanierungen und Erweiterungen immer wieder an neue Anforderungen angepasst wurden, spiegeln sie dennoch die pädagogischen und betrieblichen Grundüberlegungen ihrer Entstehungszeit. Gleichzeitig hat sich die Raumnutzung wie in allen Lebensbereichen verändert, der Raumbedarf hat zugenommen.

Im eingangs erwähnten Beispiel des Schulhauses Bühl ist der zunehmende und sich wandelnde Raumbedarf in erster Linie durch die deutliche Reduktion der Klassengrössen, durch eine leichte Reduktion der Anzahl der Klassen und durch die Aufhebung nicht mehr benötigter Spezialräume (Zeichensäle) aufgefangen worden. Das Raumangebot ist aber für eine Schule mit 21 Klassen und diversen Zusatzangeboten knapp, hilfreich wären insbesondere Gruppenräume. Die Untersuchung der bestehenden Schulhäuser hat gezeigt, dass viele von ihnen Raumdefizite aufweisen, was sie aber nicht daran hindert, ein modernes Schulangebot bereitzustellen. Teilweise dürften die einschränkenden Rahmenbedingungen sogar der Auslöser für innovative Ideen sein.

Firstly, the Fachstelle für Schulraumplanung der Stadt Zürich [Office for School Design and Planning of the City of Zurich] has studied the space allocation programs of twenty-nine new schools planned or actually constructed in the canton of Zurich.[6] Secondly, space allocation programmes were captured and analyzed for the school buildings presented in the second part of this book. When the present essay was written, data were available for eight projects from Switzerland, including a private school. The state of the data does not permit of representative conclusions concerning the total space available per class. However, it is possible to draw inferences concerning the sizes of different types of rooms.

An analysis of average room sizes in the projected or newly constructed school buildings shows that the average space available per class for classrooms and group rooms stands at 88 square metres for the primary level (22 facilities) and 95 square metres for secondary level I (14 facilities). The average size of a new multi-purpose space is approximately 170 square metres, while that of a library is about 120 square metres. It is clear that, on average, the rooms that were studied in the planned or newly constructed school buildings are larger than the corresponding rooms in existing school buildings. In addition, they are larger than they are required to be by the guidelines. [fig.4]

On average, the 'new' classrooms (including group rooms) are more than fifteen square metres larger per class than the existing ones. The difference is larger at secondary level I than it is at the primary level. A similar picture emerges for multi-purpose spaces and libraries. The size of these rooms is dependent, however, on the size of the school and the external uses planned for them. This explains the wide variations.

It is likely that the increased floor areas are a reaction to the changed framework conditions. Larger classrooms make possible and support a variety of forms of teaching and learning. Libraries and multi-purpose spaces allow for many different uses, and they are central elements in the design of many modern schools. They are often intended to be used by both the school and the neighbourhood, and their dimensions are selected accordingly.

New demands are also emerging for kindergartens and day-care spaces. These are only partially reflected in the new school buildings, because the discussions are still in the beginning stages.[7]

### Conclusion and Open Questions

The existing school buildings were built in large part within the last 150 years. Despite the fact that they have been updated time and again to meet new demands in the context of redevelopment efforts and expansions, they still reflect the basic

---

7 Zu den Anforderungen der Grundstufe vergleiche beispielsweise: Bildungsdirektion des Kantons Zürich: Räume der Grundstufe, Zürich 2003

6 Fachstelle für Schulraumplanung der Stadt Zürich, Neue Schulbauten im Kanton Zürich: Vergleich von Raumtypen (Zurich, 2004).

7 For further information on preschool requirements, see, for example, Bildungsdirektion des Kantons Zürich, Räume der Grundstufe (Zurich, 2003).

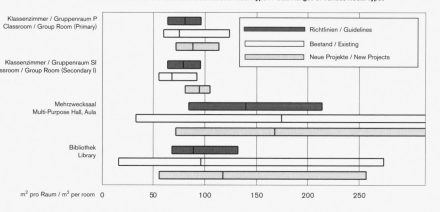

**Bandbreiten für die Grössen verschiedener Raumtypen / Size Ranges of Various Room Types**

Klassenzimmer / Gruppenraum P
Classroom / Group Room (Primary)

Klassenzimmer / Gruppenraum SI
Classroom / Group Room (Secondary I)

Mehrzwecksaal
Multi-Purpose Hall, Aula

Bibliothek
Library

Richtlinien / Guidelines
Bestand / Existing
Neue Projekte / New Projects

m² pro Raum / m² per room   0     50     100    150    200    250

fig.4 Grösse verschiedener Raumtypen. Es wird zwischen den in den diskutierten Richtlinien enthaltenen Vorgaben, dem aktuellen Bestand und den in den letzten Jahren gebauten und geplanten Projekten unterschieden. Die Balken geben die Bandbreite (Minimum, Mittelwert und Maximum) der in den jeweiligen Untersuchungen ermittelten Raumgrössen an. Quelle: Vgl. Fussnoten 4 bis 6

Sizes of different types of rooms. The chart differentiates among the figures contained in the guidelines discussed, actual rooms and projects planned and constructed in recent years. The bars indicate the bandwidth (minimum, average and maximum) of the room sizes ascertained by the relevant studies. Source: see footnotes 4 through 6

Auch in Zukunft werden weder in den bestehenden noch in den neu zu bauenden Schulhäusern sämtliche Raumanforderungen der Schule erfüllt werden können. Die bestehenden Raumstrukturen und die knappen Finanzen der öffentlichen Hand stehen dem entgegen. Trotzdem sind vielerlei Möglichkeiten zur Optimierung des vorhandenen Raums im Hinblick auf neue Anforderungen gegeben. Dabei sollten folgende Fragen bedacht werden: Wie lassen sich die oft reichlich vorhandenen Zirkulationsflächen vermehrt als Lernorte und zur Förderung der Schulgemeinschaft nutzbar machen? Wie lässt sich die Schule stärker in die Verantwortung für eine verbesserte Raumnutzung einbinden? Gibt es Möglichkeiten zur Aufhebung oder Umnutzung von Spezialräumen? Kann die Zahl der zu unterrichtenden Klassen reduziert werden? Wie weit können die Klassenzimmer für zusätzliche Nutzungen geöffnet werden?

pedagogical and operational approaches that held sway when they were built. At the same time, the use of space has changed, just as it is has in all other areas of life. Space requirements have increased.

In the case of the Bühl School, which was mentioned at the beginning of this essay, growing and evolving space requirements have primarily been met by a significant reduction in class sizes, a light reduction in the number of classes and the abolition of special teaching rooms that are no longer needed (drawing rooms). However, the space on offer is tight for a school with twenty-one classes and various additional offerings. Group rooms would be especially useful. The examination of existing school buildings has shown that many of them exhibit shortages of space, which does not prevent them, however, from presenting a full range of modern school offerings. In part these constricting framework conditions might even be catalysts for innovative ideas.

In future too it will not be possible to fulfil all of the spatial requirements of the schools, whether in existing school buildings or in those that have yet to be built. The existing structures and the state's tight budget stand in the way. Nevertheless, there are many opportunities to optimise the existing space in order to meet new demands. The following questions should be considered as this process goes forward: How can the circulation areas that are often so abundant be made more useful as learning spaces and for the promotion and support of the school community? How can the school be brought to exercise greater responsibility for an improved use of space? Are there possibilities for the abolition of special teaching rooms or their conversion to new uses? Can the number of classes be reduced? To what extent can the classrooms be opened to supplementary uses?

Adrian Scheidegger

# 13 Fragen zur Beurteilung
# von Schulbauprojekten

Pädagogische Anforderungen an Schulraumprojekte sind nicht quantifizierbar. Um ihren Einbezug in Schulraumprojekte zu gewährleisten, wurde eine Liste von Fragen zusammengestellt. Die Fragen sollen in den Planungs- und Realisierungsprozess einbezogen werden und damit die Einhaltung pädagogischer Mindestanforderungen gewährleisten. Die Gewichtung der einzelnen Anforderungen hängt vom konkreten Einzelprojekt ab.

### Anregende Gestaltung

1.  Ermöglicht die Architektur eine helle und freundliche Gestaltung der Räume und der offenen Bereiche innerhalb des Gebäudes?

2.  Ist die Anordnung der Schulzimmer und der offenen Bereiche übersichtlich?

3.  Können die verschiedenen Unterrichtsräume durch eine entsprechende Umgestaltung andere Funktionen übernehmen?

4.  Regen Architektur und Umgebung zu altersgemässem Lernen, Spielen und Bewegung an?

5.  Bieten Gebäude und Umgebung Anregungen für das Sehen, das Hören, das Fühlen und das Tasten?

6.  Bieten die Pausenzonen (innen und aussen) sowohl grossräumige Spielflächen als auch Rückzugsmöglichkeiten und Nischen?

7.  Regen die Innen- und Aussenräume aktive Beziehungen zur Natur sowie aktives Gestalten und Verändern bestimmter Bereiche an?

### Flexibilität der Raumnutzung

8.  Ist innerhalb der verschiedenen Räume ein kurzfristiger Wechsel zwischen verschiedenen Lehrformen möglich?

9.  Können die Räume langfristig an veränderte Rahmenbedingungen angepasst werden?

10. Sind die Räume auch für nichtschulische Zwecke geeignet?

### Gestaltungsmöglichkeiten für SchülerInnen und Lehrkräfte

11. Bietet die Architektur den SchülerInnen und Lehrkräften die Möglichkeit, Klassenzimmer und offene Bereiche flexibel zu gestalten?

12. Bieten Architektur und Umgebung einen gestalterischen Spielraum an, um den verschiedenen Bereichen ein jeweils eigenes Gesicht zu geben?

13. Ermöglicht das Projekt eine aktive Mitgestaltung naturnaher Elemente durch die SchülerInnen und LehrerInnen?

Adrian Scheidegger

# 13 Questions for Assessing School Construction Projects

Educational demands on school building projects are not quantifiable. Proceeding from this assumption, a list of questions was compiled to ensure that such demands are taken into account in school planning projects. These questions should be included in the planning and implementation process to ensure that educational demands are satisfied. The importance attached to individual demands will depend on the nature of the project in question.

## Stimulating design

1.  Does the architecture allow for the creation of well-lit friendly rooms and open areas inside the building?

2.  Are the classrooms and open areas clearly arranged?

3.  Are the individual classrooms flexibly designed to allow their conversion to other uses?

4.  Do the architecture and the surroundings stimulate the pupils to learn, play and move as befits their age group?

5.  Do the building(s) and surroundings stimulate the senses of sight, hearing and touch?

6.  Do the schoolyards and recreational areas (inside and outside) provide spacious play areas, as well as niches and places to withdraw to?

7.  Do the interiors and exteriors encourage pupils to cultivate an active relationship to nature and design and to change certain areas?

## Flexible room use

8.  Is it possible to change from one form of teaching to another at short notice?

9.  Can the rooms be adapted to changes in overall conditions in the long term?

10. Are the rooms also suitable for non-school activities?

## To what extent can pupils and teachers influence the design?

11. Does the architecture give pupils and teachers a chance to redesign the classrooms and open areas flexibly?

12. Do the architecture and surroundings give users sufficient scope to modify the various areas and give them an individual appearance?

13. Does the project allow pupils and teachers to participate actively in designing the natural elements?

Das 2004 fertig gestellte Schulhaus Im Birch
von Peter Märkli liegt mitten im Entwicklungsgebiet
Zentrum Zürich-Nord. Foto: Georg Gisel

The Im Birch School (Peter Märkli, 2004)
is situated in the newly planned district of
Zentrum Zürich-Nord. Photo: Georg Gisel

Peter Ess

# Zürcher Erfahrungen

### Ein Boom im Schulhausbau

Die Stadt Zürich erlebt gegenwärtig einen Boom im Schulhausbau. Nach Jahren baulicher
Windstille kumulierten sich die Bedürfnisse. Wachsende Schülerzahlen in manchen Quartieren,
vermehrter Raumbedarf durch die Blockzeiten, neue Unterrichtsformen, über Jahre zurück-
gestellte Unterhaltsarbeiten an den Gebäuden und andere Faktoren überlagern sich: In den
Jahren 1998 bis etwa 2007 werden 18 Schulhaus-Erweiterungen und -Neubauten realisiert.
Dies entspricht dem Schulraum für etwa 2'500 bis 3'000 Schulkinder und einem Investitions-
volumen von rund 600 Millionen Franken. Es ist absehbar, dass nach dieser intensiven
Bauperiode wieder eine ruhigere Phase folgen wird.

Schulhäuser prägen ihren Standort. In vielen Stadtquartieren sind sie die einzigen
öffentlichen Gebäude und besitzen im städtebaulichen Gefüge einen hohen Stellenwert, der
nach architektonischer Qualität verlangt. Schulhäuser sind der Ort, an dem Kinder erstmals eine Öffentlichkeit ausserhalb der Familie kennen lernen. Die Räumlichkeiten der eigenen
Schule vergisst man nie: Nach Jahrzehnten noch kann man jedes Detail genau beschreiben.
Schulen sind daher ohne Zweifel auch wichtige Lernorte für räumliche Wahrnehmungen, für das
Licht- und Farbempfinden, für die Erfahrung von Räumen der Gemeinschaft und des Rück-
zugs. Auch deshalb gelten für Schulhäuser hohe räumliche und gestalterische Anforderungen.

Lehrerinnen und Lehrer benötigen ein Umfeld, das ihren Unterricht unterstützt. Im
heutigen Schulalltag wechseln Gruppenarbeit, Werkstattunterricht oder Projektlernen
mit traditionellen Lehr- und Lernformen im Schulzimmer. Dafür ist ein qualitätsvolles und
vor allem flexibles Raumangebot bereitzustellen.

Anforderungen an die Schulanlagen, die über den Unterricht hinausgehen, gewinnen
immer mehr an Bedeutung. Beschränkt sich bisher die öffentliche Nutzung vor allem auf die
Sportanlagen, werden in Zukunft ausserschulische Betreuungsaufgaben wie Schülerclubs
und Mittagstische immer mehr zum Regelfall werden. Öffentliche Freizeit- und Kulturangebote
werden die ausserschulische Nutzung ergänzen.

### Unsicherheiten der Schulentwicklung

Als in den späten neunziger Jahren die Welle von Schulerweiterungen und neuen Schulanlagen die Stadt Zürich erfasste, fehlte nach langen Jahren des Stillstands im Schulhausbau
die Erfahrung einer kontinuierlichen Praxis. Die Herausforderung bestand für uns darin,
im Vorfeld der Projektentwicklungen in einem iterativen Prozess zwischen Pädagoginnen und
Pädagogen sowie Architektinnen und Architekten und Projektentwicklern auszuloten, welche
Anforderungen eine Schulanlage zu erfüllen hat, die nachhaltig und langfristig — das heisst
für etwa zwei Generationen — geplant werden soll. Wir hatten herauszufinden, wie moderne
Schule funktioniert und welche räumlichen Gegebenheiten dafür erforderlich sind. Die
Diskussion wurde durch mehrere Unsicherheiten erschwert: Erstens existieren unterschiedliche
Zeithorizonte von Gebäudezyklus und pädagogischen Konzepten, zweitens fehlen die Grund-
lagen zur Beurteilung von Kosten und Nutzen in schulischen Belangen, und drittens sind die
Kenntnisse von Pädagogen und Baufachleuten im jeweils anderen Fachbereich nur schwach
entwickelt. Für den erfolgreichen Dialog ist es wichtig, dass jede Disziplin die fachliche
Zuständigkeit in ihrem eigenen Bereich behält und dennoch die andere versteht.

Voraussetzung für eine den Ansprüchen genügende Projektentwicklung und ganz besonders
für einen Architekturwettbewerb ist, dass die Bauherrschaft die funktionalen Erfordernisse
kennt und ein eindeutiges Raumprogramm aufstellt. Noch bis vor wenigen Jahren stellte
dies kein Problem dar, denn seit dem Bestehen eines öffentlichen Bildungswesens (im Kanton
Zürich seit den dreissiger Jahren des 19. Jahrhunderts) hatte sich die Grundstruktur der
Schulen wenig verändert. Das Programm von Klassenzimmern, Singsaal und Turnhalle war vorge-
geben, und es galt nur, diese Raumgruppen mit Hilfe gut gestalteter Verbindungsbereiche

Peter Ess

# The Zurich Experience

## The Boom in School Construction

The city of Zurich is currently experiencing a boom in school construction. Cumulated needs are now asserting themselves. Growing numbers of pupils in specific districts, greater room requirements following the introduction of core times, new teaching approaches, years of postponing much-needed maintenance work, and a host of other factors have come together. Since 1998, many extensions and new schools have been completed, and their total number is expected to rise to about eighteen by 2007. They will provide space for around 2,500 to 3,000 pupils at an investment volume of approximately 600 million Swiss francs. There are clear signs that this period of building activity will be followed by a quieter phase.

Schools leave their mark on their surroundings. In many districts, the school is the only public building, and it has a pre-eminent status in its urban environment. This situation calls for high-quality architecture. It is at school that a child first encounters public life outside the family. We never forget our old school rooms. Decades later, we can still describe them down to the last detail. Schools are, therefore, without any doubt, important places for learning and developing spatial perception, for experiencing light, colour, community and retreating. Consequently, very tough requirements are placed on schools with respect to both space and design. Teachers need an environment that positively supports their teaching. During a normal day's teaching, group work, instruction in workshops, and projects alternate with traditional forms of teaching and learning. Consequently rooms and room arrangements are needed that are not only flexible, but also meet the highest demands on quality. Demands are increasingly being placed on school buildings which go far beyond the framework of the normal teaching situation. Whereas public use of schools was formerly restricted to the playing fields, extra-curricular care in school clubs and lunch rooms will tend to become the norm in the future. Public leisure and cultural facilities will be provided to extend the range of extra-school activities.

## Uncertainties in Planning and Constructing Schools

When the City of Zurich became caught up in a wave of school-extension and new-school construction in the late 1990s, it became evident that many years of stagnation had atrophied practical experience in this field. We found ourselves faced with the challenge of identifying what precise demands school design had to meet. This necessitated an iterative process between educators, architects and project developers before it was even possible to start developing a project. Furthermore, schools had to be planned to fulfil these requirements on a sustainable and long-term basis — for, say, two generations. We had to learn how a modern school functions and to ascertain its spatial requirements.

Discussion was complicated by a number of uncertainties: firstly, building cycles and educational concepts have different time horizons; secondly, there is no established basis for assessing costs and benefits in the case of schools; thirdly, educators and building experts know too little about one another's fields. A successful dialogue presupposes that each discipline retains its competence in its own field but still understands the other party.

The prerequisite for a project development scheme that does justice to the demands placed upon it — and especially for an architectural competition — is that the client knows the functional requirements of the building and prepares a distinct room plan. Until recently, this was quite simple, because the basic structure of schools had hardly changed since public education was first introduced in Zurich in the 1830s.

zu einer gelungenen Gesamtanlage zu verschmelzen. Dies hat sich in den letzten Jahren stark verändert. Die pädagogischen Ansätze sind einem raschen Wandel unterworfen; unterschiedliche Konzepte werden gleichzeitig gelebt. Schulteams müssen auf Anforderungen der Eltern, technologische Entwicklungen und aktuelle pädagogische Tendenzen rasch reagieren können. Dazu brauchen sie wandelbare Gebäudehüllen.

### Zürcher Grundsätze

Aufgrund der Erfahrungen der letzten Jahre haben wir für die Schulraumentwicklung folgende Rahmenbedingungen festgelegt:

— Schulanlagen werden nicht für spezifische pädagogische Konzepte entwickelt. Sie müssen vielmehr unterschiedliche Lehr- und Lernformen ermöglichen.
— Ausgangspunkt ist nach wie vor das Klassenzimmer. Allerdings muss es so flexibel angelegt werden, dass vielfältige Lernarrangements für Kleingruppen und klassenübergreifende Unterrichtsprojekte kombiniert werden können.
— Frei benutzbare, gemeinsame Vorbereiche von zwei bis vier Schulzimmern sind insbesondere in grossen Schulanlagen wichtige Identifikationsorte für Schülerinnen und Schüler (Klassencluster) und weisen ein grosses Nutzungspotenzial auf. Dabei sind die feuerpolizeilichen Anforderungen (Fluchtwege) so zu lösen, dass diese Bereiche ohne Einschränkungen möbliert und eingesetzt werden können. Dem finanziell grösseren Aufwand steht eine qualitativ wesentlich hochwertigere Raumnutzung gegenüber.
— Die Gemeinschaftsbereiche (Turnhalle, Mehrzwecksaal, Mensa, Bibliothek, ausserschulische Betreuungsbereiche) sind räumlich so zu organisieren, dass sie ausserhalb der Unterrichtszeit von anderen Personengruppen genutzt werden können.
— Die Aussenbereiche (Pausen- und Spielplätze) stehen als Grün- und Freiflächen auch dem Quartier zur Verfügung.

### Was darf es kosten?

Ein sensibler Punkt in der Projektentwicklung ist die Frage nach den angemessenen Kosten. Die Finanzknappheit der öffentlichen Hand ist kein vorübergehender Zustand, sondern politisches Programm und wird uns auch in den nächsten Jahren begleiten. Mit ihrem grossen Investitionsvolumen steht die Schule nun unverhofft im Blickpunkt der Öffentlichkeit und in Konkurrenz zu anderen Bedürfnissen, sei es im Kultur- oder Gesundheitsbereich. Neue Fragen sind zu beantworten: Mit wie viel Aufwand erzielt die Schule welche Wirkung? Was können wir mit den verfügbaren Mitteln realisieren? Welche Prioritäten setzen wir? Andere Akteure — beispielsweise im Gesundheitswesen — sind inzwischen in der Lage, solche Fragen zu beantworten. Der Schulbereich steht dagegen erst am Anfang und kann allein mit dem Hinweis, dass durch räumliche Einschränkungen die pädagogische Qualität leide, nicht mehr überzeugend argumentieren. Auf der anderen Seite hilft die Aufforderung, billiger zu bauen und technische Standards zu senken, nicht weiter. Die Effekte sparsamen Bauens sind leider begrenzt: Unsere Auswertung aktueller Bauten zeigt ein Sparpotenzial von etwa 5 bis maximal 10 Prozent. Die wesentlichen Sparmöglichkeiten liegen deshalb in der optimalen Ausnützung des bestehenden Raums und in der Reduktion der Flächenansprüche bei neuen Bauten, sei es durch effizientere Bewirtschaftung oder durch Doppelnutzung von Räumen (etwa für Schule und Freizeit).

### Nachhaltigkeit

Nachhaltigkeitsstandards werden in der Stadt Zürich zwischen dem Stadtrat und dem Amt für Hochbauten als Baufachorgan der Stadt festgelegt. Grundhaltungen in Bezug auf die Bauökologie sind ebenso definiert wie die Anforderungen an die Dauerhaftigkeit der Materialien, ihre Alterungsfähigkeit, haptische und optische Qualitäten oder Unterhaltsaspekte. Für Neubauten ist der schweizerische Minergie-Standard verbindlich, der Grenzwerte für den Energieverbrauch bei Beleuchtung und Heizung definiert. Diese Standards bedingen eine

There was a routine program which included classrooms, a music (singing) room and a gymnasium. The only requirement was that these rooms be combined with a well-planned system of corridors to create a well-functioning whole. However, the situation has changed dramatically over the past few years. Educational approaches have undergone rapid transformation. Nowadays, a broad spectrum of concepts is applied simultaneously. School teams must be able to respond quickly to parents' demands, technological developments and the latest trends in education. In order to do so, they need flexible building envelopes.

### The Principles Underlying School Planning and Construction in Zurich

Proceeding from our experience over the past few years, we have established the following preconditions for planning schools:

- Schools should not be planned to meet the requirements of one-sided educational conceptions. Instead, they must allow for diverse forms of teaching and learning.
- The point of departure is always the classroom. This must be designed to ensure maximum flexibility, so that a variety of learning arrangements for small groups and inter-class teaching projects can be combined.
- Freely available common anterooms for two to four classrooms (clusters of classes) are not only important places where pupils can feel at home, they also contain enormous potential. The fire-safety requirements (escape routes) must be fulfilled in such a way that these areas can be furnished and used without restriction. The far greater potential for high-quality room use makes up for the higher cost.
- The common areas (gymnasium, multifunctional hall, canteen, library, extra-school care facilities) are to be arranged in such a way that they can be used by other groups of people outside normal school hours.
- The external areas (schoolyards and playgrounds) are available to the neighbourhood as green areas and open spaces.

### Is There a Cost Limit?

The question of reasonable costs is a sensitive issue. The shortage of public funds is not just a passing fad, but the consequence of a political programme that will still affect us in the years to come. As school construction requires huge investments, the school has suddenly found itself in the public eye and in competition with other needs, as for instance in the areas of culture or health. New questions have to be answered. How much do we need to invest in a school to achieve which result? What can we do with the funds available? Which priorities shall we set? Other agents, in the field of health care, for instance, are able to answer such questions. However, in the sector of school education the situation looks very different, for the responsible authorities are only just beginning to examine these questions. It will no longer do to argue that the quality of education suffers when rooms are inadequate. Nor does it help matters when people demand that construction costs and technical standards be lowered. The effects of lowering construction costs are, unfortunately, limited, and our assessment of existing buildings reveals that the potential saving amounts to 5 to 10 per cent at most. The greatest saving potential therefore lies in using existing space optimally and reducing new buildings' spatial requirements, whether by more efficient management or by making space available for dual use (for both school and leisure purposes, for example).

### Sustainability

In the city of Zurich, sustainability standards are set by the city council and the municipal building department. These bodies define the preconditions for ecologically sound building and the requirements relating to the sustainability of mate-

sehr sorgfältige Planung von Lüftungs- und Beleuchtungsanlagen, die den Schülerinnen und Schülern zugute kommt. Die technischen Nachhaltigkeitsstandards stehen im Dialog mit der Schulseite nicht zur Debatte. Dagegen sind Fragen nach dem Nutzungsspielraum und der Anpassungsfähigkeit an sich verändernde pädagogische Anforderungen ein gemeinsames Anliegen bei der Projektevaluation.

Nachhaltigkeit beinhaltet aber auch den sorgfältigen Umgang mit bestehenden älteren Schulanlagen, welche fast immer von hoher architektonischer Qualität sind und in vielen Fällen unter Denkmalschutz stehen. Auch hier gilt es, das Mögliche vom Wünschbaren zu unterscheiden und mit Respekt und Sorgfalt an das bauliche Erbe heranzugehen. Mit einer Vielzahl kleinerer Eingriffe können baukünstlerisch wertvolle Gebäude Schritt für Schritt ruiniert werden. Bei jedem Eingriff in die bestehende Substanz sind daher die Herkunft und der Zeitgeist des Gebäudes ebenso wie seine Zukunftsperspektive zu klären.

**Architektonische Verantwortung**

Die Stadt Zürich verlangt von ihren Bauten hohe städtebauliche und architektonische Qualität – dieser Anspruch steht nicht im Widerspruch zu den Forderungen nach Funktionalität, Kostenbewusstsein und Nachhaltigkeit. Unsere Partner haben Anspruch darauf, dass ihre funktionalen Anliegen in hoher Qualität umgesetzt werden. Schulfachleute sind in den Wettbewerbsjurys vertreten und bringen ihr Wissen und ihre Erfahrungen in den Auswahlprozess ein. Die architektonisch-städtebauliche Umsetzung des Projekts ist danach Sache der Bauseite.

Auf dem Weg vom Projekt zum fertigen Bau kommt man nicht umhin, laufend Güterabwägungen zwischen pädagogischen und anderen Anliegen vorzunehmen. Als Baufachorgan der Stadt Zürich übernehmen wir in diesem Prozess jedoch die Verantwortung, dass die Projekte nicht verwässert werden, sondern in ihrer Prägnanz erhalten bleiben.

**Fazit**

In städtebaulicher Hinsicht hat sich zweifellos ein Wandel vollzogen. Schulanlagen stellen nicht mehr, wie bis zu Beginn des 20. Jahrhunderts, die politischen Errungenschaften des Bürgertums und seines Bildungsverständnisses dar. Schulhäuser sind aber nach wie vor wichtige Orte der Quartiersöffentlichkeit und somit Teile eines funktionierenden sozialen Gemeinwesens, das sich eben auch in seinen Bauten repräsentiert sieht.

In funktionaler und architektonischer Hinsicht stehen Schulbauten kaum mehr für ein bestimmtes pädagogisches Konzept. Vielmehr müssen Schulen räumlich starke und vielseitig verwendbare räumliche Gebilde sein, in denen unterschiedliche, möglicherweise heute noch unbekannte pädagogische Konzepte inszeniert werden können – vergleichbar mit einem Theater, in dem im Lauf der Zeit ganz unterschiedliche Stücke aufgeführt werden.

Die Forderung nach dem kindlichen Massstab oder nach Kleinteiligkeit im Sinne der Pavillonschulen hat, jedenfalls im städtischen Kontext, an Relevanz verloren. Die Areale sind beschränkt, die Bedürfnisse gross. Anstelle von einzelnen Schulhäusern werden daher vermehrt «Schulstädte» entstehen, die es subtil zu differenzieren gilt. Einerseits sind sie städtebaulich in den grossmassstäblichen Kontext einzubinden, andererseits sind sie so zu strukturieren, dass es auch den jüngsten Schülerinnen und Schülern gelingt, sich zu orientieren.

Diese Qualitäten vereinigt das Schulhaus Im Birch, das der Architekt Peter Märkli in Zürich-Nord erbaut hat. Die grösste in Zürich je gebaute Schulanlage wird im Sommer 2004 in Betrieb genommen. Wir werden mit Interesse verfolgen, wie die Anlage von der Schule in Beschlag genommen und bespielt wird.

rials, their sensitivity to ageing, their haptic and optical qualities, and their maintenance. The Swiss Minergie Standard, which lays down the energy consumption limits for lighting and heating, applies to all new buildings. These standards demand that ventilation and lighting systems be planned with considerable care so that they have a beneficial effect on pupils. The sustainability standards are not a subject of discussion with the school management. Questions of flexible use and adaptability to changing educational requirements, on the other hand, are a matter for joint discussion during project evaluation.

Sustainability also means adopting a sensitive approach to older schools, which are often excellent works of architecture and frequently listed as protected buildings. Here too, it is important to distinguish between what is possible and what is desirable, and to treat our architectural heritage with respect and care. The combined effect of a great number of minor changes can, over the course of time, destroy a valuable work of architecture. Before any work is done on an old building, it is always necessary to clarify its origin, Zeitgeist and prospects for the future.

## Architectural Responsibility

The city of Zurich requires that its buildings meet high architectural and planning standards. This demand in no way contradicts the requirements of functionality, cost-consciousness and sustainability. Our partners have a right to buildings which fulfil their functional requirements. School experts are represented on competition juries and bring their knowledge and experience into the selection process. The building department will then take care of the implementation of the project and its architectural design.

From the project to the completed building, one must continually weigh up the respective conflicting needs of education and other areas. We at the Municipal Building Department of the city of Zurich are responsible at all times for making sure that projects are not watered down but retain their original character.

## Summary

In terms of schools' urban presence, things have certainly changed. Modern school buildings, unlike those constructed in the early twentieth century, no longer embody the political gains and educational conceptions of the middle classes. Even so, they remain important public places within the district and thus form part of a well-functioning community which sees itself represented in its buildings.

Both functionally and architecturally, school buildings have more or less ceased to stand for a particular view of education. Instead, they now have to be robust and adaptable, offering a variety of uses. They must be designed so that diverse educational concepts — including, perhaps, some as yet unknown — can be realised there, rather like a theatre, where very different plays are performed over the course of time.

The demand for a scale commensurate to children or for small units (as found in the pavilion schools) is no longer relevant, at least not in an urban context. Space is limited and needs are great. Where, at one time, single school buildings were constructed, there is now a growing tendency to build 'school cities' which call for highly differentiated design. On the one hand, schools have to be integrated into the larger urban context; on the other hand they need to be structured so that even the youngest children can find their way around in them.

These qualities are combined in the Im Birch School, designed by the architect Peter Märkli, in Zürich Nord. The largest school complex ever to be built in Zurich opens its doors in summer 2004. We shall follow, with great interest, the way the school occupies and uses the complex.

Elisabeth Gaus
**Schulbesuch/school visit**

**Tagesschule Bungertwies, Zürich**

Das Schulhaus mit der zentralen Halle wurde 1970 von den Architekten Häfeli, Moser und Steiger erbaut. Es ist heute eine geleitete Tagesschule: Lehrpersonen und Hort-Mitarbeitende arbeiten im Team und beziehen die Eltern mit ein. Moderner Schulbetrieb findet in einem Haus statt, das zu seiner Zeit für ganz andere Bedürfnisse erbaut wurde.

**Day School, Bungertwies, Zurich**

The school building, which has a central hall, was built by the architects Häfeli, Moser and Steiger in 1970. The school is now open the whole day: the teaching- and day-care centre staff work as a team and involve the parents in their work. A modern school is now run in a building originally erected to satisfy very different needs.

**Brigitte Harder,** Schulleiterin

Mir gefällt hier besonders die grosse Halle, auch wenn wir darin ein Lärmproblem haben. Die Halle ist ein sichtbares Zentrum: Da finden sich die SchülerInnen morgens vor dem Unterricht ein, da begegnet man sich, da wird gegessen. Die Eltern kommen in die Halle, begegnen sich beim Warten auf ihre Kinder, sehen andere Kinder, HortnerInnen und LehrerInnen. Gerade darum habe ich dieses Haus gerne.

Doch es braucht auch Raum für Begegnungen im kleinen Rahmen, Raum für die Aufbewahrung von Material, damit Sorgfalt möglich wird. Das Haus ist etwas überfüllt. Was fehlt, sind Nischen zum Lernen in kleinen Gruppen, kleine Zusatzräume, wo ungestört in Ruhe etwas erarbeitet werden kann. In meinem Büro bin ich etwas zu sehr abgeschirmt, ich möchte lieber zentraler sein, umgeben von Glas und mit einer offenen Türe für alle.

**Brigitte Harder,** headmaster

I particularly like the big hall, despite all the problems with the noise. The hall is a visible centre: the children gather there in the mornings before lessons. It's also used as a canteen. The parents meet one another in the hall while they're waiting for their children; they see other children, carers and teachers. That's why I'm so fond of this building.

But you also need space for meeting people on a smaller scale, space for storing material, so that you can work conscientiously. This building is a bit overcrowded. What we need are some niches where kids can work in small groups, and additional, small rooms where you've got the peace and quiet you need to work things out. I'm too cut off from things in my office. I'd like to be more central, surrounded by glass, with an open door.

**Mädchen**

Das Schulhaus gefällt uns sehr gut, wir möchten kein anderes haben. Es hat zwei Pausenplätze und sieht lässig aus, es ist nicht zu gross und nicht zu klein und hat lässige Kinder. Wir haben hier mehr Freizeit als in anderen Schulen, da wir Blockzeiten und einen Hort haben. Nur die Knaben stören uns manchmal.

**Girls**

We love the building and wouldn't want a different one. It has two schoolyards and looks pretty cool. It's not too big, and not too small - and the kids are cool. We have more free time here than they do at other schools, because we have core times and a care centre. But the boys really get on our nerves sometimes.

**Buben**

In der Pause bin ich am liebsten auf der Hängematte, mache Versteckis oder Fangis auf der Wiese, bei den Bäumen. Mir gefällt auch der grosse Pausenplatz und dass es einen Hort hat. – Mir gefallen die Scherenschnitte am Schulhaus. Ich gehe da sehr gerne in die Schule, auch wenn der Weg weit ist. Wir kennen da eigentlich alle, nicht nur die eigenen LehrerInnen. – Mir gefällt es auch, weil es hier Zmittag und Znüni gibt. Uns stört es nicht, dass wir so viele Kinder sind, wir machen ja Zehner-Gruppen.

**Boys**

What I like doing most during the break is lying in the hammock, playing hide-and-seek in the field and among the trees. I also like the big schoolyard and the fact that there's a care centre. - I like the cut-out silhouettes on the side of the building. I really like going to school here, even though I have a long way to go. Everyone knows everyone else — you don't just know your own teachers and that's that. - I also like the fact that we have midday meals and tea breaks here. It doesn't bother us that there are so many children here, because we're all in groups of ten.

Photos: Claudia Caprez

**Maria**

Dies ist mein drittes Schulhaus. Am liebsten spiele oder lese ich im Hort. Hier gefällt es mir besser wegen der Tagesschule, dem Essen, den guten HortleiterInnen und Lehrpersonen.

Als ich das erste Mal hier war, staunte ich ob der Bemalung; unterdessen habe ich mich daran gewöhnt. Wenn ich Geld hätte, würde ich die Räume vergrössern. Wir haben viele Stühle, die haben im Klassenzimmer kaum Platz.

**Maria**

This is my third school. What I like best is playing or reading in the care centre. I like it much more here because of the day school, the food, the good carers and the teachers.

The first time I came here I was astonished by the painting. But now I've got used to it. If I had the money, I'd make all the rooms bigger. We've got loads of chairs, so there's hardly any space in the classrooms.

**Michèle Grumbach,** Lehrerin

Dieses Schulhaus gefällt mir wegen der offenen Gänge und Türen, der Sicht in die Halle und dem gemeinsamen Essen mit den Kindern. Grössere und luxuriösere Schulräume wären manchmal schön, jedoch auch nur Hülle. Es geht um den Inhalt, um das Kind und sein Denken, alles andere ist nicht so wichtig. Heute haben zum Beispiel einige Kinder auch vor der Türe gerechnet.

Wir im Team haben hier vor vier Jahren das offene Lernen entdeckt. Wesentlich für uns war der gemeinsame Entschluss, neue Ideen umzusetzen. Anfangs war es schwierig, doch heute merken wir, dass die Kinder viel besser formulieren können und einander auch besser zuhören.

**Michèle Grumbach,** teacher

What I like about this building are the open corridors and doors, the fact you can look into the hall, having meals with the kids. Sometimes I think it would be nice if we had bigger and more luxurious classrooms, but that's just the packaging. The important thing is content, the children and what they think. The rest isn't so important. Today, for instance, some of the children sat outside the door doing arithmetic.

Those of us in the team here discovered open learning four years ago. The important thing for us was making decisions together, putting new ideas into practice. It was difficult at first, but now we can see that the children are able to formulate things much better, and have got better at listening to one another.

**Beatrice Di Pizzo,** Präsidentin des Elternforums

Die Kinder verbringen in einer Tagesschule sehr viel mehr Zeit als in einer anderen Schule. Der Schulbau ist zwar mit einer Küche und Essplätzen eingerichtet, jedoch längst nicht optimal. Von Elternseite wird über Aggressionen beim Mittagstisch in der Halle berichtet, die nicht der Erziehung zugeschrieben werden können, die etwas mit der Atmosphäre des Baus zu tun haben.

Der Ersatz des Kachelbodens und kleinere architektonische Interventionen würden vermutlich einiges verbessern und das Schallproblem mindern. Dies sind jedoch Details angesichts dessen, was die Schulleiterin und das Team mit viel Phantasie aus dem Vorgefundenen gemacht haben.

**Beatrice Di Pizzo,** president of the parents' forum

The children spend far more time in a day school than they do in a normal school. Even though the building has a kitchen and dining tables, it's still nowhere near perfect. Parents have spoken of rough behaviour in the hall at lunchtime, which you can't put down to the children's education - it must have something to do with the atmosphere created by the building.

Replacing the tiled floor and making a few other small architectural changes would probably improve things and help counteract the noise problem. But these are little things when you think of all the school head and the team have done so far, with a lot of imagination, to this building.

Ich würde die Turnhalle renovieren, da sie nicht wasserdicht ist.
Ich würde das Schulhaus anmalen, grau gefällt mir nicht.
Ich würde das Schulhaus vergrössern, eine Halle zum Spielen anbauen.
Ich würde mehr Spielgeräte auf den Pausenplatz stellen — eine Schaukel — eine Rutschbahn.
Ich möchte auch drinnen herumrennen können.
Ich möchte weniger strenge Lehrer und Lehrerinnen.

I would renovate the gymnasium because it leaks.
I would paint the school building because I don't like grey.
I would make the school bigger, add a hall for playing in.
I'd put more play equipment in the schoolyard — a swing and a slide, for example.
I wish I could run around inside too.
I wish the teachers weren't so strict.

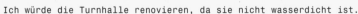

Peter Eberhard, Urs Meier

# Lern-Räume:
# Pädagogik und Architektur im Dialog

**«Die Schule selbst soll eine liebliche Stätte sein, innen und aussen eine Augenweide. Drinnen sei ein helles, reines Zimmer, ringsherum mit Bildern geschmückt. Draussen aber sei bei der Schule zunächst ein freier Patz ... aber auch ein Garten, wohin man die Schüler bisweilen schicken soll und wo man ihre Augen sich am Anblick der Bäume, Blumen und Kräuter weiden lassen soll.»**
Jan Amos Comenius: «Didacta Magna» (1632)

Schon zu einer Zeit, als Lernen noch mechanische Dressur war, der Stoff meistens formalistisch aufbereitet und frontal vorgetragen wurde, dachte Comenius (1592–1670) darüber nach, wie man Lernräume gestalten könnte. Das Lernen, so nahm er schon damals an, hinge nicht nur von der Lehrperson oder den Fähigkeiten der Schülerinnen und Schüler ab, sondern eben auch von der Architektur: dem Ort, an dem gelernt wird, und zugleich dem Umfeld, in dem Bildung Raum gegeben wird. Damit ist das Verhältnis zwischen Architektur und Pädagogik angesprochen.

Wer der Frage nachgehen will, in welchen Räumen Menschen in Zukunft lernen sollen und wie die räumliche Konzeption das Lernen unterstützen soll, muss sich der Bildung, genauer: den aktuellen pädagogischen Auffassungen, die selbstständiges Lernen fördern, zuwenden. Lernen ist heute Annäherung und Recherchieren, Bewegung und Perspektivenwechsel, Re-Konstruktion und Infragestellung, Üben und Forschen.

Lehrende inszenieren und choreographieren Unterricht, sie schaffen die Atmosphäre, in der Lernen möglich wird, und kreieren Realitätsbezüge, die die Diskrepanz zwischen Lebens- und Schulerfahrungen verkleinern. Dazu benötigen sie die Unterstützung der Architektur.

Das Verhältnis zwischen Architektur und Pädagogik muss über einen Dialog zwischen diesen Disziplinen verhandelt werden. Diesen Dialog bestreiten Urs Meier, Erziehungswissenschaftler und Dozent an der Hochschule für Gestaltung und Kunst, Zürich, und Peter Eberhard, Architekt und Leiter des Departements Lehrberufe für Gestaltung und Kunst an der HGKZ.

**Urs Meier** In den letzten Jahren habe ich verschiedene Architektenteams bei Schulhaus-Wettbewerben beraten und begleitet. Dabei ist mir aufgefallen, dass Architektur und Pädagogik unterschiedliche Denkweisen und andere Theorien und Terminologien aufweisen. Manchmal haben wir uns entsprochen, oft aber auch widersprochen. Müsste es nicht das Ziel sein, die gegenseitigen Sprachen und Theorien besser zu verstehen oder eine neue gemeinsame Terminologie zu entwickeln? Dazu meine Frage: Wie denkt der Architekt? Was muss ich von der Architektur wissen, um das Handeln des Architekten zu verstehen?

**Peter Eberhard** Zur Entwicklung einer gemeinsamen Sprache ist ein tieferes Verständnis für die Disziplin des Gesprächspartners notwendig. Zum Beispiel dürfte der Architekt oder die Architektin nicht mehr vom Schulhausbau sprechen, sondern müsste die Sicht der anderen Seite einnehmen: Lernräume und Lernorte werden benötigt, also muss von «Lernortgestaltung» oder vom Gestalten von Lernwelten die Rede sein.

Der Architekt denkt in einem bestimmten Muster, er hat seine Denkfiguren. Es geht ihm um ein Werk, das bestimmte Aufgaben erfüllen muss und eine bestimmte Form haben wird. Die zentrale Kategorie für die Architektin ist der Raum. Sie schafft Räume für Handlungen und unterschiedliche Funktionen; Räume müssen Bedürfnisse befriedigen. Das entstandene «Gebilde» steht in einem städtebaulichen Kontext und in der Tradition des Schulhausbaus. Zum Entwurf gehören weiter die Gestaltung der Umgebung, das Festlegen der Raum- und Baustruktur sowie der Innenausbau bis hin zur Wahl des Mobiliars.

Der Architekt hat ein Raumprogramm zu erfüllen, ökonomische Anforderungen zu berücksichtigen, Auflagen der Feuerpolizei und Denkmalpflege einzubinden, kantonale Richtlinien des Schulhausbaus umzusetzen und Ähnliches mehr. Ihm geht es darum, ein Bauwerk zu schaffen, welches hohen ästhetischen Anforderungen genügen muss und das gegenüber vergleichbaren Werken

Peter Eberhard, Urs Meier

# Spaces for Learning:
# Education and Architecture in Dialogue

**The school itself should be a lovely place, a feast for the eyes both within and without. Within, there should be a bright, clean room adorned all round with pictures. Without, however, there should be an open space next to the school … but also a garden, where the children should be sent from time to time to feast their eyes on the sight of trees, flowers and herbs.**

Jan Amos Comenius, *Didacta magna* (1632)

At a time when learning still took the form of rote training and material was usually prepared formalistically and presented in lecture format, Comenius (1592–1670) thought about how one might go about designing spaces for learning. He assumed even then that learning depended not only on the teacher and the abilities of the pupils, but also on architecture, the place where people learn and at the same time the environment where education is given the space it needs to unfold. Thus he broaches the subject of the relationship between architecture and educational theory.

In order to explore the question of the spaces in which people should learn in the future and the ways in which the conception of space might support the learning process, it is necessary to turn one's attention to education, or more precisely, the current pedagogical views that promote autonomous learning. Learning today means approaching and investigating, moving, changing perspectives, re-constructing and placing things in question, practising and exploring.

Teachers stage and choreograph instruction. They create the atmosphere in which learning becomes possible, and they create connections with reality that reduce the discrepancy between life experiences and scholastic ones. In order to be able to do so, they need the support of architecture.

The relationship between architecture and educational theory must be negotiated by means of a dialogue between the two fields. This challenge is met below by Urs Meier, an educator and lecturer at the Hochschule für Gestaltung und Kunst in Zurich, and Peter Eberhard, an architect and director of the departement Lehrberufe für Gestaltung und Kunst at the HGKZ.

**Urs Meier** In recent years I have advised and accompanied various teams of architects as they participated in school building competitions. I have noticed that architecture and education have different ways of thinking and different theories and terminology. Sometimes we agreed, but often we disagreed. Shouldn't our objective be to develop a better understanding of our respective languages and theories or to develop a new, shared vocabulary? Hence my question: How do architects think? What must I know about architects in order to understand the way they act?

**Peter Eberhard** In order to develop a common language, each of the parties to the dialogue must have a deeper understanding of the other's field. For example, the architect should stop referring to school construction and design and adopt the other side's perspective. What is required is spaces and places for learning. The conversation should thus refer to 'learning place design' or the design of 'learning worlds'.

Architects think according to a particular pattern. They have their conceptual models. At issue for them is to design a building that must fulfil certain tasks and one that will have a particular form. The central category for architects is space. They create spaces for actions and different functions; spaces must satisfy needs. The resulting structure exists in an urban context and within the tradition of school construction and design. The design of the environment, the definition of the spatial structure and the structure of the buildings and the interior design, up to and including the choice of furnishings, also form part of the overall design.

bestehen kann. Mit dem eigentlichen Lern- und Handlungsprozess der Nutzer und Nutzerinnen setzt er sich nur am Rande auseinander. Die Beschäftigung mit dem wünschenswerten pädagogischen Ambiente kommt dabei zu kurz.

**Urs Meier** Mir fällt auf, dass die Lehrperson eigentlich ähnlich strukturiert denkt wie der Architekt. Was für den Architekten das Zusammenspiel von Raum, Funktion, Form und Konstruktion ist, ist für die Lehrperson das Verhältnis zwischen Zielen, Inhalten, Methoden und Medien. Alle diese Dimensionen des Lehr-Lerngeschehens beeinflussen sich wechselseitig. Veränderungen in einem dieser vier Eckpunkte haben zwangsläufig Wechselwirkungen mit den anderen zur Folge.

Wenn nun aus der Sicht der Pädagogik zunehmend von der Psychologie der «Lernumgebung» oder von «Lernlandschaften» gesprochen wird, geht dies über dieses «magische Viereck» hinaus. Mit diesen Begriffen kommt das gesamte Umfeld des Lernens in den Blick: die Architektur, die Raumgestaltung, das Mobiliar, die multimediale Ausstattung, die Regeln des Umgangs, das Arbeitsklima, die Lernatmosphären, die Lernenden und Lehrenden.

Die Architektur sieht sich vor die Schwierigkeit gestellt, dass Unterrichten heute nicht mehr einzig auf ein Schulzimmer mit fixen, auf Wandtafel und Lehrerpult ausgerichteten Bankreihen beschränkt ist, sondern «Lernräume» oder «Lernlandschaften» benötigt, in denen Lernende Informationen abrufen, Projekte realisieren, Ideen gestalten und Probleme lösen, aber auch einem systematisch aufgebauten Unterricht folgen können. Im Vordergrund steht die Kooperation unter den Schülerinnen und Schülern, der Teamgeist und forschendes Lernen. Lernwelten in Schulen sollen zum Verweilen einladen und Angebote und Herausforderungen zum Lernen bieten, die zur selbständigen Auseinandersetzung verlocken und die Freude am Lernen steigern. Bei Schulbesuchen ist mir in den letzten Jahren zunehmend aufgefallen, dass Lernende neben dem Klassenzimmer auch andere Räume vielfältig zu nutzen beginnen: Nebenräume, Gänge, Treppenhäuser, Nischen, unterschiedlichste bequeme und unbequeme Sitzgelegenheiten, Einzel- und Gruppenarbeitsplätze, Mediotheken und Fachbibliotheken. Sie alle werden zum Lesen, Diskutieren und Ausruhen genutzt.

**Peter Eberhard** Zu erwähnen sind ferner unterschiedliche Raum- und Nutzungsvorstellungen: Lehrende und Lernende, Mitglieder der Behörden, der Hausdienst, externe Benutzer und Architekten haben unterschiedliche Raumauffassungen und nehmen Räume unterschiedlich wahr. Problematisch ist dabei, dass über Lernräume keine gemeinsamen Grundvorstellungen vorhanden sind. Der Architekt geht aber selbstverständlich davon aus, dass Lehrerinnen und Lehrer das gleiche Raumverständnis haben wie er. Dass der Mensch aber je nach Altersstufe, Sozialisierung und Rolle ein anderes Raumverständnis und andere Raumbedürfnisse hat, ist den Architekten wenig bewusst.

Auch den Lehrenden ist zu wenig klar, wie Raum wahrgenommen wird: Dazu gehören die physischen Voraussetzungen des Wahrnehmenden, sein Bewegungsverhalten, Raumvorbilder und -erfahrungen, Prägungen und Lernerfahrungen sowie soziale Begebenheiten. Solche Aspekte der Raumwahrnehmung sind meines Wissens in ihrer Komplexität und in ihrem Zusammenspiel nicht genau erforscht und dargestellt. Das Raumverständnis und das Formulieren von Raumbedürfnissen baut auf dem Wissen über Raumwahrnehmung auf.

Auch das Verhältnis von Raumatmosphäre und Lernortgestaltung wird in der Architektur zu wenig thematisiert. Beides wird durch die Lichtführung, Farben, Materialien und Oberflächen, also durch die Innenarchitektur beeinflusst. Manchmal beobachte ich aber auch, dass Lehrpersonen es nicht verstehen, das vorhandene architektonische Potenzial eines Lernraumes optimal zu nutzen. Räumliche Gegebenheiten werden oft schlecht genutzt.

**Urs Meier** Bedeutet das nicht, dass Raumgestaltung zu einem Thema der Ausbildung von Lehrpersonen werden müsste und Lernortgestaltung zum Inhalt der Architektur? Die Voraussetzung dafür ist das Verstehen und Interpretieren der Architektur; die Lehrperson muss mit Licht umgehen können, die technische Infrastruktur verstehen lernen und das Mobiliar sinnvoll einsetzen können — mit anderen Worten: mit den zur Verfügung stehenden Mitteln Lernatmosphäre schaffen lernen. In der Raum-Organisation sind Unterschiede durchaus möglich, denn meiner Meinung nach ist es wichtig, Räume so gestalten zu lernen, dass sie die Schülerinnen und die

The architect must implement a space allocation program, consider economic requirements, meet the requirements of the fire police and the preservation of historic buildings and monuments, implement cantonal guidelines concerning school construction and design and the like. He or she is concerned to create a work that must meet high aesthetic standards and one that can hold its own against comparable buildings. He or she only takes a marginal interest in the actual learning process and activities of the buildings' users. In the process, attention to the desirable pedagogical ambience loses out.

**Urs Meier** It strikes me that teachers actually think in a rather similar pattern as do architects. What the interplay of space, function, form and construction is for the architect, the relationship among goals, content, methods and media is for the teacher. All these dimensions of the teaching and learning process influence one another. Changes to any one of these four cornerstones necessarily have repercussions for the others.

When theorists of education speak — as they increasingly do — about 'learning landscapes' or the psychology of the 'learning environment', that is something that extends beyond this 'magic quadrangle'. With these concepts, the whole environment of learning comes into view: the architecture, the interior design, the furnishings, the multimedia equipment, the rules of interaction, the working atmosphere, the atmospheres for learning, the learners and teachers.

Architecture confronts the difficult fact that today, instruction is no longer exclusively limited to a schoolroom with fixed rows of benches that face the blackboard and the teacher's lectern. Instead, it requires 'learning spaces' or 'landscapes', in which learners can retrieve information, execute projects, shape ideas and solve problems, but also follow a systematic course of instruction. Cooperation among the pupils, team spirit and exploratory learning take centre stage. 'Learning worlds' in schools should invite the children to linger; they should offer them opportunities and challenges that tempt them to grapple with material independently and increase their joy in learning.

On my visits to schools in recent years, I have been increasingly struck by the fact that learners are beginning to make varied use of other rooms in addition to the classroom, including side rooms, corridors, stairways, niches, a great variety of comfortable and uncomfortable seats, individual and group workplaces, as well as media and specialised libraries. The children use all of these for reading, conversing and resting.

**Peter Eberhard** I would also like to mention the issue of differing notions of space and the use of space. Teachers and learners, members of government, caretakers, external users and architects have different conceptions of space and perceive spaces differently. What is problematic in this is that there are no shared basic notions with respect to learning spaces. Architects, however, naturally assume that teachers conceive of space the same way they do. Architects are relatively unaware of the fact that human beings have different conceptions of space and different space-related needs according to their age, their socialisation and their role.

Teachers also lack an adequate understanding of the way space is perceived. The perception of space depends on the physical equipment of the perceiver, how much they move and the way they move, their previous spatial models and spatial experiences. To my knowledge, these aspects of spatial perception have not been researched precisely and described in their complexity and interplay. The understanding of space and the formulation of space-related needs build on the knowledge and understanding of spatial perception.

Architects also pay too little attention to the relationship between atmosphere and the design of learning spaces. Both are influenced by illumination, colours, materials and surfaces, in short by interior design. Sometimes, however, I also notice

Schüler zu vielfältigen Lernaktivitäten anregen. Die räumliche Gestaltung kann sich auf das Wohlbefinden und die Lernbedingungen der Lehrenden und Lernenden positiv auswirken. Die Interaktion zwischen Benutzern und Architekten muss intensiviert werden, damit das gegenseitige Verständnis gefördert wird.

**Peter Eberhard** Die Veränderungen in der Bildungslandschaft, vor allem die Einführung der «teilautonomen Schulen», verlangen in Zukunft eine veränderte Interaktion zwischen Planenden und Erziehenden. Der Blick auf das Schema unten zeigt uns, dass bisher ein Zusammengehen zwischen Pädagogik und Architektur nur bedingt stattgefunden hat und dass vor allem Lehrpersonen noch zu wenig befragt und einbezogen wurden.

**Traditionell**                                              **In Zukunft**

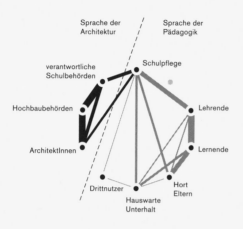
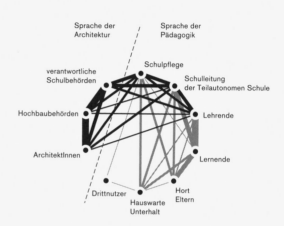

Durch das Einführen der geleiteten Schulen kommen neue Gesprächspartner ins Blickfeld, die sich in den Dialog zwischen Architektur und Pädagogik einbringen müssen. Die Schulleitung der teilautonomen Schulen muss sich zusammen mit ihrem Team in den Planungsvorgang einschalten und ihre Bedürfnisse an die Lernortgestaltung anmelden. Mit anderen Worten wird es in Zukunft mehr Personen mit einem pädagogischen Hintergrund geben, die auf der Ebene der Architektur mitreden müssen. Im gleichen Zuge ist der Architekt durch die neuen Verhältnisse herausgefordert, sich vermehrt auf pädagogische Anliegen einzulassen.

**Urs Meier** Meine Vorstellung wäre es aber, dass Architekten sich vermehrt für Bildung interessieren und Lehrende sich vermehrt mit Architektur auseinander setzen. Beide müssen sich mit den Denkvorstellungen und den Handlungsmöglichkeiten des jeweils anderen befassen. So könnten zum Beispiel Architektinnen und Architekten, die an Schulhausbau-Wettbewerben teilnehmen, vermehrt Lehrende und Lernende einbeziehen und mit ihnen zusammen Lernlandschaften für die Zukunft entwickeln. Eine andere Möglichkeit wäre, im Rahmen der jeweiligen Ausbildungen über interdisziplinäre Module das Verhältnis zwischen Raum, Raumorganisation und Lernen zu thematisieren. Als Sofortmassnahme sind Weiterbildungskurse für Interessierte anzubieten.

that teachers do not understand how to make best use of the available architectural potential of a learning space. They often take inadequate advantage of spatial features.

**Urs Meier** Doesn't that mean that interior design should be incorporated into teacher training and the design of learning spaces made a part of the study of architecture? The prerequisite for this is the understanding and interpretation of architecture. Teachers must be able to work with light, they must understand the technical infrastructure and they must be able to make meaningful use of the interior furnishings. In other words, they must learn to create the atmosphere for learning by making use of the means at hand. Differences are entirely possible in the area of spatial organisation, because I believe it is important to learn to design spaces so that they stimulate the pupils to embark upon a variety of learning activities. Interior design can have a positive impact on the well-being and learning conditions of teachers and learners. The interaction between users and architects must be intensified in order to promote mutual understanding.

**Peter Eberhard** The changes in the educational landscape, especially the introduction of 'semi-autonomous schools', require that planners and educators interact in a different way in the future. A look at the schema on the left will show that architecture and educational theory have thus far only worked together to a limited extent and that teachers above all are still not asked what they think and included enough.

**traditional**

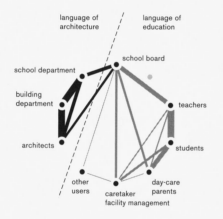

**future**

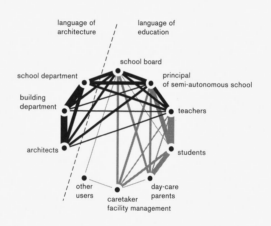

With the introduction of directed schools, new discussion partners are making their appearance, and they must be included in the dialogue between architecture and educational theory. Together with their team, the headmasters of the semi-autonomous schools must enter the planning process and signal their needs. In future, in other words, there will be more people with a background in education who will have to participate in the architectural discussion. At the same time, these new conditions challenge the architect to take a greater interest in educational concerns.

**Urs Meier** What I envision, however, is a situation where architects take a greater interest in education, and teachers concern themselves to a greater extent with architecture. Each must explore the thought processes and possibilities for action of the other. Thus, for example, architects who participate in school building competitions might involve teachers and learners to a greater extent and develop learning landscapes for the future together with them. Another possibility would be to treat the relationship of learning, space and spatial organisation in interdisciplinary modules within the existing training curricula in each field. As a measure that can be implemented immediately, continuing education courses should be offered for those who are interested.

Freilichtunterricht im Wald gibt es seit
1904 in Berlin-Charlottenburg, seit 1914 in
Zürich an der Biberlinstrasse. Foto: BAZ

Health and nature: Open-air instruction
in the forest has existed since 1904
in Berlin-Charlottenburg, and since 1914
in Zurich's Biberlinstrasse.

# 100 Jahre Reformdiskussion

Die Geschichte des Schulhausbaus im 20. Jahrhundert ist eine Abfolge von pädagogischen Diskussionen, die immer wieder neu mit moralischem Impetus und reformerischem Wahrheitsanspruch geführt wurden. Zentrale Themen und Fragestellungen der heutigen Debatte wurden bereits vor 100 Jahren formuliert und bestimmten über Jahrzehnte die Auseinandersetzungen.

## Sauberkeit und Disziplin

Seit den dreissiger Jahren des 19. Jahrhunderts konstituierte sich die allgemeine und obligatorische Volksschule als nationalstaatliche Institution und erfasste sehr rasch die ländliche wie die städtische Jugend aller Schichten und beider Geschlechter. Im Rahmen des bürgerlichen Gleichheitsprinzips vermittelte die Schule im 19. Jahrhundert nicht nur kognitive Lerninhalte, sondern in hohem Mass auch normierende und disziplinierende Erziehungsziele. Für den Bau von Schulhäusern lieferte die sozialmedizinische Hygienebewegung die wichtigsten Impulse. Ärzte formulierten Normen, die den notwendigen «Luftraum» pro Kind definierten, genügend Licht und eine gerade Haltung in der Sitzbank anstrebten. Die Verordnung über das Volksschulwesen des Kantons Zürich zum Beispiel verlangte 1900 mindestens 1 Quadratmeter Schulzimmerfläche pro Kind und eine Raumhöhe von 3,50 Meter. In seinem umfassenden Werk über den Schulhausbau in der Schweiz fasste Henry Baudin 1907 die wesentlichen Themen im Zeichen der Hygienebewegung zusammen.[1] Die Schule sollte ein Ort der Sauberkeit sein und Hygiene zum Erziehungsinhalt machen: Seit 1893 wurden in Stadtzürcher Schulen Brausebäder (Schulduschen) eingebaut, um die Kinder an regelmässiges Baden zu gewöhnen. Zu den Forderungen der Hygienebewegung gehörte auch die Pavillonschule, die schon 1904, beim Ersten Internationalen Kongress für Schulhygiene in Nürnberg, der ungesunden «Schulkaserne» gegenübergestellt wurde.[2] [fig. 1/2/3]

## Reformpädagogik und Psychoanalyse

Unter den Teilnehmern dieses Nürnberger Kongresses war der Hygieniker Friedrich Erismann, damals Vorsteher des Stadtzürcher Gesundheitswesens. In seinem Bericht in der schweizerischen «Zeitschrift für Schulgesundheitspflege» führte er den Begriff der «Erziehungshygiene» ein und damit ein neues Verständnis von Kindheit, Schule und Unterricht in einem viel weiteren Sinn. Es handle sich darum, so Erismann, die «möglichst gesunde, harmonische Entwicklung des Körpers und des Geistes beim Einzelnen» zu fördern. Er forderte eine Schule, die neben der Entwicklung der intellektuellen auch die der körperlichen und schöpferischen Kräfte anstrebt.[3]

1  Henry Baudin, Les constructions scolaires en Suisse, Genf 1907

2  Bericht über den 1. Internationalen Kongress für Schulhygiene, Nürnberg 1904

3  Friedrich Erismann in: Zeitschrift für Schulgesundheitspflege, 1904, S. 361–385

Karin Dangel, Daniel Kurz

# A Century of Discussion on Reform

The history of schoolhouse construction in the twentieth century is a succession of pedagogical discussions, led time and again with moral force and the reformer's claim to truth. Central themes and questions of the debate today were already formulated a hundred years ago and determined disagreements over the decades.

## Cleanliness and Discipline

From the 1830s onwards, the general and compulsory *Volksschule* [primary and secondary school] became established as an institution of the nation state and spread quite rapidly to encompass the rural as well as urban youth from all classes and both genders. In the context of the principle of equality as citizens, the school in the nineteenth century conveyed not only cognitive learned content, but also a high measure of normative and disciplinary educational goals. The socio-medical hygiene movement was the source of the most important ideas in the construction of schoolhouses. Doctors formulated norms that defined the necessary 'breathing space' per child and strived for sufficient light and an upright seating position. The regulations for *Volksschulen* in the canton of Zurich, for example, required in 1900 that there be at least one square metre of classroom area per child with a height of 3.50 metres. In his comprehensive 1907 work on schoolhouse construction in Switzerland, Henry Baudin summarised the essential themes of the hygiene movement.[1] The school was to be a place of cleanliness and to make hygiene a topic of education: Beginning in 1893, school showers were built in schools in the city of Zurich so as to accustom children to regular bathing. Also among the demands of the hygiene movement was the pavilion school, which was already promoted as an alternative to the unhealthy 'school barracks' in 1904 at the Erster Internationale Kongress für Schulhygiene [First International Congress for School Hygiene] in Nuremberg.[2] [fig.1/2/3]

## Reform Pedagogy and Psychoanalysis

Among the participants at this Nuremberg congress was the hygienist Friedrich Erismann, then director of the health authority of the city of Zurich. In his report in the Swiss *Zeitschrift für Schulgesundheitspflege,* he first introduced the term 'educational hygiene' *(Erziehungshygiene),* and with it a new and greatly broadened understanding of childhood, school and instruction. According to Erismann, 'educational hygiene' was about promoting the 'development of the body and spirit of the

1  Henry Baudin, Les constructions scolaires en Suisse (Geneva, 1907).

2  Bericht über den 1. Internationalen Kongress für Schulhygiene (Nuremberg, 1904).

fig.1    Schulhygiene: Schulduschen in
         La Chaux-de-Fonds.

         Bild aus Henry Baudin, 1907


         School hygiene: School showers in
         La Chaux-de-Fonds.

         From: Henry Baudin, 1907

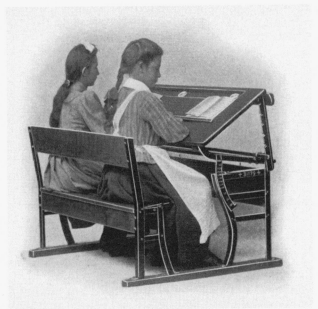

fig.2    Schulhygiene: Verstellbare Pulte
         sorgen für gerade Haltung.

         Bild aus Henry Baudin, 1907


         School hygiene: Adjustable desks
         provide for upright posture.

         From: Henry Baudin, 1907

fig.3    Die Geometrie des Schulzimmers:
         Schulbänke und Katheder im **Schulhaus Riedtli**
         in Zürich 1908.

         Foto: Baugeschichtliches Archiv der
         Stadt Zürich (BAZ)


         The geometry of the classroom:
         School benches and lecturer's desk at
         the **Riedtli School,** 1908.

         Photo: Baugeschichtliches Archiv der Stadt
         Zürich (BAZ)

Dieser Einsicht lag eine neue Achtung und Wahrnehmung des Kindes zugrunde, die zentral für die Reformpädagogik der Jahrhundertwende war. Sie fasste das Kind als aktives Subjekt und die Schule als Institution auf, in der Interesse als Triebkraft der kindlichen Aktivität im Vordergrund steht. Dahinter verbarg sich eine radikale Kritik an der Schule des 19. Jahrhunderts. Die «Pädagogik vom Kinde aus» wurde zum Schlagwort. Sowohl das sozialkritische Engagement der Schwedin Ellen Key, die das anbrechende 20. Jahrhundert zum «Jahrhundert des Kindes» erklärte, als auch die aus dem kindlichen Lernverhalten abgeleiteten Theorien von Maria Montessori oder die Demokratisierung der Schule nach John Dewey wurzeln in diesen Grundsätzen.

Einen neuen Zugang zur Kindheit eröffnete zur gleichen Zeit die Psychoanalyse nach Sigmund Freud, die in der Zürcher Klinik Burghölzli von Eugen Bleuler und C. G. Jung bereits um 1900 praktiziert wurde. Die Übertragung von Freuds Gedankengut auf die Schweizer Pädagogik war weitgehend das Verdienst des Psychoanalytikers und Pfarrers Oskar Pfister, der ab 1912 als Redaktor bei den «Berner Seminarblättern» mitarbeitete. In einem 1923 erschienenen Artikel in der «Schweizerischen Pädagogischen Zeitschrift» stellte Pfister dem normierenden «Methodismus» der alten Pädagogik eine individualistische Behandlung des Kindes gegenüber, die das Kind in seiner Eigenart erkennt und seine Seelennöte ernst nimmt.[4] Pfister forderte eine Pädagogik, die auf dem Wissen über die unbewussten Geistesprozesse beruht und neben den intellektuellen Fähigkeiten «sorgfältigste Gemütspflege» fördert. Gemäss dem Grundsatz, wonach der grösste Teil der Erziehung vom Kind selbst geleistet werden müsse, sollte sich der Lehrer vom Schulmonarchen zum selbst lebenslang Lernenden entwickeln. Der Lehrer wird zum Mitarbeiter des Kindes und ist nicht nur Wissensvermittler, er regt kindliche Interessen an und fördert intellektuelle und moralische Bedürfnisse.

### Von Stil keine Spur, Gott sei Dank!

Reformwillen erfasste um 1900 nicht nur die Pädagogik, sondern ebenso die Welt der Kunst und Architektur. Der Historismus des 19. Jahrhunderts wurde – ganz ähnlich wie dessen Pädagogik – als schematisch und gemütslos kritisiert. Die 1905 gegründete Heimatschutzbewegung setzte sich für eine neue, sachliche Baukultur ein, die mit Farben, natürlichen Materialien und handwerklicher Sorgfalt Räume gestaltet. Das Heimatstil-Schulhaus sollte ein Gesamtkunstwerk werden, das den kindlichen Geschmack bilden hilft. Zur Eröffnung des Schulhauses Riedtli schrieb die Zürcher Wochen-Chronik 1908: «Mit ausgesuchtem Raffinement gingen die Architekten darauf aus, überall durch grösste Einfachheit, mit den bescheidensten Mitteln, vornehme Wirkung zu erzielen und damit den guten Geschmack der Kinder heranzubilden, ihnen durch beständige Anschauung einen Massstab des Schönen beizubringen, sie dazu anzuleiten, das Hässliche zu verwerfen. Wenn wir ehrlich

individual in as healthy and harmonious a manner as possible'.[3] He called for a school that would strive not only for the development of intellectual powers but also for that of physical and creative powers. This insight was based on a new respect for and view of the child that was central to the reform pedagogy of the *fin de siècle*. It viewed the child as an active subject and the school as an institution at the fore of which was the child's interest as the driving force behind his or her activity. Implicit in this was a radical critique of the nineteenth-century school. 'Child-centred education' became a slogan. Rooted in these principles were the socially critical engagement of the Swedish reformer Ellen Key, who at the start of the twentieth century declared it to be the 'century of the child', the theories of Maria Montessori drawn from the learning behaviour of children and the democratisation of the school by John Dewey.

A new approach to childhood was opened at the same time by Sigmund Freud's psychoanalysis, which was already practised in 1900 at the Klinik Burghölzli in Zurich by Eugen Bleuler and Carl Gustav Jung. The transmission of Freud's ideas into Swiss pedagogy was in many respects due to the psychoanalyst and pastor Oskar Pfister, who beginning in 1912 worked as editor of the *Berner Seminarblätter*. In a 1923 article in the *Schweizerische Pädagogische Zeitschrift*, Pfister contrasted the normative 'methodism' of the old pedagogy to treating a child as an individual, recognizing the child in its distinctiveness and taking seriously its mental anguish.[4] Pfister called for a pedagogy making use of the knowledge of unconscious spiritual processes and promoting not only intellectual abilities but also 'highly thorough emotional care'. According to the principle that the greater part of the education of a child must be achieved by the child itself, the teacher should evolve from school monarch to life-long learner. The teacher becomes the child's co-worker. He not only conveys knowledge, but also stimulates childlike interests and supports intellectual and moral needs.

### 'No Trace of Style, Thank God!'

The will to reform in 1900 extended not only to pedagogy, but also to the worlds of art and architecture. The historicism of the nineteenth century was criticised — much as was its pedagogy — as schematic and unfeeling. The Heimatschutzbewegung [preservation movement], founded in 1905, engaged itself on behalf of a new, functional culture of building, one which would design spaces with colours, natural materials and careful craftsmanship. The 'Heimatstil' [early modern] schoolhouse was to be a total work of art, one that would help shape children's taste. At the opening of the Riedtli Schoolhouse in 1908, the *Zürcher Wochen-*

---

4  Oskar Pfister in: Schweizerische pädagogische Zeitschrift, 1923, S.97ff., 129ff., 161ff. und 193ff.

---

3  Friedrich Erismann in: Zeitschrift für Schulgesundheitspflege (1904), pp.361–85.

4  Oskar Pfister in: Schweizerische pädagogische Zeitschrift (1923), pp.97ff., 129ff., 161ff. and 193ff.

fig.4 «Von Stil keine Spur»: Freie Volumen-
gruppierung am **Heimatstil-Schulhaus Riedtli**
in Zürich, Bischoff + Weideli, 1908.

Foto: BAZ

'No trace of style': Free grouping of volumes
at the early-modern *(Heimatstil)* **Riedtli
School** in Zurich, Bischoff + Weideli, 1908.

Photo: BAZ

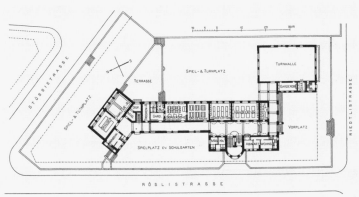

fig.5 Grundriss ohne Symmetriezwang: Im **Schulhaus
Riedtli** ergänzen Handfertigkeitsräume, eine
Schulküche, ein Demonstrations- und ein
Sammlungszimmer, vier Klassenzimmer für den
Arbeitsunterricht sowie Singsaal, Bibliothek
und Zeichensaal das Raumangebot — «kurz
alles, was zum Tip-Top eines modernen Schul-
hauses gehört».

Plan Schweiz. Bauzeitung Bd. 54, 1909

Ground plan without forced symmetry: In the
**Riedtli School,** handicraft rooms, a school
kitchen, an assembly room, four classrooms for
work teaching, a singing hall, library and
arts hall make up the available spaces — 'in
short, everything that belongs in a tip-top
modern schoolhouse'.

Plan: Schweizerische Bauzeitung 54 (1909)

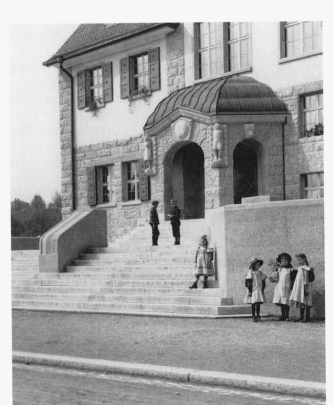

fig.6 Kunst im Dienst der Erziehung:
**Schulhaus Hans Asper** in Zürich von
Friedrich Fissler, 1910.

Foto: BAZ

Art in the service of education:
**Hans Asper School** in Zurich by
Friedrich Fissler, 1910.

Photo: BAZ

sein wollen, müssen wir zugeben, dass es nach all den Jahrzehnten unerträglicher Geschmacklosigkeiten höchste Zeit ist, beim Baue von Schulhäusern in einer neuen Generation den Sinn fürs Schöne zu wecken.»[5] [fig.4/5/6]

Einem ähnlichen Erziehungsziel folgte das Reformprojekt der «Arbeitsschule», die neben kognitivem Wissen auch praktische Erfahrungen und Fertigkeiten vermittelt und Grundlagen für handwerkliche Berufe lehrt. Die Revision des Unterrichtsgesetzes im Kanton Zürich und der neue Lehrplan aus dem Jahr 1905 trugen diesem Aspekt Rechnung. Neben den Hauptfächern Lesen, Schreiben und Rechnen enthielt der neue Lehrplan auch Stoffpläne für Realien, für die Kunstfächer Zeichnen, Werken, Gesang und Turnen sowie für den Handarbeitsunterricht. Die spezialisierten Unterrichtsräume gehörten seither zum Raumprogramm jedes Schulneubaus. [fig.5]

Insgesamt war um 1910 im Schulhausbau ein Standard erreicht, der im Wesentlichen bis in die Zeit nach dem Zweiten Weltkrieg bestimmend bleiben sollte. Die einbündige Anlage mit einseitig an einen Längskorridor gereihten Schulzimmern kommt der Forderung nach einer guten Belichtung und Belüftung der Innenräume ebenso entgegen wie die breiten, zu eigentlichen Pausenhallen ausgeweiteten Korridore, die dem kindlichen Bewegungsdrang Raum geben und zum Tummeln und Spielen einladen. Eine wichtige Auswirkung der Reformen war die Reduktion der Klassengrössen und damit der Schulzimmerflächen. Neben dem traditionellen Schulhof stand immer öfter eine «Spielwiese» für Sport und freie Bewegung zur Verfügung.

### «Schulbauten sind pädagogische Angelegenheiten»

Die Architektur-Avantgarde der dreissiger Jahre nahm die Reformdiskussionen der Jahrhundertwende wieder auf und verband sie mit ihrem eigenen typischen Formenvokabular. Die Licht- und Luftbegeisterung der klassischen Moderne spiegelt sich in der Schwerelosigkeit der Architektur. Glas, Öffnung, helle Farben, Dachgärten, Terrassen waren die Merkmale. Die Architekten sahen sich als Vollstrecker der objektiven Bedürfnisse ihrer Zeit. Gerade der Schulbau bot sich als Anwendungsbereich der modernen Bestrebungen an, denn in diesem Bereich konnten die Architekten sich als verantwortungsvolle Erzieher und Sozialärzte besonders überzeugend in Szene setzen. Doch gerade im Schulhausbau zeigt sich sehr deutlich, dass das Neue Bauen Erkenntnisse umsetzte, die die vorangegangene Generation bereits formuliert hatte.

1932 zeigte das Zürcher Kunstgewerbemuseum die Ausstellung «Der neue Schulbau», die der Hygieniker Wilhelm von Gonzenbach, der Architekt Werner M. Moser und der Pädagoge Willi Schohaus in interdisziplinärer Zusammenarbeit konzipiert hatten. Sie postulierte die Grundsätze des Neuen Bauens. Nach der Devise «form follows function» sah sie das Schulhaus des Neuen Bauens als Zweckbau, der sich aus seiner Bestimmung heraus entwickelt und als Antwort auf die neuen pädagogischen Konzepte versteht. [fig.7/8/9]

5  Zürcher Wochen-Chronik, 10 (1908), S.461

*Chronik* wrote: 'With exquisite refinement, the architects have sought, through the use throughout of great simplicity and modest materials, to achieve an elegant effect and in so doing to educate the good taste of the children, to teach them through the constant contemplation of a standard of the beautiful, to guide them to reject the ugly. To be honest, we must confess that, after so many decades of unbearable tastelessness, it is high time to awaken the sense for the beautiful in a new generation through the construction of schoolhouses.'[5]

A similar educational goal was pursued by the reform project of the 'work school' (*Arbeitsschule*), which conveyed practical experience and skills alongside cognitive knowledge and taught fundamentals for craft careers. The revision of the education law (*Unterrichtsgesetz*) in the canton of Zurich and the new curriculum of 1905 took this aspect of reform into account. In addition to the main subjects of reading, writing and arithmetic, the new curriculum also contained specific syllabi for general knowledge, for the art subjects of arts, crafts, singing and gymnastics, and for needlework as well. Specialised classrooms belonged thenceforth to the spatial design of every newly constructed school. [fig.5]

By 1910, a comprehensive standard was reached in schoolhouse construction that remained essentially unchanged and authoritative until the period after the Second World War. The single-depth structure with a row of classrooms down one side of a longitudinal corridor addresses the call for good lighting and ventilation of inner rooms as well as that for broad corridors, expanded into break halls that allow space for the childlike urge for movement and invite romping and playing. An important consequence of the reforms was the reduction in class sizes and with it classroom areas. Alongside the traditional schoolyard, a playground for sports and free movement became increasingly common.

### 'School Structures Are Pedagogical Matters'

The architectural avant-garde of the 1930s resumed the reform discussions of the turn of the century and connected them to its own specific formal vocabulary. The classical modernist enthusiasm for light and air was reflected in the weightlessness of the architecture. Glass, openings, bright colours, rooftop gardens and terraces were defining traits. The architects saw themselves as fulfilling the objective needs of their time. School construction in particular offered itself as an area of application for modernist endeavours, as it was in this area that architects could draw attention to themselves most convincingly as responsible educators and social healers. Yet it was exactly in the field of school construction that it was particularly clear that the high modernist (*Neues*

5  Zürcher Wochen-Chronik 10 (1908), p.461.

fig.7　«Aufwand für das Kind?» Polemik gegen die Kasernenbauweise an der Zürcher Schulbau-ausstellung 1932. Im Bild die **Freiluftschule** in Amsterdam von Johannes Duiker (1927–1930).

Bild aus: Das Kind und sein Schulhaus, 1932

'Extravagance for the child?' Polemic against the barracks construction method at the Zurich school construction exhibition in 1932. Depicted is the **Open-Air School** in Amsterdam by Johannes Duiker (1927–1930).

From: Das Kind und sein Schulhaus, 1932

Vorschlag für ebenerdige Anlage mit Austritt auf offenen Gartenhof.

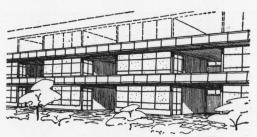

Vorschlag für mehrgeschossige Anlage mit Austritt aus Klassenzimmer in gedeckte Hallen.

fig.8　Vorschläge für die Pavillonbauweise mit zweiseitiger Belichtung (oben) und mehrge-schossiger **Freiluftschule** (unten) von Alfred Roth.

Bild aus: Das Kind und sein Schulhaus, 1932

Suggestions for the pavilion method of building with lighting from two sides (above) and multi-level **Open-Air School** (below) by Alfred Roth.

From: Das Kind und sein Schulhaus, 1932

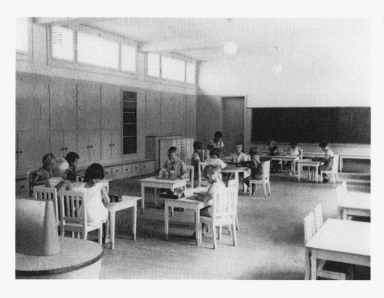

fig.9　Zweiseitig belichteter Kindergarten mit beweglichem Mobiliar an der Ausstellung «Das Kind und sein Schulhaus» 1932.

Foto: Museum für Gestaltung und Kunst, Zürich

Kindergarten lit from two sides with movable furnishings at the exhibition *Das Kind und sein Schulhaus,* 1932.

Photo: Museum für Gestaltung und Kunst, Zurich

Der Architekturkritiker Peter Meyer fasste die Erkenntnis der Ausstellung in der Forderung nach einer
«kindertümlichen» Schulhausarchitektur zusammen,
die nicht die Repräsentation, sondern das Kind in den
Mittelpunkt stellt und an ihm ihren Massstab nimmt:
«Eine ausgesprochen bescheidene, menschlich gütige,
allem pompösen Scheinwesen abgeneigte Haltung
scheint deshalb heute den Lehrern und Architekten, die
sich mit der Frage des Schulbaus abgeben, die allein
richtige.»[6] Anstelle von Monumentalität und Grösse
seien das Stille und der unmittelbare Zugang zur Natur,
zu Bäumen, Gärten und Wiesen zu suchen.

Als ideale Schulform propagierten die Ausstellungs-
macher 1932 die kleinmassstäbliche Pavillonbauweise.
Sie versprach, dem Kind eine überschaubare Welt sowie
eine intensive Beziehung zur Natur und zur unmittelbaren Umgebung des Schulhauses zu bieten, und sie erlaubte eine bessere, nämlich zweiseitige Belichtung der
Klassenzimmer. Mit dem Kindergartenhaus Wiedikon
realisierten die Architekten Hans Hofmann und Adolf
Kellermüller 1928–1932 die erste Pavillonanlage in
Zürich und eine der frühesten in der Schweiz.[7] [fig.9/10]

### Äusserliche Modernität

Das «Neue Bauen» prägte in den dreissiger Jahren
die architektonische Erscheinung der meisten neuen
Schulhäuser in der Schweiz. Die Formensprache der
horizontal ausgedehnten Baukörper war betont schlicht
und nüchtern. Grosse Fensteröffnungen gliederten die
glatten Fassaden, Flachdach und auf Pilotis ruhende,
überdeckte Pausenhallen im Erdgeschoss wurden Marken-
zeichen der neuen Architektur. Die Disposition der
Grundrisse und das Raumprogramm unterschieden sich jedoch wenig von den Schulbauten der Heimatstil-Zeit:
Zweiseitig belichtete Klassenzimmer und Pavillon-Schul-
häuser setzten sich noch nicht durch. [fig.11/12]

Eine Forderung der Ausstellung von 1932 fand jedoch
sehr schnell Eingang in die Schulbaupraxis: das bewegliche Mobiliar. Tisch und Bank wurden jetzt voneinander getrennt, um eine erhöhte Beweglichkeit der
Schüler und Schülerinnen zu ermöglichen. Die Stadt
Zürich begann in den dreissiger Jahren mit der An-
schaffung beweglicher Möbel — in ländlichen Gegenden
blieben die alten schraubstockartigen Schulbänke vielerorts jedoch bis in die sechziger Jahre im Gebrauch.

In der Zeit nach dem Zweiten Weltkrieg fanden die
Forderungen von 1932 breitere Anerkennung. Wesentliche
Impulse für den Schulhausbau lieferte nun Albert
Heinrich Steiner, der 1943 bis 1957 als Zürcher Stadtbaumeister amtierte. In seiner Ägide wurden insgesamt
65 Schulhäuser, Turnhallen und Kindergärten gebaut,
projektiert oder in Auftrag gegeben, darunter 25 grosse
Neubauten.[8] Steiner stellte den Schulhausbau in den
grösseren Rahmen des Städtebaus. Die frühzeitige pro-
spektive Planung und Sicherung grosszügiger Schulareale
ermöglichte in den Neubauquartieren der Nachkriegszeit
eine grossräumige Anlage der Schulhäuser und Sport-
flächen. Die Schulanlagen wurden jetzt inmitten weiter

*Bauen*) movement was only implementing findings that
had already been formulated by the prior generation.

In 1932, the Zurich Kunstgewerbemuseum mounted
the exhibition *Der neue Schulbau* [The New School
Building], which had been conceived in interdisciplinary collaboration between the hygienist Wilhelm
von Gonzenbach, the architect Werner M. Moser and
the pedagogue Willi Schohaus. They postulated
the fundamentals of high modernism. According to the
motto of 'form follows function', they saw the
schoolhouse of high modernism as a structure which
was to be understood as a response to new pedagogical concepts. [fig.7/8/9]

The architecture critic Peter Meyer summarised
the vision of the exhibition as a call for a 'childlike' (*kindertümlich*) schoolhouse architecture, one
that took its standards from the child and placed
not representation but the child in the centre:
'A markedly modest attitude, one of human goodness
and that eschews all pompous falseness, therefore
seems the only right one to teachers and architects
concerned today with the question of school construction.'[6] In lieu of monumentality and size,
tranquillity and direct access to nature, trees,
gardens and meadows were to be sought.

In 1932, the exhibition organisers propagated
the small-scale pavilion building method as the
ideal form for a school. The form promised to offer
children an easily grasped world as well as an
intensive relationship to nature and to the direct
surroundings of the schoolhouse, and the form also
allowed classrooms a better, namely a two-sided,
exposure to light. With the kindergarten house
Wiedikon, the architects Hans Hofmann and Adolf
Kellermüller realised in 1928 to 1932 the first pavilion structure in Zurich and one of the first
in Switzerland.[7] [fig.9/10]

### External Modernity

The high modernist movement characterised the
architectural appearance of most new schoolhouses
in Switzerland in the 1930s. The formal language of
the horizontally long main body was emphatically
simple and sober. Large window openings subdivided
the straight façades; flat roofs and covered break
halls resting on pillars on the ground floor were
the hallmarks of the new architecture. The arrangement of the ground plan and the spatial design
varied little, however, from the schoolhouses of the
*Heimatstil* period: classrooms lit from two sides
and pavilion schoolhouses had not yet caught on.
[fig.11/12]

One demand of the 1932 exhibition was adopted
quickly into the praxis of school construction, however: movable furnishings. Table and seat were now
separated from one another so as to make possible
greater freedom of movement for the pupils. The city
of Zurich began to acquire movable furniture in

---

6 Peter Meyer in: Werk 5 (1932), S.129

7 Arthur Rüegg, Hermann Kohler (Hg.), Kindergartenhaus Wiedikon 1928–32. Denkmalpflegerische
  Erneuerung, Zürich 2003

8 Ruedi Weidmann in: Das öffentliche Bauwesen in
  Zürich, 4. Band (1907–1957), Zürich 2000, S.102ff.

6 Peter Meyer in: Werk 5 (1932), p.129.

7 Arthur Rüegg and Hermann Kohler, eds.,
  Kindergartenhaus Wiedikon, 1928–32:
  Denkmalpflegerische Erneuerung (Zurich, 2003).

fig.10 Das **Kindergartenhaus Wiedikon** in Zürich von Hans Hofmann und Adolf Kellermüller (1928–1932) fasst acht Pavillons mit Glasfassade und seitlichen Oberlichtern zu einer Anlage zusammen, die ausserdem einen Hort und einen Gemeindesaal enthält.

Foto: Hans Finsler, 1932

The **Wiedikon Kindergarten** in Zurich by Hans Hofmann and Adolf Kellermüller (1928–1932), a single construction comprised of eight pavilions with glass façades and skylights at the sides, and containing an after-school care centre and community hall as well.

Photo: Hans Finsler, 1932

fig.11 Moderne Architektur, traditioneller Grundriss: **Schulhaus Kappeli** in Zürich-Altstetten von A. + H. Oeschger 1937.

Foto: BAZ

Modern architecture, traditional ground plan: **Kappeli School** in Zurich-Altstetten by A. + H. Oeschger 1937.

Photo: BAZ

fig.12 **Schulhaus Kappeli.** Bewegliches Mobiliar verändert den Schulalltag in Zürich ab 1932.

Foto: BAZ

**Kappeli School.** Moveable furniture was introduced in Zurich schools after 1932.

Photo: BAZ

Grünanlagen konzipiert, angebunden an verkehrsfreie Grünzüge, welche wie Finger in die besiedelten Gebiete hineingriffen.

Steiner prägte den Begriff des altersgerechten Schulhaustypus nach dem Grundsatz «Kleine Häuser für kleine Kinder – grosse Häuser für grosse Kinder». So empfahl er den Schulpavillon mit höchstens sechs Klassenzimmern für die Unterstufe, das Normalschulhaus mit 12 Klassen für die Mittelstufe und das Grossschulhaus mit 18 Klassenzimmern für die Oberstufe.[9] Die Konzeption des Schulhauses wandelte sich vom isolierten Grossbaukörper zum Komplex verschiedener Einzelbauten. Der Verzicht auf repräsentative Gesten war Programm; oft traten die Schulbauten zur Strasse hin kaum in Erscheinung. Mit dem Schulhaus Propstei in Schwamendingen realisierte die Stadt Zürich 1946 die erste grössere, in Pavillons aufgelöste Schulanlage.

### Die fünfziger Jahre – gesichertes Wissen

Mit dem V. Internationalen Kongress für Schulbaufragen und Freilufterziehung, der 1953 in der Schweiz abgehalten wurde, und mit der gleichzeitigen Ausstellung «Das neue Schulhaus» im Zürcher Kunstgewerbemuseum gelang es den Schweizer Wegbereitern des modernen Schulbaus – dem Architekten Alfred Roth und dem Pädagogen Willi Schohaus – ihre Anliegen wirksam zu legitimieren. Die stark beachtete Ausstellung machte die Erkenntnisse des Neuen Bauens zum weithin verbindlichen Standard im schweizerischen Schulhausbau. [fig. 13/14/15]

Die an der Ausstellung gezeigten Schweizer Schulen erfüllten zwar alle baulichen Anforderungen der Hygiene, der Lichtführung und der konstruktiven Sorgfalt, die an eine moderne Schule gestellt werden können. Sie wirkten jedoch im internationalen Vergleich auffallend bieder und detailverliebt. Vor allem aber waren Programmpunkte wie Freizeitbetreuung der Schüler, Mittagstisch oder Veranstaltungssäle – in Grossbritannien selbstverständlich – in der Schweiz völlig unbekannt; selbst Räume für den Gruppenunterricht blieben noch jahrzehntelang ein unerfülltes Postulat.

Funktionale und pädagogische Anliegen bestimmten den Kanon der für die fünfziger und sechziger Jahre verbindlichen Normen. Das räumliche Konzept ging stets vom Klassenzimmer als Grundeinheit aus, das mit 55 bis 65 Quadratmetern (rund 2 Quadratmeter pro Kind) knapp dimensioniert blieb. Eine möglichst quadratische Grundform des Raums und zweiseitiges Tageslicht waren erforderlich, um das bewegliche Schulmobiliar in unterschiedlicher und wechselnder Art anzuordnen. Zusätzlich zu einer grosszügigen, meist nach Südosten orientierten Fensterfront sorgten entweder rückwärtige Fensterbänder oder Oberlichter für eine ausgeglichene Beleuchtung des gesamten Raums. Architektinnen und Architekten entwickelten raffinierte Erschliessungssysteme, um diese Anforderungen auch in mehrgeschossigen Schulhäusern zu verwirklichen: Duplex-Erschliessungen mit je zwei Klassenzimmern an einer Treppe waren häufig. Mit ihnen entfielen die langen Korridore.

the 1930s, although the old, vice-like school-desks remained in use in many rural areas into the 1960s. The demands of 1932 won broader recognition in the period after the Second World War. Albert Heinrich Steiner, who served from 1943 until 1957 as the Zurich director of urban planning, was the source of important impulses for schools construction. Under his aegis, a total of 65 schools, gymnasiums and kindergartens were built, planned or commissioned, including 25 large new buildings.[8]

Steiner situated schoolhouse construction in the larger context of urban planning. Prospective planning well in advance of construction and the securing of generous sites of land for schools made possible expansive school facilities and sports fields in the newly constructed areas of the post-war period. School structures were now conceived amidst larger green areas, connected to greenswards free of traffic that extended like fingers into populated areas.

Steiner characterised the notion of types of schoolhouse construction according to age along the principle of 'little houses for little children – big houses for big children'. He thus recommended the school pavilion with at most six classrooms for the lower primary school, the normal school-building with twelve classrooms for the upper primary (Mittelstufe) schools and the large school with eighteen classrooms for the secondary schools (Oberstufe).[9] The conception of the school changed from that of an isolated single main body to a complex of various individual buildings. Avoiding imposing public gestures was programmatic; school buildings were often hardly visible at all from the street. With the Propstei School in Schwamendingen of 1946, the city of Zurich realised the first large-scale school structure broken up into pavilions.

### The 1950s: Secured Knowledge

At the Fifth International Congress for School Construction and Open-Air Education, held in Switzerland in 1953, and with the simultaneous exhibition Das Neue Schulhaus [The New School] at the Zurich Kunstgewerbemuseum, the Swiss innovators of modern school construction – the architect Alfred Roth and the pedagogue Willi Schohaus – succeeded in legitimating their work effectively. The highly regarded exhibition made the findings of the high modernism the widely held standard for Swiss school construction.

The Swiss schools shown at the exhibition did indeed fulfil all of the architectural requirements for hygiene, the use of light and the care in construction that could be asked of a modern school. In international comparison, however, they seemed conspicuously conservative in design and obsessed with detail. In particular, programmatic

9 Alfred Roth: Das Neue Schulhaus,
   1. Auflage, Zürich 1950

8 Ruedi Weidmann in: Das öffentliche Bauwesen in
   Zürich (1907–1957) (Zurich, 2000), pp.102ff.

9 Alfred Roth, Das Neue Schulhaus, 1st ed.
   (Zurich, 1950).

fig.13 Im Zeichen Pestalozzis: Die Ausstellung «Das Neue Schulhaus» 1953 in Zürich. Im Hintergrund ein 1:1-Modell eines modernen Klassenzimmers.

Foto: Museum für Gestaltung und Kunst, Zürich

Under the sign of Pestalozzi: the exhibition *Das Neue Schulhaus* [The New School] in Zurich in 1953. In the background: a 1:1 model of a modern classroom.

Photo: Museum für Gestaltung und Kunst, Zurich

fig.14 **Pavillonschulhaus Chriesiweg** in Zürich-Altstetten von Cramer, Jaray, Paillard (1954–1957). Im Anschluss an die Schulhausbau-Ausstellung 1953 schrieb die Stadt Zürich einen Wettbewerb für ein innovatives Schulhaus aus.

Foto: Peter Grünert

**Chriesiweg Pavilion School** in Zurich-Altstetten by Cramer, Jaray, Paillard (1954–1957). On the occasion of the schoolhouse construction exhibition of 1953, the city of Zurich also announced a competition for an innovative schoolhouse.

Photo: Peter Grünert

fig.15 **Chriesiweg:** Ausgewählt wurde ein Pavillonschulhaus mit Oberlichtern, Gruppenraum und Gartenhöfen, das Anklänge an die **Munkegaard-Schule** von Arne Jacobsen, Kopenhagen (1956) erkennen lässt.

Foto: Peter Grünert

**Chriesiweg:** A pavilion schoolhouse with skylights, group space and garden courtyards was selected, echoing the **Munkegaard School** by Arne Jacobsen, Copenhagen (1956).

Photo: Peter Grünert

## Modernität und Reformstau

Die intensive Schulbaudiskussion der fünfziger und sechziger Jahre war bestimmt von der Diskrepanz zwischen pädagogischer Reformdiskussion und architektonischer Aufbruchstimmung einerseits und dem beharrlichen Reformwiderstand der Institution Schule andererseits. Forderungen nach Gruppenunterricht und einer Schule, die das lernende Kind in den Mittelpunkt stellt, wurden schon an der Schulbau-Ausstellung 1953 erhoben und häufig wiederholt, fanden aber in der schulischen Praxis wie in den Bauprogrammen wenig Echo.

Da ein sehr grosser Teil der Schulbauten über Wettbewerbe vergeben wurde, finden sich dagegen selbst in ländlichen Gemeinden ab etwa 1955 Schulen von höchster Ausdruckskraft und zuweilen kompromissloser Modernität. Die «Solothurner Schule» um Fritz Haller, Franz Füeg und Barth & Zaugg strebte nach Öffnung und formaler Abstraktion im Mies'schen Sinn; eine ähnliche Tendenz bildete sich in der Westschweiz um Architekten wie Jean-Marc Lamunière und Paul Waltenspuhl. Sinnlichere Ansätze verfolgte in Zürich Ernst Gisel: Den gleichmässig hellen und glatten Räumen der klassischen Moderne setzte er ein Spiel von hell und dunkel, hoch und niedrig entgegen. Backstein und Beton brut waren seine bevorzugten Ausdrucksmittel. [fig. 16/17/18]

Den reformerischen Anspruch fasst Roland Gross, Architekt zahlreicher innovativer Schulbauprojekte, im Rückblick so zusammen: «Wir wollten durch die Architektur die Pädagogik verbessern und durch sie die Welt.» Während die Raumprogramme in jenen Jahren wenig differierten, suchten Architektinnen und Architekten nach neuen Ausdrucksformen und alternativen Grundrissformen für das Klassenzimmer. Immer wieder gelang es Einzelnen, moderne Anliegen wie Freiluft-Schulräume, Gruppen-Arbeitsbereiche oder offene Arbeitszonen in ihre Entwürfe zu schmuggeln. Sitzstufen im Freien verwiesen auf die Möglichkeit zur Diskussion oder zu spontanem Theaterspiel. In wenigen Fällen liessen sich grössere Säle oder eine öffentliche Bibliothek in der Schule unterbringen. [fig. 19/20]

## Systembau und Gesamtschule

Nicht didaktische, sondern gesellschaftliche Fragestellungen waren es schliesslich, die die Schule kurz vor 1968 aus ihrem Dornröschenschlaf weckten. Zwei Jahrzehnte der Hochkonjunktur hatten das Land verändert. Der Arbeitsmarkt war ausgetrocknet, und der Ruf nach «Aktivierung der Begabtenreserve» liess die hohen Hürden zwischen akademischen und beruflichen Ausbildungsgängen fragwürdig erscheinen — nicht nur aus demokratischer Sicht, sondern auch im Interesse der nationalen Wettbewerbsfähigkeit. In der Zeitschrift «Werk» forderte Lucius Burckhardt 1967 durchlässigere Selektionsverfahren und neue Lehrmethoden, die auf die moderne Teamarbeit und lebenslanges Lernen vorbereiteten. Für Sentimentalitäten, so Burckhardt, bleibe keine Zeit. Grössere und zentralisierte Schulanlagen seien das Gebot der Zukunft: «Gegenwärtig passen sich die

matters like leisure activities for pupils, lunches and event halls — all a matter of course in Great Britain — were wholly unknown in Switzerland; even spaces for group instruction were to remain a largely unfulfilled need for decades to come.

Functional and pedagogical matters determined the canon of the binding norms of the 1950s and 1960s. The spatial concept always began with the assumption of the basic unit of the classroom, which remained, at 55 to 65 square metres (about 2 square metres per child) tightly dimensioned. An as-square-as-possible basic form for the space and daylight from two sides were needed so that the movable school furnishings could be placed in as many places as possible. In addition to a generous front window, usually oriented to the southeast, the well-balanced lighting of the entire space was assured either by rear lines of windows or by sky lights. Architects developed ingenious access systems so as to be able to realise these requirements in multiple level schoolbuildings as well: Duplex developments with two classrooms to a staircase were a frequent solution. With their appearance vanished the long corridors with their strong smell of floor polish and discipline.

## Modernity and the Sluggishness of Reform

The intensive discussion of school construction in the 1950s and 1960s was characterised by the discrepancy between pedagogical reform discussions and an architectural mood eager for new departures on the hand, and by the dogged resistance to reform by the school as an institution on the other. At the school construction exhibition in 1953 and frequently thereafter, calls were made for group teaching and a school with the learning child as its focus, but these found little resonance in educational praxis and the building programs.

Since a very large proportion of school buildings were awarded via competitions, schools appeared, from around 1955 on, of the highest expressiveness and occasionally uncompromised modernity, even in rural communities. The 'Solothurn School' by Fritz Haller, Franz Füeg and Barth & Zaugg strived for openness and formal abstraction in the manner of Mies van der Rohe; similar tendencies were represented in western Switzerland by architects like Jean-Marc Lamunière and Paul Waltenspuhl. In Zurich, Ernst Gisel pursued a more sensual approach: He contrasted the at once bright and clean spaces of classical modernism with an interplay of light and dark and high and low. Brick and exposed concrete were his preferred means of expression.

Roland Gross, the architect of numerous innovative school construction projects, summed up the reformist project in this way: 'Through architeture, we wanted to change education, and through education the world.' While spatial designs varied little

fig.16 Britisch inspiriert: Die **Schulanlage Riedenhalde** in Zürich-Affoltern von Roland Gross
(1957–1959). Der viergeschossige Bau der
Oberstufe ist windflügelartig um eine zentrale
Treppenhalle angeordnet. Die Klassenzimmer
sind doppelseitig belichtet.

Foto: Walter Binder

British-inspired: The **Riedenhalde School**
in Zurich-Affoltern by Roland Gross
(1957–1959). The four-level secondary
school building is arranged around
a central staircase like a weathervane.
The classrooms are lit from two sides.

Photo: Walter Binder

fig.17 **Riedenhalde:** Je zwei Klassen der Unterstufe
haben einen gemeinsamen Vorraum, der für beide
als Gruppenraum zur Verfügung steht.

Grundriss: Werk 1 (1962)

**Riedenhalde:** Every two primary classes
share a foyer that is available as a common
group room.

Plan: Werk 1 (1962)

fig.18 Die Klassenzimmer sind doppelseitig belichtet,
die Möbel in Gruppen frei angeordnet.
Schlichte und natürliche Materialien charakterisieren den Raum.

Foto: Walter Binder

The classrooms are lit from two sides. The
furniture is freely arranged. Simple and
natural materials are characteristic of the
design.

Photo: Walter Binder

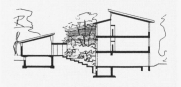

fig.19 Freilicht-Bühne in der **Schule Parc Geisendorf**
in Genf von Georges Brera + Paul Waltenspuhl
(1952–1956). Die durchdachte Schnittlösung
ergibt zweiseitig belichtete Klassenzimmer und
einen abgetreppten Innenhof.

Schnitt und Foto: Werk 6 (1957)

Open-air theatre at the **Parc Geisendorf
School** in Geneva, by Georges Brera + Paul
Waltenspuhl (1952–1956). The well
thought-out sectional solution yields
classrooms lit from two sides and a
terraced inner courtyard.

Section and photograph from Werk 6 (1957)

neuen Lehrmittel noch den bestehenden Schulhäusern an, so wie man zu Anfang des Jahrhunderts Automotoren in kutschenartige Gefährte einbaute.»[10]

Die Schule stand bald von allen Seiten unter Beschuss: Die ständische Abschottung der Bildungs- und Ausbildungsgänge wurde als undemokratisch und ineffizient entlarvt, und daraus ergab sich die Forderung nach durchlässigeren Modellen für die Sekundarstufe. Neue technische Hilfsmittel wie das Sprachlabor, Lernprogramme oder Schulfernsehen schienen ungeahnte neue Möglichkeiten für den Unterricht zu bieten. Die antiautoritäre Pädagogik verunsicherte die Lehrerinnen und Lehrer in ihrer Rolle. Gruppendynamik wurde zu einem Schlagwort, das auch die Unterrichtsrealität veränderte.

Die Reform der Oberstufe im Sinn vermehrter Chancengleichheit führte zur Planung von gross angelegten Schulzentren. Mit der Gesamtschule war ein Begriff gefunden, der die unterschiedlichsten Reformwünsche auf einen Schlag zu erfüllen versprach: «Demokratisierung, Chancengleichheit, Differenzierung und Individualisierung des Unterrichts, Technisierung, neue Formen, neue Inhalte.»[11] Seit den fünfziger Jahren hatte man in den USA mit «open plan schools» experimentiert. Die Forscher der New Yorker Educational Facilities Laboratories propagierten Schulen in der Form grosser, kaum gegliederter aber hoch flexibler Hallen, die statt Klassenzimmern Raum für unterschiedliche Gruppenkonstellationen boten. In Schweden und Dänemark, später auch in Deutschland, wurden Gesamtschulen ähnlichen Typs seit den sechziger Jahren erprobt.[12]

In den Architekturzeitschriften verschob sich das Interesse von architektonischen Fragen zu Begriffen wie Struktur, Prozess, Programm, Projektmanagement, Kostenplanung, Systembauweise, Flexibilität, Anpassungsfähigkeit und anderen, ähnlich abstrakten Werten. Die Möglichkeit, angesichts des raschen und unvorhersehbaren Wandels überhaupt Architektur im herkömmlichen Sinn zu entwerfen, wurde fraglich: Unter dem Titel «Schulbetriebsgebäude: Anpassbare Hüllen für den Unterricht» kapitulierten Berner Architekten 1971 vor der architektonischen Herausforderung und kamen zu dem Schluss: «Die Form darf sich nicht mehr aus den heutigen Anforderungen ableiten: deshalb undifferenzierter Grossraum, der so weit als möglich frei organisiert werden kann.»[13] [fig. 21/22]

### Schulhausbau ist Städtebau

Der Reformaufbruch der siebziger Jahre war kurz: Die 1973 beginnende Wirtschaftskrise setzte dem Glauben an technische Lösungen ein schnelles Ende. «Small is beautiful», hiess die neue Devise. Auf die Welle des Babybooms folgten jetzt jährlich schrumpfende Schülerjahrgänge. Die Schulreform begab sich auf den langen Marsch durch die Institutionen. Erneuerungen kamen in den folgenden Jahren eher von den Rändern her, von kleinen Experimenten und Schulversuchen, und erfassten von da aus allmählich den Mainstream.

in those years, architects looked for new forms of expression and layout for the classroom. Individuals succeeded time and again in smuggling modern projects like open-air school spaces, group work areas and open working zones into their designs. Outdoor seating pointed out the possibility for discussion or spontaneous theatre. In a few cases, large auditoriums or a public library could be housed in a school.

### Modular Construction and the Comprehensive School (*Gesamtschule*)

It was not didactic but rather social questions that finally awakened the Sleeping Beauty of Swiss schools shortly before 1968. Two decades of economic boom times had changed the country. The job market was dry, and the call for the 'activation of the talent reserve' brought the high hurdles between academic and professional plans of study into question — not only in view of democratic ideals, but also in the interest of national competitiveness. In the journal *Werk* in 1967, Lucius Burckhardt demanded more transparent processes of selection for school placement and new teaching methods that would prepare pupils for modern teamwork and lifelong learning. There was no time left, Burckhardt maintained, for sentimentalities. Larger and more centralised school facilities were the way of the future: 'Presently, the new means of teaching are still being adapted to the existing schools, much like auto engines were put into coach-like vehicles at the start of the century.'[10]

The school was soon under attack from all sides: The corporate separation of the various plans of study were debunked as undemocratic and inefficient, and out of that critique came the call for more porous models for schooling at the secondary level (*Sekundarstufe*). New technical aids like language labs, learning programs and school television seemed to offer undreamt-of new possibilities for instruction. Anti-authoritarian pedagogy challenged the teacher's self-definition. Group dynamics became a slogan that changed the reality of teaching.

The reform of secondary (*Oberstufe*) schooling to increase the equality of opportunity led to the planning of large-scale school centres. In the comprehensive school (*Gesamtschule*), a term was found that promised to fulfil at once the most various reform agendas: 'Democratisation, equality of opportunity, differentiation and individualisation of teaching, the introduction of new technologies, new forms, new subjects.'[11] Beginning in the 1950s, there had been experiments in the USA with 'open-plan schools'. Researchers at educational facilities laboratories in New York propagated schools in the form of large, barely structured but highly flexible interiors that in place of classrooms offered space for various group constellations. Total schools of a

10  Lucius Burckhardt: Schulhäuser,
    in: Werk 7 (1967), S.393

11  Zur Planung von Gesamtschulen,
    in: Werk 2 (1970), S.77

12  SAMSKAP — ein schwedisches Schulbauprogramm für
    «offene» Schulen, in: Werk 1 (1975), S.73

13  Arbeitsgruppe für rationelles Bauen:
    Bauliche Hülle für veränderbare Unterrichtsformen,
    in: Werk 8 (1971), S.512—513

10  Lucius Burckhardt: Schulhäuser,
    in: Werk 7 (1967), p.393.

11  Zur Planung von Gesamtschulen,
    in: Werk 2 (1970), p.77.

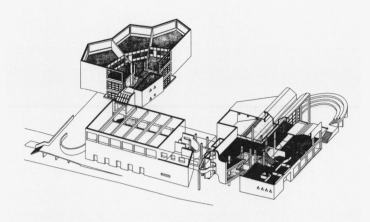

fig.20 Die Schule als sozialer Treffpunkt: **Primar-schule und Gemeinschaftszentrum Loogarten** in Zürich-Altstetten von J.Naef und E.Studer (1971–1975). Fächerförmige Anordnung fünfeckiger Klassenzimmer mit beweglichen Glaswänden zur Treppenhalle.

Plan: Werk-archithese 13–14 (1978)

The school as social meeting point: **Loogarten Primary School and Community Centre** in Zurich-Altstetten by J. Naef and E. Studer (1971–1975). Fan-shaped arrangement of pentagonal classrooms with movable glass walls onto the stairway.

Isometric view from: werk-archithese 13–14 (1978)

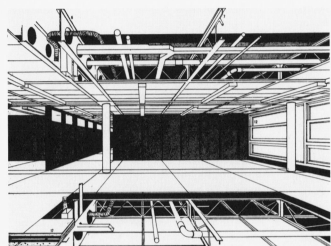

fig.21 Das Stahl-Bausystem CROCS (Centre de Rationalisation et d'Organisation des Constructions Scolaires, Lausanne) verspricht um 1969 Baurationalisierung, maximale Flexibilität und technische Infrastruktur in Analogie zum Bürobau.

Plan: Werk 8 (1971)

In 1969, the CROCS (Centre de Rationalisation et d'Organisation des Constructions Scolaires, Lausanne) steel building system promised building rationalisation, maximum flexibility and a technical infrastructure analogous to that of office construction.

Plan: Werk 8 (1971)

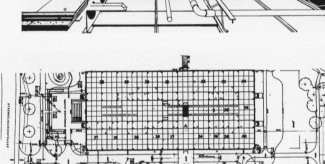

fig.22 Demokratische Grossstruktur: Das **Bildungs-zentrum Zofingen** von Metron (1972–1978). Hoch flexible Anlage aus vorfabrizierten Elementen, die unter anderem Gymnasium, Berufsschulen, Mediathek und Mensa enthält.

Plan: Metron Architektur AG, Brugg

Large democratic structure: the **Zofingen Education Centre** by Metron (1972–1978). Highly flexible facility made from prefabricated elements, including secondary and *Gymnasium* school, professional schools *(Berufsschulen),* media library and canteen.

Plan: Metron Architektur AG, Brugg

In der Zeitschrift «Werk» schritt der Kunsthistoriker Stanislaus von Moos 1978 zur Generalabrechnung mit dem zu Ende gehenden Jahrzehnt. In seinen Augen war «der Schulbau der letzten Jahre in der Schweiz von den technologischen Trivialmythen von Flexibilität und Systembauweise tyrannisiert» worden.[14] Begriffe der Architektur, des Städtebaus und der öffentlichen Repräsentation seien dabei verloren gegangen. In seinem Vergleich von zehn neueren Schulbauten ignorierte von Moos bewusst die schulischen Vorzüge und Mängel der vorgestellten Bauten und fragte stattdessen danach, welche Bedeutung Architekten der Schule im Kontext der Siedlung, der Stadt oder der Landschaft zumessen.[15] [fig. 23/24]

Neue Ansätze in diesem Sinn fand von Moos in den Bauten der Tessiner «Tendenza», in den Schulen von Livio Vacchini (Locarno, Ai Saleggi, 1972–1977), Mario Botta (Morbio Inferiore, 1972–1977) und Tita Carloni (Stabio, 1968–1974). Die Architektinnen und Architekten der Tendenza leiteten den Entwurf nicht linear aus der Funktion ab, sondern primär aus dem Studium des Orts, seiner Morphologie und Geschichte und ihrer Auffassung vom Städtischen. Der öffentliche Charakter des Gebäudes war für sie der Kern seiner Identität und seiner demokratischen Legitimation. [fig. 25]

Die Entwurfsansätze der Tendenza nahmen um 1970 die Entwicklungen voraus, die zwanzig Jahre später auch die übrige Schweiz bestimmten. Die zeitliche Verspätung ergibt sich vor allem aus der Tatsache, dass in den achtziger Jahren angesichts sinkender Schülerzahlen fast keine neuen Schulbauten entstanden. Dies änderte sich recht überraschend in den frühen neunziger Jahren. Zwei Gründe waren dafür ausschlaggebend. Einerseits führten mehrere Schweizer Kantone grundlegende Schulreformen durch, andererseits war die sprunghafte Zuwanderung von schulpflichtigen Kindern das Ergebnis eines erleichterten Familiennachzugs und politischer Umwälzungen in Osteuropa. [fig. 26]

Der Kanton Basel-Stadt beschloss 1988 eine Schulreform, die unter anderem die Einführung einer Orientierungsschule beinhaltete und die – entgegen den ursprünglichen Prognosen – einen erheblichen Ausbaubedarf nach sich zog. Zahlreiche Neu- und Erweiterungsbauten mussten in kurzer Zeit geplant und erstellt werden. Die Basler Baubehörden orientierten sich dabei bewusst mehr an den alten Schulbauten aus der Zeit um 1900 als an den Schulen der Nachkriegszeit, denn «beim Umbau der Schulräume für die Anforderungen der Schulreform erwiesen sich die ältesten Bauten als die anpassungsfähigsten».[16] Diese Schlussfolgerung ist umso überraschender, als die traditionelle Raumdisposition einem sehr modernen Schulverständnis gegenübersteht, das auf «Möglichkeiten selbstständigen, werkstattartigen Arbeitens» basiert. Die Basler Schulbauinitiative der neunziger Jahre brachte der Schweiz eine lange nicht mehr gekannte Intensität in der Auseinandersetzung mit Schulhausarchitektur. Neben der zentralen Frage nach der städtebaulichen Einordnung auf eng begrenzten

similar type were put to the test from the 1960s on in Sweden and Denmark, and later also in Germany.[12]

In architectural journals, interest shifted from architectural questions to terms such as structure, process, program, project management, cost planning, systematic construction methods, flexibility, adaptability and other, similarly abstract values. In view of rapid and unpredictable change, the possibility to continue to design architecture at all in the traditional sense became open to question: Under the title 'Operating Buildings for Schools: Adjustable Shells for Instruction', architects gave in to the architectural challenge in 1971, arriving at the conclusion: 'Form may no longer be derived from today's requirements: therefore the unstructured large room, which can be organised as freely as possible.'[13]

## A Contextualist Approach

The burst of reform in the 1970s was brief: The economic crisis that began in 1973 put a swift end to the belief in technological solutions. 'Small is beautiful' was the new motto. Following the wave of the baby boom came annually shrinking classes of new pupils. School reform set out on the long march through the institutions. In the years that followed, renewal most often came from the edges, through small trials and educational experiments, and from there gradually took over the mainstream.

In the journal Werk, the art historian Stanislaus von Moos set out in 1978 to undertake a general reckoning of the closing decade. 'Swiss school construction', he found, had 'been tyrannised in recent years by the technological pulp mythology of flexibility and modular construction methods'.[14] Concepts of architecture, urbanism and public representation had been correspondingly abandoned. In his comparison of ten recent school buildings, von Moos consciously ignored the educational advantages and disadvantages of the buildings presented, enquiring instead as to what meaning the architects had given schools in the context of the city and the landscape.[15]

Von Moos found new design approaches in buildings by the Ticino 'Tendenza', in schools by Livio Vacchini (Locarno, Ai Saleggi, 1972–1977), Mario Botta (Morbio Inferiore, 1972–1977) and Tita Carloni (Stabio, 1968–1974). The architects of the Tendenza did not derive their designs linearly from function, but instead primarily from the study of the place, its morphology and history and their conception of the urban. For these architects, the public character of the building was the core of its identity and its democratic legitimation.

The Tendenza's approach to design in 1970 anticipated developments that would be central to school construction in the rest of Switzerland twenty years

14  Stanislaus von Moos in: werk-archithese
    13–14 (1978), S.26

15  Ebd., S.16

16  Bruno Chiavi in: Architektur für Basel
    1990–2000. Baukultur eines Kantons,
    Basel 2001, S.33

12  SAMSKAP – ein schwedisches Schulbauprogramm
    für 'offene' Schulen, in: Werk 1 (1975), p.73.

13  Arbeitsgruppe für rationelles Bauen:
    Bauliche Hülle für veränderbare Unterrichts-
    formen, in: Werk 8 (1971), pp.512, 513.

14  Stanislaus von Moos in: Werk 13–14 (1978) p.26.

15  Ibid., p.16

fig.23 Die Schule als kleine Stadt. **Primarschule Ai Saleggi** in Locarno von Livio Vacchini (1969–1979). Die funktional-modernen Schulräume der «wachsenden» Schulanlage verbinden sich in den gedeckten Gassen mit klassischen Formen wie dem Bogengang.

Foto: Werk 7 (1976)

The school as small town. **Ai Saleggi Primary School,** Locarno by Livio Vacchini (1969–1979). The functional-modern school spaces of the 'growing' school facility are connected by covered paths with classic forms such as the arcade.

Photo: Werk 7 (1976)

fig.24 Die Typologie von Strasse, Platz und Haus definiert die Struktur der Schulanlage.

Plan: Werk 7 (1976)

The school's structure is based on the typology of street, square and house.

Plan: Werk 7 (1976)

fig.25 Einen Ort entwerfen: **Scuola Media** (Gesamtschule) in Morbio Inferiore von Mario Botta (1975).

Foto: Alo Zanetta

Designing a place: **Scuola Media** (comprehensive school) in Morbio Inferiore by Mario Botta (1975).

Photo: Alo Zanetta

Arealen fällt an den Basler Schulhäusern die Sorgfalt
in Fragen der Lichtführung, der Farbigkeit und Materialisierung auf, die diese Schulbauten auf ein aussserge-
wöhnlich hohes Niveau erhebt. [fig.27/28]

In den Kantonen Zürich und Zug begann der bauliche
Nachholbedarf einige Jahre später. Auch hier über-
lagerten sich demografische Entwicklungen mit neuen
schulischen Bedürfnissen: Zusätzliche Räume für den
Sport, die (Quartier-)Kultur, den Gruppenunterricht und
klassenübergreifende Projekte, für Hort und Mittagstisch, musikalische Erziehung und die Schulleitung waren
gefordert. Die Flächenansprüche an die Klassenzimmer
sind gewachsen und liegen heute bei rund 4 Quadratmetern
pro Kind. In beiden Kantonen finden sich zahlreiche
Versuche, spezifische neue Raumstrukturen für die
vielfältigen Nutzungsformen moderner Schulen zu finden.
Dabei überrascht es wenig, dass die Themen — wie auch
die baulichen Lösungen — in der Geschichte des europäischen Schulhausbaus nicht zum ersten Mal zum Vor-
schein kommen.

later. The delay resulted predominantly from the
fact that, owing to sinking numbers of pupils, almost no new school buildings were created in the
1980s. This changed quite surprisingly in the early
1990s. There were two decisive reasons for this.
First, multiple Swiss cantons implemented fundamental school reforms. Second, the sharp rise in the
immigration of school-age children resulted from
eased rules for family reunification and political
upheaval in eastern Europe.

The city of Basel adopted a school reform in
1988 containing, among other things, the introduction of a new type of secondary school (Orientierungsschule), which occasioned — contrary to the
original prognoses — a considerable need for building. Numerous projects for new expansion had to
be planned and carried out over a short period of
time. The Basel building authorities oriented
themselves consciously more towards the old turn-of-
the-century school buildings than to the schools
of the post-war period, since 'the oldest buildings
proved to be the most adaptable in the reorgani-
sation of school spaces to meet the requirements of
the school reform'.[16] This conclusion is all the
more surprising because the traditional spatial plan
is contrasted with a highly modern understanding
of the school, one based on 'the possibilities for
workshop-like, independent work'. The school building initiative in Basel in the 1990s returned to
Switzerland a long-unknown intensity of engagement
with school architecture. In addition to the central
question of urbanistic integration of new designs
on tightly limited areas, the Basel schoolhouses
also prompted the questions of lighting, coloration
and choice of material, all of which were treated
exceptionally in these school buildings. [fig.27/28]

In the cantons of Zurich and Zug, the need to
catch up on building began some years later. Here,
too, new educational needs overlaid demographic developments: Additional spaces were needed for
sports, (neighbourhood) culture, group instruction
and projects spanning multiple classes, lunch and
after-school care, musical education and school
administration. The claims on space in the classroom
had grown too. Today they are around 4 square metres
of classroom area per child. Many new designs in
the two cantons aim at finding specific new spatial
structures for the diverse forms of use of modern
schools. It is not surprising that they raise questions — as well as the structural solutions — that
were discussed at earlier stages of the history of
European schoolhouse construction.

16  Bruno Chiavi: 'Schulreform und Schulbauten',
    in: Architektur für Basel, 1990—2000:
    Baukultur eines Kantons (Basel 2000), p.33.

fig.26 Die Schule bleibt im Dorf: Die Primarschule
in **Duvin**, Graubünden, von Gion Caminada
(1995), integriert sich durch den Massstab
und die traditionelle Holzbauweise in den
Dorfkern, dem sie ein neues Zentrum bietet.

Foto: Lucia Degonda

The school remains in the village: Through
its scale and traditional wood construction,
the Primary School in **Duvin**, Graubünden,
by Gion Caminada (1995) integrates into the
village core, which it gives a new centre.

Photo: Lucia Degonda

fig.27 Schulbau als Stadtreparatur: Die Erweiterung
der **Dreirosen-Schule** in Basel von Morger +
Degelo (1994–1996) besetzt die Kante des
Blockrands und schützt sich selber vor dem
Strassenlärm. Mit der Schule entstanden
29 Wohnungen und die unterirdische Dreifachturnhalle.

Foto: Bau- und Planungsamt Basel

School construction as urban repair: The
expansion of the **Dreirosen School** in Basel
by Morger + Degelo (1994–1996) occupies
the edge of the city block and protects
itself from street noise. Also built with
the school were 29 flats and a triple
underground sports hall.

Photo: Bau- und Planungsamt Basel

fig.28 **Dreirosen-Schule:** Die Dreifachturnhalle
liegt unter dem Pausenplatz.

Foto: Bau- und Planungsamt Basel

**Dreirosen School:** triple underground
sports hall

Photo: Bau- und Planungsamt Basel

Martin Schneider
**Schulbesuch/school visit**

**Jürg Willimann,** Primarlehrer

Der entscheidende Vorteil ist, dass das Haus aus
dem 19. Jahrhundert stammt und für heutige Verhältnisse
sehr grosse Klassenzimmer aufweist. Lehrerkollegen be-
neiden uns um unsere «Ballsäle». Wir können auch überall
Zeichnungen aufhängen und Nägel einschlagen.

Dafür können wir die Fenster nur zum Lüften öffnen:
Täglich brausen 70'000 Autos und Lastwagen am Schulhaus
vorbei. Unterricht bei offenem Fenster ist undenkbar.

Der Grossteil der Kinder spricht als Muttersprache
türkisch, albanisch, kroatisch, tamilisch, portugiesisch
oder spanisch. Untereinander sprechen sie fast aus-
schliesslich deutsch. Ihren unterschiedlichen Erfahrungshintergrund bringen sie ins Schulleben ein, auch in
den Unterricht: zum Beispiel im Fach Mensch und Umwelt.

In unserem Schulhaus reagieren wir auf die He-
terogenität der Kinder, indem wir den Unterricht auf
allen Ebenen individualisieren. Dank der Grösse
der Klassenzimmer können die Kinder einzeln, mit Partnern
oder in Gruppen gleichzeitig nebeneinander an ver-
schie-densten Themen arbeiten. Das ist zwar ein grosser
Vorteil für das Erreichen unserer Ziele, das Engagement der Lehrperson ist aber letztendlich trotzdem viel
entscheidender als optimale Raumbedingungen.

Ich war in meinem Berufsleben schon Architekt,
später Dozent an der Hochschule für Gestaltung und
Kunst, die Arbeit als Primarlehrer ist aber die bisher
anspruchvollste und spannendste Herausforderung.

**Jürg Willimann,** primary school teacher

The great advantage is that the building dates
from the 19th century and has very big classrooms by
today's standards. The colleagues are envious of
our 'ballrooms'. We can hang up paintings and knock
in nails wherever we want.

But there is one drawback: we can only open the
windows when we want to air the rooms. Every day,
70,000 cars and lorries zoom past the school. It would
be impossible to teach with the windows open.

Most of the children speak either Turkish, Al-
banian, Croatian, Tamil, Portuguese or Spanish. They
almost always talk to one another in German. They
bring their different experiences and backgrounds into
the school, and that includes the lessons too, like
in the subject 'Man and the Environment'.

At our school, we respond to the heterogeneity of
the children's experiences with individualised
teaching at all levels. Thanks to the size of the
classrooms, children can work alongside one another on
the most diverse subjects alone, with partners,
or in groups. Although this is a great advantage
when it comes to achieving our goals, ultimately the
personal commitment of the teachers is far more
important than having optimal room conditions.

I first worked as an architect, and then as a
lecturer at the University for Design and Art. But for
me, my present job has easily been the most demanding
one and the most exciting challenge so far.

**Schule und Schülerclub Nordstrasse, Zürich**

1892 wurde das Haus als Gemeindeschule von Wipkingen erbaut.
Die Klassen zählten damals bis 50 Kinder. Die Schule liegt heute direkt
an der Westtangente, der lärmigsten Transitstrasse in der Stadt.
Bis zu 70 Prozent der Kinder sind fremdsprachig.

Schon seit 1980 ist die Schule ein Schülerclub: Hort, Schule
und Eltern arbeiten in der Betreuung der Kinder eng zusammen. Ziel der
Lernkultur im Schülerclub ist es, die besonderen Bedürfnisse der
Kinder zu erfassen und zu fördern. Integrative und differenzierende
Lernangebote und Unterrichtsformen prägen den schulischen Alltag.

**Nordstrasse School and School Club, Zurich**

In 1892 the building was constructed as Wipkingen Municipal
School. There were more than fifty children to a class. The school
now stands right next to the western by-pass, the noisiest through
road in the town. Up to 70 per cent of the children speak a
foreign language.

Since 1980, the school has served as a pioneer school club:
the day-care centre, the school and the parents closely co-operate
in taking care of the children. The school club has a 'learning
culture' that involves noting and nurturing the children's particular needs. A feature of the school's daily activities is its
integrative and differentiated approach to teaching.

**Antonio Di Roma,** Hauswart

Mir gefällt das Schulhaus, weil es ein Altbau ist. Die grosse
Raumhöhe ist sehr angenehm und die Atmosphäre ist belebter;
nicht so steril wie in einem Neubau. Es gibt aber keinen Lift.
Der Reinigungswagen, die Putzmaschine und andere schwere Geräte
müssen immer von Hand mit zwei bis drei Personen transportiert
werden. Die Gangfläche ist beschränkt, was für die Zwischen-
und Hauptreinigung der Schulzimmer mehr Umstände ergibt, da die
Zimmer nicht alle auf einmal ausgeräumt werden können. Die
Kinder sind sehr lebhaft. Sie kommen aus 25 bis 30 Nationen, was
eine grosse Vielfalt an Charakteren ergibt. Was ich nicht
toleriere, ist zu wildes Geschrei im Haus. In den hohen Räumen
hallt es enorm. Trotzdem: der Altbau lässt mir und der Schule
mehr Möglichkeiten für die Benützung als ein Neubau.

**Antonio Di Roma,** caretaker

I like the school because it's in an old building. It's
very nice having high ceilings, and the atmosphere is more
lively. It's not as sterile as a new building. But there's
no lift. The cleaning trolley, the cleaning machine and other
heavy equipment have to be taken up by hand with the help
of two or three other people. The corridor is rather confined,
which creates a number of problems when it comes to doing
the minor or main cleaning work in the classrooms, because you
can't always clear out the rooms in one go. The kids are a
lively bunch. They come from about twenty to twenty-five different countries, so you've got a wide variety of different
types. What I can't stand is screaming and shouting — it
echoes incredibly in these high rooms. Even so, there's a lot
more me and the school can do in this old building than we
could in a new one.

**Begüm,** Schülerin

Ich arbeite am liebsten für mich selber an meinem Arbeitstisch. In der Gruppe wird es mir meistens zu laut und ich mache zu viele Fehler. Zu Hause arbeite ich immer am Boden. In der Pause bin ich am liebsten auf dem Pausenplatz. Das Haus gefällt mir gut, ich fühle mich sehr wohl, da es ein Altbau ist. Eine grosse Bibliothek mit vielen Büchern würde ich mir wünschen. Heute sind alle Bücher im Singsaal in Schränken eingeschlossen.

**Begüm,** schoolgirl

I most like working on my own at my desk. I usually find it too noisy in the group and I make too many mistakes. At home I always work on the floor. During the break, I like being in the schoolyard best. But I like the building, I feel good here because it's an old building. I wish we had a big library with lots of books. At the moment, all the books are locked up in cupboards in the music room.

Photos: Claudia Caprez

**Remo,** Schüler

Ich arbeite gerne in der Gruppe und gerne für mich alleine. Wenn ich in der Gruppe arbeite, muss ich nicht immer alles selber wissen. Dafür kann ich mich alleine besser konzentrieren. Auch ich arbeite zu Hause meist am Boden. Jede zweite Woche ist Fussball auf dem Pausenplatz, dann bin ich am liebsten am Spielen. Sonst bin ich lieber in der Pausenhalle mit meinen Freunden. Später möchte ich Fussballspieler oder Sportreporter werden.

**Remo,** schoolboy

I like working both in the group and on my own. When I'm working in the group I don't always need to know everything myself. On the other hand, I can concentrate better when I work alone. I also generally work on the floor when I'm at home. Every other week we play soccer in the schoolyard. Then I always like to be out there playing. Otherwise I like being in the recreation hall with my mates. One day I want to be a footballer or a sports reporter.

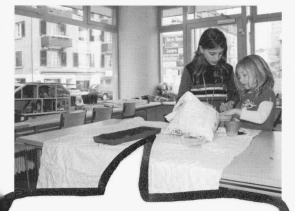

**Frau Charlotte Walder,** Hortleiterin

Im Hort sind die Kinder in der unterrichtsfreien Zeit, vor allem über Mittag und am späten Nachmittag. Die meisten kommen zwei oder drei Tage in der Woche. An den anderen Tagen sind sie zu Hause oder bei befreundeten Familien. Die Jugendlichen legen viel Wert auf ihre eigenen Mädchen- und Knabenräume. Im Keller können sie laute Musik hören und sich am Boxsack austoben. Das Essen wird von der Stadtküche angeliefert, beim Abwaschen müssen die Kinder mithelfen.

**Charlotte Walder,** head of the day-care centre

The children come to the care centre when there are no lessons, particularly at midday and in the afternoon. Most of them come two or three times a week. They spend the other days at home or with families they are friends with. The young people are very keen on having their own girls' and boys' rooms. They can hear loud music in the basement and get rid of their pent-up energy on the punchbag. Meals are supplied by the municipal kitchen. The children have to help with the washing up.

**Barbara Custer,** Schulleiterin

Das Alter dieses Hauses gibt uns viele Freiheiten. Einen Neubau würden die Architekten am liebsten unbenutzt sehen. Die grossen Zimmer, die einst für 50 Kinder konzipiert wurden, sind für den heutigen Gebrauch fast schon ideal. Der Unterrichtsstil kann dadurch sehr vielfältig gestaltet werden. Nutzungsänderungen sind einfach: Aus dem Klassenzimmer wird ein Mittagshort, später vielleicht eine Bibliothek oder ein Kindergarten.

Der Schülerclub bietet Freizeitangebote für die Kinder kombiniert mit Tagesbetreuung. Als ergänzende Angebote führt die Schule Mittags- und Abendhorte für die Schüler. Einer liegt vis-à-vis in einem umgenutzten Ladenlokal. Die Hortleiterinnen und die Lehrkräfte arbeiten in Unterricht und Betreuung der Kinder sehr eng zusammen.

**Barbara Custer,** headmaster

Because this school is in an old building it gives us a lot of scope. If it were a new building, the architects would probably be happiest if nobody used it. The large rooms, which were once conceived for fifty to seventy children, are almost ideal for today's use. They allow you a wide range of different approaches to teaching. It's no problem reassigning uses: the classroom is turned into a midday care centre; later on it might serve as a library or a kindergarten.

The school club offers leisure activities for the children in con-junction with day care. On top of that, the school offers midday and evening care for the pupils. One of the centres is in an unused shop opposite. The carers and the teachers co-operate closely in caring for the children.

a æ b

c ç d

e f g

h i j

k l m n

ñ o œ

p q r

s t

u û v w

x y z

31 Schulbauten und Projekte
31 School Buildings and Projects

Schlüssel zu den Raumbezeichnungs-Nummern:
siehe Umschlagsklappe hinten

Key to room function number code:
see back cover flap

Ostansicht/east elevation

Westansicht/west elevation

Südansicht mit Park/south elevation, with park

**Schulanlage Im Birch**
**Im Birch School**
Zürich-Oerlikon, Switzerland
Peter Märkli, Zürich

Text: Daniel Kurz, Photo: Georg Gisel

## Die Schulstadt

Im städtebaulichen Entwicklungsgebiet Zentrum Zürich-Nord entsteht nach einer städtebaulichen Planung der neunziger Jahre ein neuer Stadtteil mit gemischter Nutzung. Der Bevölkerungszuwachs macht ein für schweizerische Verhältnisse aussergewöhnlich grosses Schulhaus notwendig. 800 Kinder in 36 Klassen, vom Kindergarten bis zur Sekundarstufe, werden die Schule Im Birch besuchen. Die gemeinsamen Infrastrukturen wie Sporthalle, Mensa und Bibliothek sind in ihrer Art und Grösse einmalig. Die neue Schule nimmt den grossen Massstab

## The School City

In the urban-development area of Zentrum Zürich-Nord, a new mixed-use district is being created on the basis of an urban-planning concept dating from the 1990s. A growing population necessitated a school unusually large by Swiss standards. Eight hundred children in thirty-six classes — from kindergarten age to secondary school level — will attend Im Birch Comprehensive. The shared facilities such as the sports hall, canteen and library are unique in both scale and type. Although the new school is designed to match the grand scale of the new district, it does so with-out being monumental. The secondary school, the

Klassenbereich (Cluster) im Bau/
classroom area (cluster) under construction

Westansicht, mit neuen Wohnbauten/
west elevation, with new residential buildings

Dreifach-Turnhalle/triple sports hall

des neuen Quartiers auf, ohne monumental zu erscheinen. Sekundarschule, Primarschule und Dreifachturnhalle sind als je eigene Baukörper ablesbar, die sich zu einer Schulstadt verzahnen und unterschiedliche Aussenräume einfassen. Die räumliche Differenzierung der Anlage wird durch die Aufteilung der Baukörper und durch ein vielfältiges Netz von Verbindungswegen angelegt. Die Klassenzimmer gruppieren sich zu Clustern, die innerhalb der grossen Schule überschaubare Einheiten bilden. Um die traditionelle «Schulstube» zu öffnen, teilen sich jeweils drei oder vier Klassen eine nach aussen abgeschlossene, nach innen aber sehr offene Raumgruppe: Glas- und Glasbausteinwände dienen mehr dazu, die Klassenräume zu verbinden, als sie zu trennen, und der zentrale Arbeitsbereich

primary school and the multifunctional gymnasium, although distinct buildings, together constitute a kind of 'school city' encompassing a variety of outdoor spaces. The spatial diversity of the complex is due to the disposition of the buildings across the site and the complex network of links between them. To overcome the traditional arrangement of isolated classrooms, three or four rooms have been arranged as a group, or cluster. The clusters, in turn, form compact units within the larger school. Glass and glass-brick walls have been used in order to link rather than separate the classrooms, whilst the central

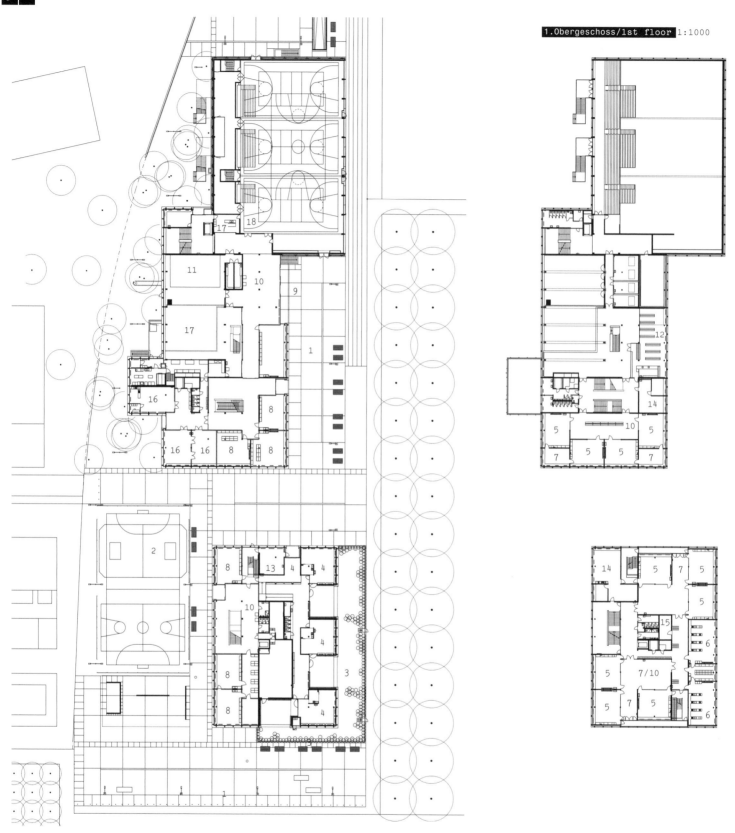

im Zentrum des Clusters erlaubt klassenübergreifende Grup-
pen- oder Projektarbeit. Auf diese Weise entsteht eine
Schule als Werkstatt. Separate Fluchtwege über aussenliegende
Treppen und Verbindungstüren zwischen den Schulzimmern
ermöglichen diese Offenheit. Ruhige Proportionen und wenige,
konsequent eingesetzte Materialien kennzeichnen den Bau:
Sichtbeton, Glasbausteine und Glas, Linol, Parkett und Travertin. Die gemeinschaftlichen Räume im Bereich von Mensa und
Mehrzwecksaal sind mit einer Wandverkleidung in Ulme aus-
gestattet.

study area in the middle of the cluster permits inter-
class group and project work, creating a school-as-work-
shop effect. The school's open character was made
possible by the separate emergency exits (complying with
fire-safety regulations) via the outside stairs and the
doors linking the classrooms. The building is characterised by its harmonious proportions and the modest number of consistently used materials: fair-faced concrete,
glass bricks and glass, linoleum, parquet flooring and
travertine. The walls of the common rooms by the canteen
and the multifunctional hall are clad in elm.

2.Obergeschoss/2nd floor 1:1000

3.Obergeschoss/3rd floor 1:1000

1:5000

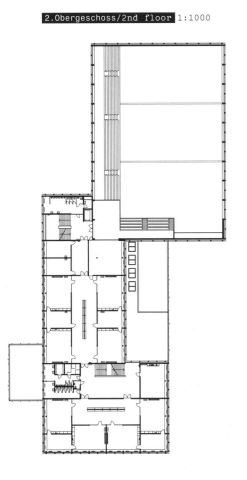

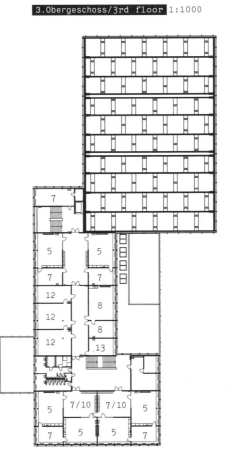

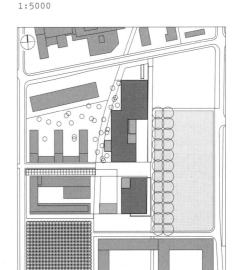

Cluster: 2.Obergeschoss, Sekundarschule/
2nd floor, secondary school 1:400

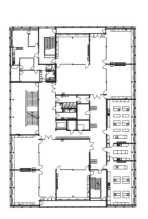

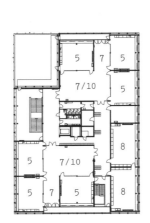

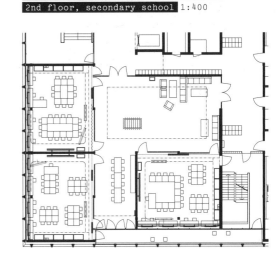

Im Birch

Primar- und Sekundarschule, Kindergarten/primary and secondary school, kindergarten
Architektur/architecture Peter Märkli, Architekt Zürich, mit Gody Kühnis, Trübbach
Landschaftsplanung/landscape architecture Zulauf Seippel Schweingruber, Baden
Wettbewerb/competition 2000 (Gesamtleistungswettbewerb)
Bauzeit/construction period 2002–2004
SchülerInnen/students 780 (Alter/age 5–16)
Klassen/classes 36 + 3 Kindergarten
Spezialangebote/special features Dreifachsporthalle, Mensa, Hort, Theatersaal/
triple sports hall, canteen, day-care centre, theatre hall
Geschossfläche (SIA 416)/total floor area 19'854 m²
Geschossfläche pro SchülerIn/floor area per student 25 m²
Rauminhalt RI (SIA 116)/volume 104'946 m³
Anlagekosten (BKP 1–9 inkl. MWSt.)/overall costs incl. VAT 66'462'000 CHF
Gebäudekosten (BKP 2 inkl. MWSt.)/net construction costs incl. VAT 53'249'000 CHF
Gebäudekosten/m² GF/net construction costs per m² floor area 2'682 CHF/m²
Gebäudekosten/m³ RI (SIA 116)/construction costs per m³ volume 507 CHF/m³
Minergiekennzahl/Minergie factor 33.4 kWh/m²a
Anmerkung/remark spezielle Sportleistungsklassen/special competitive sportclasses

Südansicht mit Turnhalle/
south elevation, with gymnasium on top

Erdgeschoss, Pausenhalle/
ground floor, break hall

Schulanlage Leutschenbach
Leutschenbach School
Zürich-Oerlikon, Switzerland
Christian Kerez, Zürich

Text: Daniela Staub, Alan Wakefield, Image: Christian Kerez

## Schulhaus und Landmarke

Leutschenbach ist eines von zwei grossen Entwicklungs-
gebieten im Norden Zürichs, für das in den letzten Jahren ein
übergeordnetes städtebauliches Leitbild erarbeitet wurde.
Hier soll neben Wohnraum, Arbeitsplätzen und zwei Parkanlagen
eine neue städtische Schulanlage mit zwölf Primarschul-
und zehn Oberstufenklassen, einem Betreuungsbetrieb und vier
Kindergärten entstehen. Am Rand eines ehemaligen Industrie-
gebiets gelegen, an dem das Quartier eine sehr heterogene
Struktur in Bezug auf Gebäudevolumen und Nutzungen aufweist,
muss das neue Schulhaus nicht nur die betrieblichen Anforderungen erfüllen, sondern sowohl innen- als auch aussen-

## School and Landmark

Leutschenbach is one of two major development areas
in the north of Zurich for which a superordinate urban-
development model has been prepared. The plans envisage
not only creating a residential area, jobs and two public
parks, but also building a new city school with twelve
primary-school, and ten upper-school classes, as well as a
day-care centre and four kindergartens. As the new school
will be situated on the periphery of a former industrial
estate, in a district structured very heterogeneously with
regard to both the scale and use of the buildings there,
it will not only have to satisfy the customary operating
requirements, but also be designed — inside and out — to

Ostansicht mit Park/east elevation, with park

Treppenhalle/stairwell

Im 4.Geschoss/4th floor

räumlich einen Ort darstellen, der sich in diesem schwierigen urbanen Kontext zu behaupten vermag. Diese Vorgabe konnte im Rahmen eines Wettbewerbverfahrens erfüllt werden. Der hohe, kompakte Baukörper des ausgewählten Projekts stellt Beziehungen zu den grossmassstäblichen Bauten der Nachbarschaft entlang der Hagenholzstrasse her. Der grosszügige Aussenraum dient nicht nur dem Schulbetrieb, sondern wird zum Abschluss der gesamten Andreas-Park-Anlage und so zu einem Naherholungsraum von übergeordneter Bedeutung für das ganze Quartier. Die im Erdgeschoss liegenden Nutzungen – Mensa und Schülerclub – treten durch die stützenfreien, raumhoch verglasten Fassaden in eine direkte Beziehung zur unmittelbaren Umgebung. Durch die Stapelung der Klassenzimmergeschosse auf drei mittleren Ebenen wird die Massstäblichkeit für die Kinder auch in diesem

assert itself in a challenging urban environment. The winning competition entry – a tall, compact building – is designed to relate to the large neighbouring buildings in Hagenholzstrasse. The school's spacious grounds not only serve the school directly, but also border on Andreas Park to create a recreational area of vital importance to the entire district. Situated behind column-free, room-high glazed façades, the functions accommodated on the ground floor – the canteen and the pupils' club – relate directly to their immediate surroundings. By stacking the classroom storeys on three middle levels, the architects have chosen a scale that remains child-friendly even for a building of this height. The gymnasium, located above

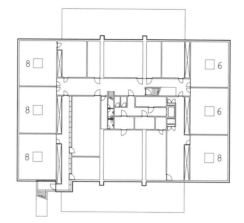

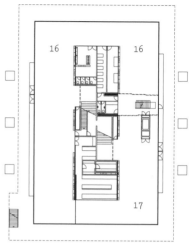

1:2500

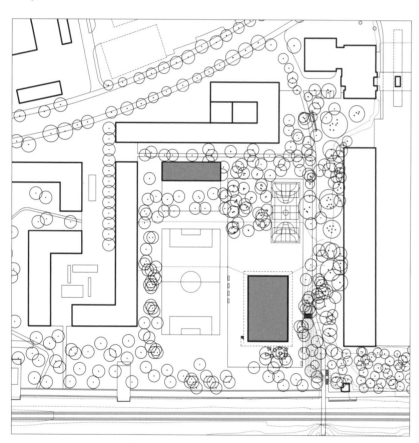

Schnitt NS/section ns 1:800

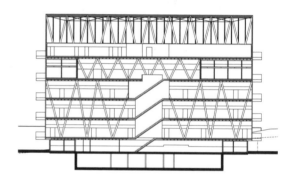

Schnitt OW/section ew 1:800

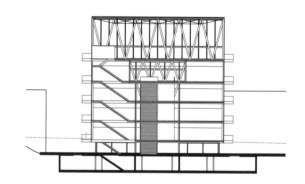

hohen Gebäude gewahrt. Über dem im vierten Geschoss angeordneten Gemeinschaftsbereich liegt die Turnhalle in prominenter Lage. Im Inneren trennt die gegenläufige Treppenanlage in der Mitte des Gebäudes das Schulhaus konsequent in einen Oberstufen- und einen Primarschulbereich. Die Schulhaustreppen bilden zusammen mit den gemeinsamen Flächen einen fortlaufenden, mehrgeschossigen Hallenraum, der für verschiedene Nutzungen wie klassenübergreifende Projektarbeit oder Ausstellungen verfügbar ist. Dank der umlaufenden Fluchtbalkone ist diese Zone uneingeschränkt möblier- und nutzbar. Durch ihre ungewöhnliche Raumhöhe, die sichtbare Konstruktion und die grossformatige Hallenverglasung erinnern die Klassenzimmer eher an Werk- und Atelierräume als an herkömmliche Schulstuben.

the fourth-floor common area, occupies a prominent position. Inside, the stairs, which have separate up and down flights in the middle of the building, neatly separate the upper school from the junior school. Together with the common areas, the staircase forms a continuous, multistorey hall that lends itself to a variety of uses, including inter-class project work and exhibitions. With its all-round fire-escape balcony, there are no limitations on the way this hall area can be furnished or used. Furthermore, the exceptional height, visible structure and large windows of the classrooms are more reminiscent of workshops or studio rooms than of traditional schoolrooms.

1.–3.Obergeschoss/1st to 3rd floors 1:800　　2.Obergeschoss/2nd floor 1:800　　5.Obergeschoss/5th floor 1:800

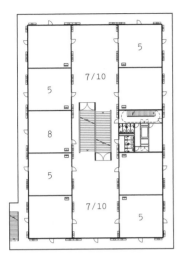
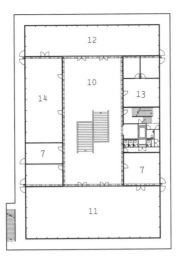
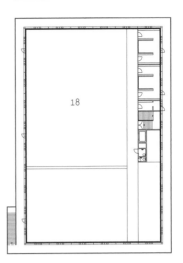

Cluster: 1.–3.Obergeschoss/1st to 3rd floors 1:250

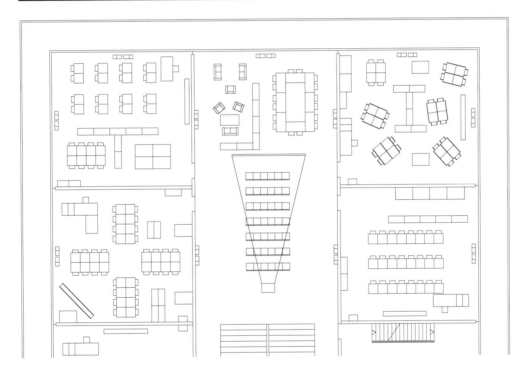

**Leutschenbach**

Primar- und Sekundarschule, Kindergarten primary and secondary school, kindergarten
Architektur architecture Christian Kerez, Architekt ETH SIA, Zürich
Landschaftsplanung landscape architecture 4d Landschaftsarchitekten, Bern
Wettbewerb competition 2003
Bauzeit construction period 2005–2007
SchülerInnen students 440 (Alter/age 7–16)
Klassen classes 22
Spezialangebote/special features Doppelturnhalle, Mensa, Hort/double sports hall, canteen, day care centre
Geschossfläche (SIA 416)/total floor area 9'723 m²
Geschossfläche pro SchülerIn/floor area per student 22 m²
Nutzfläche (SIA 416)/net area 7'594 m²
Rauminhalt RI (SIA 116)/volume 50'486 m³
Gebäudevolumen (SIA 416)/net volume 44'873 m³
Anlagekosten (BKP 1–9 inkl. MWSt.)/overall costs incl. VAT 44'160'000 CHF
Gebäudekosten (BKP 2 inkl. MWSt.)/net construction costs incl. VAT 29'385'000 CHF
Gebäudekosten/m² GF/net construction costs per m² floor area 3'022 CHF/m²
Gebäudekosten/m³ RI (SIA 116)/construction costs per m³ volume 582 CHF/m³
Minergiekennzahl/Minergie factor 31.5 kWh/m²a
Anmerkung/remark Kennzahlen ohne Kindergarten (separates Gebäude)/operating figures (data) without kindergarten (separate building)

Ostansicht mit Park/east elevation, with park

Aussenraum im Obergeschoss/outside space on the first floor

Oberstufenschulhaus Albisriederplatz
Albisriederplatz Secondary School
Zürich-Aussersihl, Switzerland
bbesw architekten, Zürich

Text: Alan Wakefield, Image: bbesw architekten

## Licht und Luft

Im Rahmen einer Gebietsaufwertung sollte das sozial benachteiligte Hardauquartier durch verschiedene Projekte eine Verbesserung der Lebensqualität erfahren. Eines dieser Projekte ist das neue Schulhaus für 12 Oberstufen- klassen, welches die heutigen Mietprovisorien ersetzen wird. Auf diese Weise soll der im Quartier ohnehin sehr anspruchs- volle pädagogische Auftrag besser erfüllt werden können. Das neue Gebäude stellt sich als regalartige Struktur, ohne Vorder- oder Rückseite, quer in den ebenfalls neu zu gestaltenden Quartierpark. Der Freiraum auf beiden Seiten des Schulhauses soll durch die Öffnungen zwischen den drei Gebäudetrakten «hindurchfliessen». Gleichzeitig sind diese Zwischenräume mittels eingehängter Plattformen

## Light and Air

A variety of projects were conceived to improve the quality of life in the socially deprived district of Hardau. One of these is the new school designed to accom- modate as many as twelve secondary school classes and replace the existing rented space. It is hoped that this will help to improve the standards of education in difficult surroundings. The new building looks rather like a cupboard, with no front or rear, inserted crosswise in the future district park. The open space on both sides of the building is supposed to 'flow' through the gaps between the three wings. Furthermore, platforms

Westansicht/west elevation

Klassenzimmer/classroom

Mehrzweckhalle/multi-purpose hall

als Aussenraumzimmer und gedeckte Pausenflächen schulisch nutzbar und machen die Umgebung erlebbar. Das Schulhaus kann von beiden Seiten des Parks her betreten werden. Das Erdgeschoss mit Mensa, Pausenhalle und Bibliothek ist der zentrale Begegnungsort der Schule. Von hier aus geht man über drei Treppenhauskerne in die Klassenzimmertürme. Die Bibliothek ist öffentlich zugänglich und kann somit dem Quartier auch ausserhalb der Unterrichtszeiten zur Verfügung gestellt werden. Die einzelnen Trakte weisen eine einfache statische Struktur mit Kernen im Zentrum und Stützen im Fassadenbereich auf.

are suspended between these gaps to create outside spaces and covered playgrounds, which can thus serve as open-air classrooms. The school can be entered from two sides. The ground floor, which contains the canteen, the recreation room and the library, not only serves as the school's central meeting place but also provides access to the classroom towers via three staircase cores. The library is open to the public, so that local residents can also use it outside school hours. The individual wings have a simple static structure with columns in the façade and central cores, thus permitting flexible partitioning of the space on the upper floors. The L-shaped form of the classrooms, dictated by the ground plan, creates the

1:5000

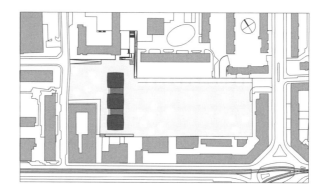

`Erdgeschoss/ground floor` 1:800

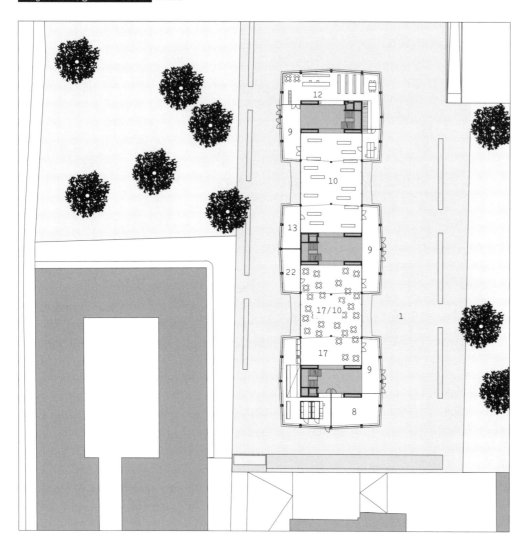

`1.Obergeschoss/1st floor` 1:800

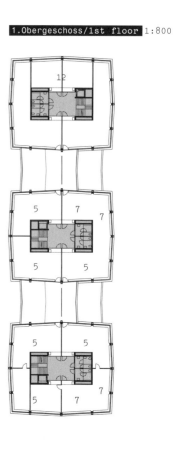

Dadurch wird in den Obergeschossen eine flexible Raumeinteilung möglich. Die sich aus dem Grundriss ergebende L-Form der Klassenräume führt zu der erwünschten räumlichen Differenzierung zwischen Klassenunterricht und Gruppenarbeit. Durch die Rahmenkonstruktion aus Betonelementen und die Füllungen aus Metall und Glas, die mit textilen Ausstellmarkisen kombiniert sind, erhält das Gebäude einen spielerisch leichten Ausdruck. Die hohe Transparenz erlaubt einen engen Bezug zwischen Unterrichtsbereich, Park und Albisriederplatz. Durchblicke und Einblicke innerhalb des Gebäudes fördern das Gemeinschaftsgefühl und sollen den Austausch unter den Nutzerinnen und Nutzern fördern.

desired spatial distinction between classroom-teaching and group-work areas. By combining a framework structure of concrete elements with metal and glass filling and awnings, the architects have given the building a playful air. Furthermore, its great transparency establishes an intimate relationship between the teaching area, the park and Albisriederplatz. The variety of perspectives inside, into and through the building, generate a sense of community and are designed to encourage interaction among the users.

Querschnitt/section 1:800    Querschnitt/section 1:800    Längsschnitt/section 1:800

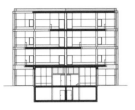

2.Obergeschoss/2nd floor 1:800    3.Obergeschoss/3rd floor 1:800    3.Obergeschoss, Klassenzimmer und Terrasse/
3rd floor, classrooms and terrace 1:250

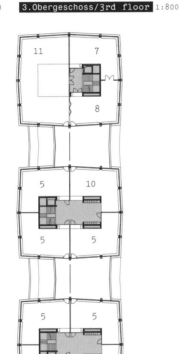

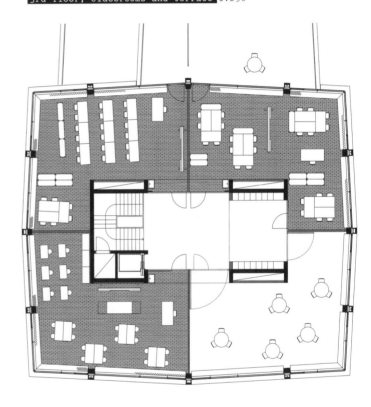

**Albisriederplatz**

Sekundarschule/secondary school
Architektur/architecture bbesw architekten eth htl, Zürich
Landschaftsplanung/landscape architecture Separater Wettbewerb/separate competition
Wettbewerb/competition 2002
Bauzeit/construction period 2005–2007
SchülerInnen/students 260 (Alter/age 12–16)
Klassen/classes 13
Spezialangebote/special features Aussenraumschulzimmer, Mensa, Quartierbibliothek/
open-air classroom, canteen, public library
Geschossfläche (SIA 416)/total floor area 6'902 m²
Geschossfläche pro SchülerIn/floor area per student 27 m²
Nutzfläche (SIA 416)/net area 4'418 m²
Rauminhalt RI (SIA 116)/volume 33'583 m³
Gebäudevolumen (SIA 416)/net volume 30'472 m³
Anlagekosten (BKP 1–9 inkl. MWSt.)/overall costs incl. VAT 33'583'000 CHF
Gebäudekosten (BKP 2 inkl. MWSt.)/net construction costs incl. VAT 22'685'000 CHF
Gebäudekosten/m² GF/net construction costs per m² floor area 3'287 CHF/m²
Gebäudekosten/m³ RI (SIA 116)/construction costs per m³ volume 675 CHF/m³
Minergiekennzahl/Minergie factor 38.3 kWh/m²a
Anmerkung/remark Sporthalle in separatem Projekt/sports hall in separate project

Heilpädagogische Schule Allenmoos II
Allenmoos II Special School
Zürich-Unterstrass, Switzerland
Scheitlin - Syfrig + Partner, Luzern

Erschliessung, Klasse und Aussenraum/access, classroom and exterior room

Text: Alan Wakefield, Image: Scheitlin-Syfrig + Partner

## Wohnen in der Schule

Die Stadt Zürich möchte im Quartier Unterstrass auf einem bestehenden Schulareal einen Neubau für eine heilpädagogische Schule sowie einen Stützpunkt für Kleinklassenunterricht realisieren. Er soll die dezentralen Pavillon- und Mietlösungen ersetzen und die wachsenden heilpädagogischen Raumbedürfnisse abdecken. Ein zentraler Aspekt des Unterrichts an dieser Schule mit geistig, körperlich und teilweise mehrfach behinderten Schülerinnen und Schülern ist das Lernen von einfachen, alltäglichen Verrichtungen. Übersichtlichkeit und Orientierung sowie Beziehung und Zuordnung zu Raum- und Kleingruppen sind wichtige Voraussetzungen für den Schulbetrieb. Das aus einem Architekturwettbewerb siegreich hervorgegangene Projekt erfüllt diese Kriterien mit besonderer Sensibilität. Der Neubau integriert sich in die weiträumige

## The Homely School

The city of Zurich wants to erect a new building for a special school as well as a centre for teaching small classes on existing school premises in the Unterstrass district. The new building is to replace the decentralised solution based on scattered pavilions and rented space and meet the growing demand for space for children requiring special education. A prime teaching goal at this school for boys and girls suffering from intellectual, physical and, in some cases, multiple disabilities is to help the children learn simple daily tasks. Compactness, a room layout giving orientation and accommodating the need for small groups of rooms and classes that users can

Innenhof, Kindergarten/inner courtyard, kindergarten

Klassenzimmer/classroom

Gartenstadtanlage. Das zweigeschossige Gebäude passt sich durch seine kubische Gliederung den bestehenden Wohnbauten an und verzahnt Innen- und Aussenraum miteinander. Den besonderen Bedürfnissen der zu unterrichtenden Kinder kommt die innere Organisation der Schulanlage entgegen. Öffentliche und privatere Bereiche sowie die verschiedenen Schulungsbereiche (Kindergarten, Kleinklassen und Heilpädagogik) erhalten ihre eigenen Gebäudeteile und sorgfältig differenzierte Aussenbereiche. Für die mit dem Schulbus ankommenden Kinder steht auf der Nordseite eine Vorfahrtsmöglichkeit zur Verfügung, die bis zur Eingangshalle reicht. Auf diese Weise haben körperlich behinderte Schulkinder kurze Verbindungswege

relate to, are qualities necessary for a school to function smoothly. The project, which won an architectural competition, fulfils all these criteria with its very sensitive solutions. The new building is integrated into the spacious garden city environment. Owing to its cubic structure, the two-storey building not only complements the neighbouring residential buildings, but also interconnects interior and exterior space. The school's internal organisation is adapted to the special needs of the pupils. Public and private areas as well as the various teaching areas (Kindergarten, small classes and special education) have been allocated distinct parts of the building and proficiently differentiated external areas. On the north side, there is an access road,

Längsschnitt/section 1:800

Querschnitt/section 1:800

Obergeschoss. Klassen mit Aussenraum
1st floor, classrooms with open-air space 1:250

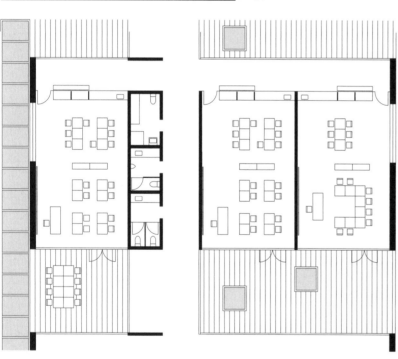

1:5000

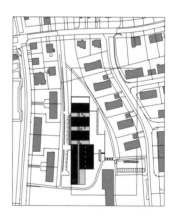

zum Schulgebäude. Vom Eingangsbereich aus können der auf der anderen Gebäudeseite gelegene Pausenplatz, das Foyer des Mehrzwecksaals, der Lehrkraftbereich, die Verpflegungs- und Aufenthaltsräume sowie das obere Geschoss erreicht werden. Der gegen Osten orientierte Kindergartenbereich im Erdgeschoss verfügt über einen separaten Zugang. Die Klassenzimmer im Obergeschoss erhalten durch die verteilte Anordnung in kleinen Gruppen mit zugehörigen Nassräumen und die vorgelagerten Dachterrassen einen wohnlichen Charakter, der zusätzlich durch die sinnliche Materialisierung unterstützt werden soll. In den Räumen mit grosser Gebäudetiefe sorgen grössere Oberlichter für genügend Tageslicht.

which goes right up to the entrance hall, for the children arriving by school bus, so that physically disabled children only have to cover a short distance to the school building. The playground on the other side of the building, as well as the foyer of the multifunctional hall, the teachers' area, the care and recreational rooms and the upper floor can be reached from the entrance area. The ground-floor kindergarten area, which faces east, has a separate entrance. Arranged in small groups with their own wet rooms and terraces, the upper-floor classrooms have a homely character, a feature underlined by their sensitive realisation. In the rooms with greater depth, large skylights ensure sufficient daylight.

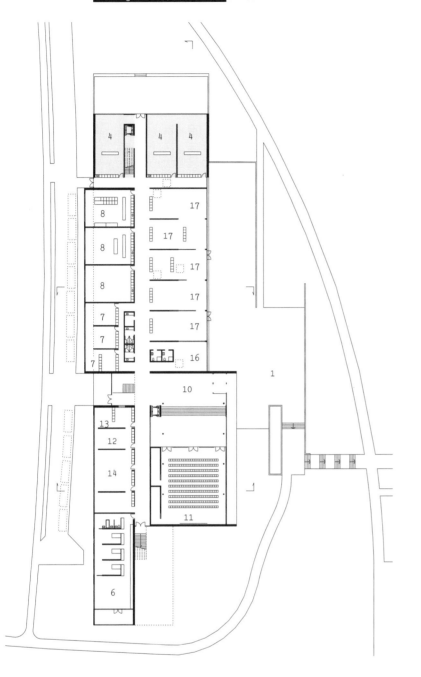

Allenmoos II
Heilpädagogische Sonderschule/remedial school
Architektur/architecture Scheitlin - Syfrig + Partner Architekten AG, Luzern
Landschaftsplanung/landscape architecture Appert + Zwahlen, Luzern
Wettbewerb/competition 2000
Bauzeit/construction period offen/open
SchülerInnen/students 130 (Alter/age 4–18)
Klassen/classes 9 HPS + 4 Kindergarten + 5 Kleinklassen/small classes
Spezialangebote/special features Ganztagesbetreuung, Sonderpädagogisches Zentrum/all-day care, remedial education centre
Geschossfläche (SIA 416)/total floor area 5'725 m²
Geschossfläche pro SchülerIn/floor area per student 44 m²
Nutzfläche (SIA 416)/net area 3'051 m²
Rauminhalt RI (SIA 116)/volume 24'770 m³
Gebäudevolumen (SIA 416)/net volume 20'640 m³
Anlagekosten (BKP 1–9 inkl. MWSt.)/overall costs incl. VAT 22'300'000 CHF
Gebäudekosten (BKP 2 inkl. MWSt.)/net construction costs incl. VAT 14'400'000 CHF
Gebäudekosten/m² GF/net construction costs per m² floor area 2'515 CHF/m²
Gebäudekosten/m³ RI (SIA 116)/construction costs per m³ volume 581 CHF/m³
Minergiekennzahl/Minergie factor 34.0 kWh/m²a

Erweiterung Schulanlage Falletsche
Falletsche School, extension
Zürich-Leimbach, Switzerland
Rolf Mühlethaler, Bern

Südwestansicht, Modell/south-west elevation, model

## The Studio Floor

The existing school in Falletsche was built in stages between 1952 and 1962 by the architect Oskar Bitterli. The buildings enclose a green area, amply planted with deciduous trees, which descends in terraces to the east and is listed as worthy of protection. Population growth in the Leimbach area has made it necessary to increase the number of rooms needed for secondary-school pupils. Furthermore, the infrastructure of the existing Falletsche school complex has become inadequate for a number of reasons (the gymnasium is too small, there is a lack of group rooms, etc.) A study was commissioned in which the project authors had to decide which parts of the existing school complex were to be demolished and replaced. The project recommended for further development envisages a new building containing eleven classrooms, a teachers'

Text: Alan Wakefield, Photo: Croci & du Fresne

## Das Ateliergeschoss

Die bestehende Schulanlage Falletsche wurde in Etappen zwischen 1952 und 1962 von dem Architekten Oskar Bitterli erbaut. Die Gebäude umfassen eine von Westen nach Osten in Stufen abfallende und mit Laubbäumen reich bepflanzte Grünanlage, die im Inventar der Gartendenkmalpflege aufgeführt ist. Das Bevölkerungswachstum im Gebiet Leimbach verlangt nach einer Vergrösserung des Raumangebotes im Oberstufenbereich. Zudem ist die Infrastruktur der bestehenden Anlage Falletsche in verschiedener Hinsicht ungenügend (zu kleine Turnhalle, fehlende Gruppenräume etc.). In einem Studienauftrag mussten die Projektverfasser entscheiden, welche Teile

Südostansicht/south-east elevation

Klassenzimmer/classroom

Nordansicht, Eingang/north elevation, entrance

Korridor/corridor

der bestehenden Schulanlage abgebrochen und ersetzt werden sollen. Das zur Weiterbearbeitung empfohlene Projekt sieht einen Erweiterungsneubau mit 11 Unterrichtsräumen, Lehrerbereich, Mehrzweckraum, Bibliothek und Doppelturnhalle vor. Der mehrfach stumpfwinklig gebrochene Baukörper erhält durch die vertikal strukturierte Fassade seine Charakteristik und fügt sich — trotz des grossen Bauvolumens — gut in die Umgebung ein. Er passt sich an die topographischen Verhältnisse des Ortes an und nimmt das bereits vorhandene Thema der Terrassierung und Geländeabstufung wieder auf. Mit Hilfe dieses Neubaus, der den heutigen Raumbedürfnissen und neuen, flexiblen Unterrichtsformen gerecht wird, kann der bestehende

area, a multifunctional hall, a library and a double gymnasium. The most characteristic feature of the building, which is repeatedly broken by obtuse angles, is its vertically structured façade. Despite its volume, the school fits in very well with its surroundings. It is adapted to the topography of the area and takes up the existing theme of terracing. As the new building satisfies both present room-space requirements and the demand for novel, flexible teaching forms, the existing school wing can still be used without major conversion work. Its location on the slope and its alternating corridor arrangement (the corridor is on the valley side on the ground floor, on the mountain side on the next, and so on) gives the classrooms a direct relationship to the outside

**Erdgeschoss/ground floor** 1:1000

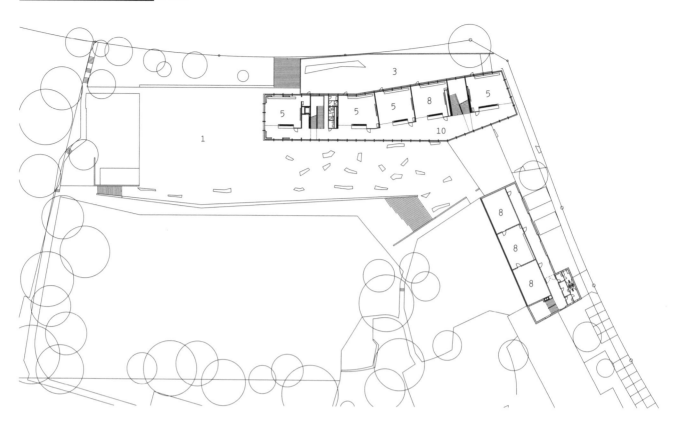

**Längsschnitt/section** 1:1000

**Querschnitt/section** 1:1000

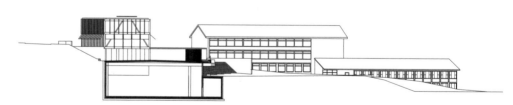

Schultrakt ohne grössere Eingriffe weiter genutzt werden. Die Lage am Hang und die wechselseitig angeordneten Korridore ermöglichen einen direkten Aussenraumbezug der Schulräume auf drei Geschossen. Durch die Ausgänge der Zimmer im Erdgeschoss wird der Korridor ohne feuerpolizeiliche Einschränkungen für den Schulbetrieb nutzbar. Der hofartige Aussenraum erweitert in der warmen Jahreszeit die Unterrichtsmöglichkeiten. Zusätzlich sorgen der Lichteinfall von zwei Seiten und die Überhöhe für Atelierstimmung in den nach Nordwest orientierten Unterrichtszimmern. Materialien wie Sichtbeton, Holzzementplatten und Glas vermitteln einen naturbelassenen und robusten Eindruck im gesamten Neubau.

on all storeys. As the rooms have exits on the ground floor, in accordance with the fire regulations, the corridor can be used unrestrictedly by the school. Use of the courtyard-like outside area broadens the scope of teaching activities during the warm weather. In addition, the light falling from two sides and the superelevation of the classrooms facing northwest create a studio atmosphere in this part of the school. Materials such as fair-faced concrete, wood-cement boards and glass give the entire building a natural and robust appearance.

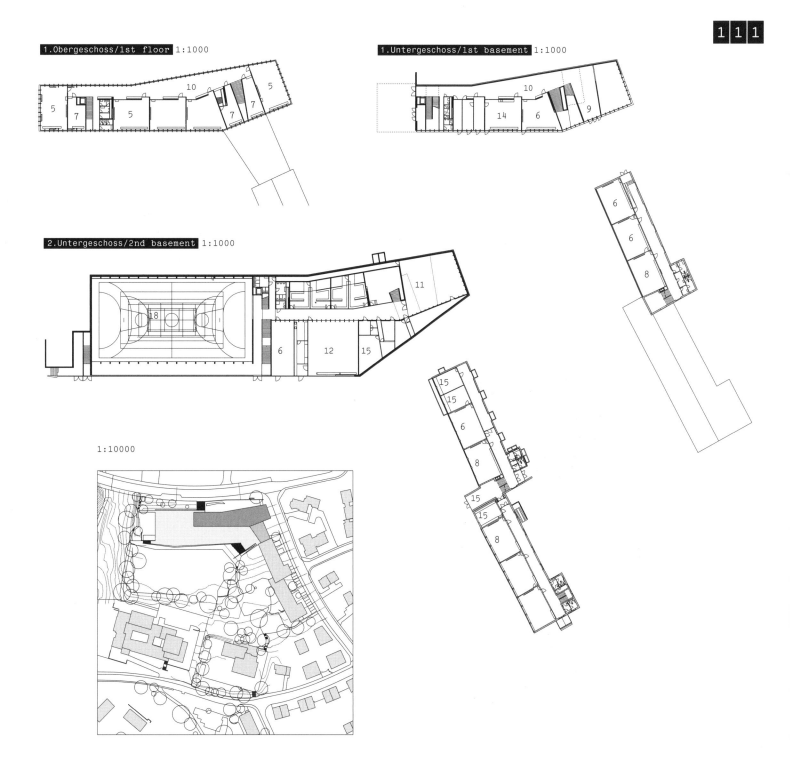

1.Obergeschoss/1st floor 1:1000

1.Untergeschoss/1st basement 1:1000

2.Untergeschoss/2nd basement 1:1000

1:10000

Falletsche
Sekundarschule/secondary school
Architektur/architecture Rolf Mühlethaler, Architekt BSA SIA, Bern
Landschaftsplanung/landscape architecture W + S Landschaftsarchitekt BSLA, Toni Weber, Solothurn
Wettbewerb/competition 2002
Bauzeit/construction period 2004-2007
SchülerInnen/students 180 (Alter/age 12-16)
Klassen/classes 9
Spezialangebote/special features Quartierbibliothek, Jugendaufenthalt/public library, youth centre
Geschossfläche (SIA 416)/total floor area 5'684 m²
Nutzfläche (SIA 416)/net area 3'260 m²
Rauminhalt RI (SIA 116)/volume 34'543 m³
Gebäudevolumen (SIA 416)/net volume 28'842 m³
Anlagekosten (BKP 1-9 inkl. MWSt.)/overall costs incl. VAT 25'368'000 CHF
Gebäudekosten (BKP 2 inkl. MWSt.)/net construction costs incl. VAT 18'885'000 CHF
Gebäudekosten/m² GF/net construction costs per m² floor area 3'322 CHF/m²
Gebäudekosten/m³ RI (SIA 116)/construction costs per m³ volume 547 CHF/m³
Minergiekennzahl/Minergie factor 30.7 kWh/m²a
Anmerkung/remark Kennzahlen beziehen sich auf Erweiterung/figures refer to extension

Erweiterung Quartierschule Scherr
Scherr Neighbourhood School, extension
Zürich-Oberstrass, Switzerland
Patrick Gmür, Zürich

Die Halle/the hall

Text: Daniel Kurz, Photo: Georg Aerni, Menga von Sprecher

### Buntes Innenleben

Das 1865 erbaute Schulhaus Scherr zeichnet sich durch seine repräsentative Lage über der Stadt und die über 100 Quadratmeter grossen Klassenzimmer aus, die einst für Klassen mit 70 Kindern gedacht waren. Auf dem knapp bemessenen Schulareal sollte ein Erweiterungsbau errichtet werden. Der Neubau ergänzt als gleichwertiges Element die beiden öffentlichen Bauten des Quartiers an prominenter Lage über der Stadt: die reformierte Kirche (1907) und eben das alte Schulhaus Scherr (1865). Auf eine bestehende L-förmige Turnhalle (1973) setzt der Entwurf einen fast quadratischen und silbern beplankten Neubau, der sich deutlich als öffentliches Gebäude zu erkennen gibt. Das Innere überrascht mit einer geräumigen, hohen

### A Colourful Interior

The old Scherr School, built in 1865, stands out due to its prominent position above the city and the size of its classrooms (each exceeding 100 square metres), originally designed to hold classes of up to seventy children. An extension was planned for construction in the confined school grounds. The new building supplements, on an equal footing, the neighbourhood's two existing public buildings at this striking location: the Reformed Church (1907) and the old Scherr School (1865). The design places an almost quadratic, silver-panelled new structure, immediately recognisable as a public building, on top of an existing L-shaped gymnasium (1973). A surprising feature of the interior is its spacious high hall, which receives light from the entrance and the sparse rooflights. With its fresh, bright colours (from the concept

Klassenzimmer/classroom

Halle, Obergeschoss/the hall, upper floor

Klassenzimmer/classroom

Altbau und Erweiterung/old building and extension

Westfassade/west façade

Halle, die Licht aus dem Eingangsbereich und durch sparsam gesetzte Oberlichter erhält. Mit ihrer frischen Farbigkeit (nach dem Konzept des Künstlers Peter Roesch) verkörpert sie die Identität des neuen Gebäudes und ersetzt als vielfach nutzbarer Raum den kleiner gewordenen Pausenplatz im Freien. Die Erweiterung hat in ihrer inneren Struktur den Charakter einer kleinen Stadt mit vielfältigen Verbindungswegen und Sichtbezügen. Die Pausenhalle entspricht dem Hauptplatz, die Gänge und Galerien den Strassen. Diese münden jeweils vor einer Gruppe von Klassenzimmern wieder in einen kleinen Platz, der von oben direktes Licht erhält. Die Klassenzimmer sind mit 68 Quadratmetern wesentlich kleiner als die im Altbau, dafür stehen separate Gruppenräume zur Verfügung. Im bewussten

developed by artist Peter Roesch), it embodies the new building's identity and, by serving as a multifunctional room, replaces the outside schoolyard, which is now too small. The extension's inner structure, with its great diversity of passageways and visual reference points, displays all the features of a small town. The hall corresponds to a town square, with passageways and galleries representing the streets. Upon encountering a group of classrooms, each of these 'streets' opens up into a small square, which receives light from above. The classrooms, which occupy an area of 68 square metres each, are far smaller than those in the old building. However, separate group rooms have been created to provide additional teaching areas. They have been deliberately set off from the public area and given the colours of white,

Gartengeschoss/garden floor 1:800

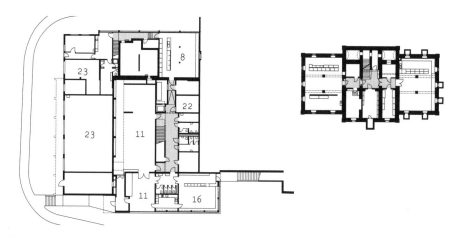

Erdgeschoss/ground floor 1:800

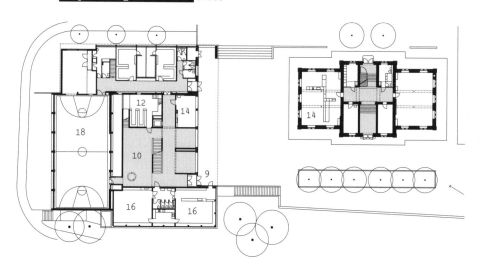

1:5000

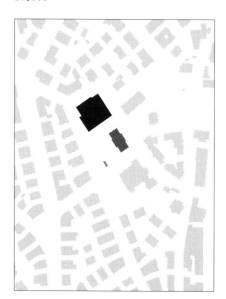

Obergeschoss/1st floor 1:800

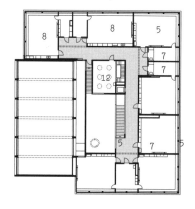

Gegensatz zum öffentlichen Bereich sind sie in den Farben Weiss, Grau und Schwarz gehalten. Diese erzeugen eine ruhige Arbeitsatmosphäre und Räume der Konzentration. Besondere Sorgfalt wurde auf die Fensterzonen gelegt, die als zusätzlicher Arbeitsplatz zur Verfügung steht. Das Raumprogramm spiegelt die veränderten Anforderungen an eine Volksschule wider: Gruppenräume, ein Mehrzwecksaal für Schule und Quartier sowie ein Tages- und Mittagshort stehen im Neubau zur Verfügung. Das Schulleitungszimmer wurde im Altbau eingerichtet, der nach denkmalpflegerischen Grundsätzen renoviert wurde.

grey and black, thus creating a peaceful working atmosphere with rooms conducive to concentrated study. Special attention has been given to the window-side areas, which provide space for additional workplaces. The room plan reflects the changing demands placed on primary schools: the new building contains group rooms, a multipurpose hall for the school and the neighbourhood, and a day-care and midday-care centre. The school management's room is housed in the old building, which has been renovated in accordance with the guidelines on preserving historical buildings.

**Ansicht/elevation** 1:800

**Querschnitte/sections** 1:800

**Längsschnitte/sections** 1:800

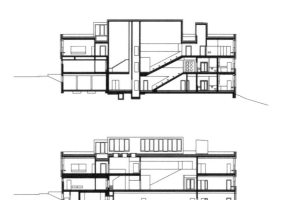

**Scherr**
Primarschule/primary school
Architektur/architecture **Patrick Gmür Architekten AG, Zürich**
Landschaftsplanung/landscape architecture **Raderschall Landschaftsarchitekten AG, Meilen**
Studien/studies **1997–1998**
Bauzeit/construction period **2001–2003**
SchülerInnen/students **100 Erweiterungsbau/extension (240 Gesamtanlage/overall complex) (Alter/age 7–12)**
Klassen/classes **5 (12 Gesamtanlage/overall complex)**
Spezialangebote/special features **Tages- und Mittagshort, Schülerclub/day-care centre, midday care centre, pupils' club**
Geschossfläche (SIA 416)/total floor area **3'210 m²**
Nutzfläche (SIA 416)/net area **1'926 m²**
Rauminhalt RI (SIA 116)/volume **16'950 m³**
Gebäudevolumen (SIA 416)/net volume **15'255 m³**
Anlagekosten (BKP 1–9 inkl. MWSt.)/overall costs incl. VAT **10'700'000 CHF**
Gebäudekosten (BKP 2 inkl. MWSt.)/net construction costs incl. VAT **8'614'000 CHF**
Gebäudekosten/m² GF/net construction costs per m² floor area **2'683 CHF/m²**
Gebäudekosten/m³ RI (SIA 116)/construction costs per m³ volume **508 CHF/m³**
Anmerkung/remark **Kennzahlen beziehen sich auf Erweiterung/figures refer to extension**

Innenhof, Kindergarten/inner courtyard, kindergarten

Text: Alan Wakefield, Image: Bildanstalt

## Campus mit Grundstufe

   Aufgrund der prognostizierten Kinderzahlen soll die bestehende Primarschulanlage aus dem Jahre 1957 vergrössert
werden. Die um einen erhöhten Pausenplatz gruppierten Gebäude
von Max Kollbrunner bilden das Zentrum eines parkartig ein-
gewachsenen Areals. Dieses ist Bestandteil der lockeren
Siedlungsstruktur des Quartiers, das einer Gartenstadt ähnelt.
Zwei gegenüber dem alten Bestand diagonal versetzt angeordnete
Baukörper verweben sich mit der bestehenden Anlage zu einem
Schulcampus mit drei präzisen Aussenbereichen: die Spielwiese
im Norden, der Park im Süden sowie der zwischen den beiden
Neubauten aufgespannte Hartplatz. Kindergarten und Schüler-
club ducken sich vor den benachbarten Reihenhäusern zu einem

## School Campus

   A projected increase in the number of children inspired the decision to extend this primary school dating
from 1957. Max Kollbrunner's buildings, grouped around
an elevated schoolyard, form the centre of a well-planted
park-like area. It is part of a spacious settlement
structure that recalls a garden city. Two buildings placed
diagonally to the old buildings interlink with the existing complex to form a school campus with three distinct
external areas: the playing field in the North, the park
in the South and a hard playground extending between
the two new buildings. The kindergarten and the pupils'
club acknowledge the neighbouring terraced houses and form
a flat, hermetic one-storey structure not unlike a pavilion. Opposite stands a multi-storey classroom wing which
conforms to the scale of the surrounding residential

Klassenzimmer/classroom

flächigen, eingeschossigen Volumen, das einem Pavillon
ähnlich ist. Demgegenüber orientiert sich der mehrgeschossige
Klassentrakt am Massstab der umliegenden Wohnblöcke. Wie im
alten Schulhaus gelangt der Eintretende auch beim neuen
Klassentrakt direkt in ein grosszügiges Treppenhaus. Bibliothek, Lehrkraftbereich, Büros und Mehrzwecksaal liegen
übereinander angeordnet auf der Platzseite gegen Norden,
während die jeweils halbgeschossig dazu versetzten Unterrichtszimmer gegen den Park nach Süden orientiert sind. Zwischen
Klassenzimmer und Korridor befindet sich eine Servicezone für
Garderoben, Nass- und Lagerräume. Die zu jedem Zimmer ge-
hörenden Materialräume ermöglichen einen Verzicht auf Schrank-
fronten und damit einen einfachen Innenausbau mit unver-
stellten, durch die Nutzer flexibel bespielbaren Wandflächen.

blocks. As with the old school, anyone going into the new
classroom wing first enters a spacious stairwell. The
north-facing library, teachers' area, offices and multi-
purpose hall are located on top of one another at one side
of the square, whilst the classrooms, which are offset
by half a floor, face the park in the south. Between the
classrooms and the corridor, a service area accommodates
both the cloakrooms and the wet and storage rooms. The
classrooms have adjoining rooms containing teaching
materials, an arrangement that obviates the need for cupboard fronts and allows for a simple interior finish
with unobstructed wall surfaces that permit flexible use.
Both the kindergarten and the pupils' club have spacious

Querschnitt/section 1:800

Erdgeschoss/ground floor 1:800

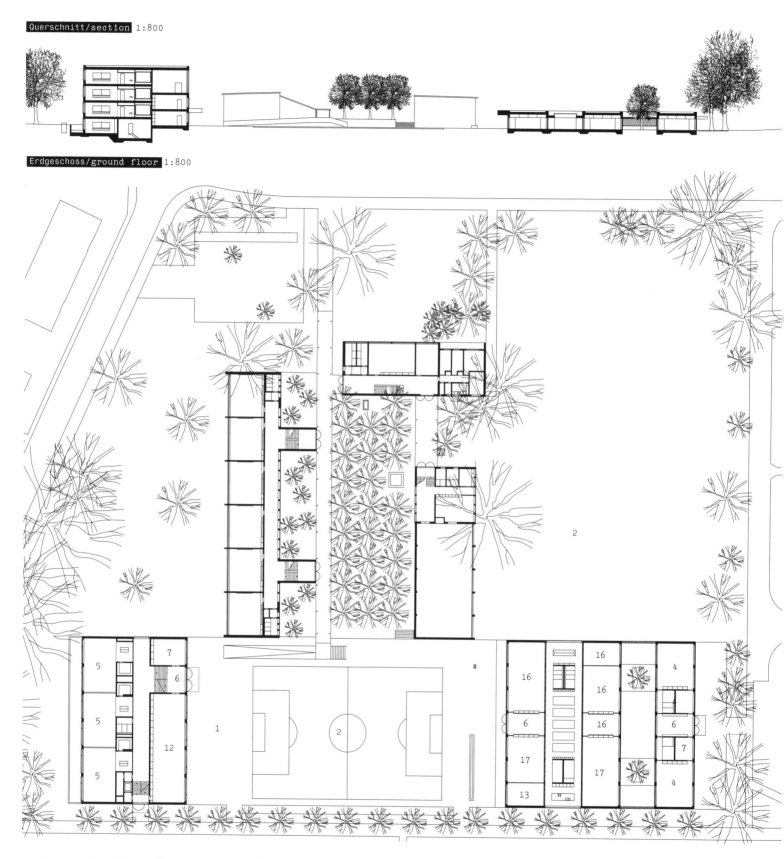

Kindergarten und Schülerclub verfügen jeweils über grosszügige Vorbereiche. Während der Schülerclub einen Aussenraum in Verbindung mit der Hartplatzfläche besitzt, ist der des Kindergartens vom Schulbetrieb abgeschirmt. Der beidseitig benutzbare, gefasste Innenhof bildet ein zugleich trennendes und verbindendes Element zwischen den beiden Trakten. Ein zenital belichteter Innenraum stellt die vielseitig nutzbare Mitte des Schülerclubs dar. Die flexible, durchlässige Gebäudestruktur lässt Potenzial für spätere schulische Nutzungsänderungen, und die Anordnung der Kindergärten ermöglicht ohne bauliche Änderungen die nachträgliche Einführung von zwei Grundstufenklassen.

anterooms. The pupils' club has access to an outside area bordering on the hard playground; the kindergarten's outside area is screened off from the school. The enclosed courtyard forms a connecting and separating element between the two wings. A top-lit interior room located at the centre of the pupils' club can be used variously. The building's flexible, permeable structure allows for future diversification of use, whilst the kindergartens are so disposed as to permit use by two elementary schools later on, without any need for structural changes to the building.

Kindergarten und Schülerclub/kindergarten and pupil's club 1:400 Erdgeschoss Schule/ground floor school 1:400

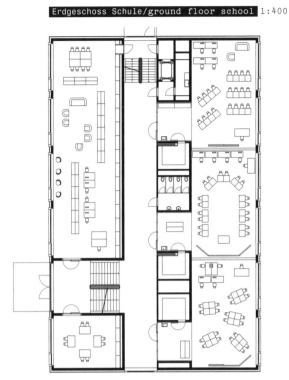

1:5000

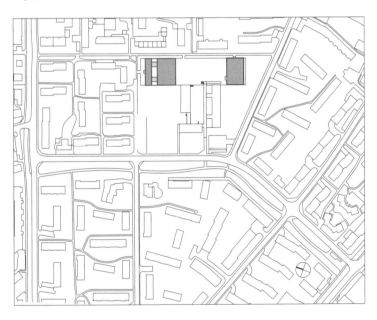

**Luchswiesen**
Grundstufe und Primarschule/primary and junior school
Architektur/architecture Covas Hunkeler Wyss Architekten ETH, Zürich
Landschaftsplanung/landscape architecture Rotzler Krebs Partner, Winterthur
Wettbewerb/competition 2002
Bauzeit/construction period 2004–2006
SchülerInnen/students 180 Erweiterungsbau/extension (400 Gesamtanlage/overall complex) (Alter/age 5–12)
Klassen/classes 7 (18 Gesamtanlage) + 2 Grundstufe
Spezialangebote/special features Schülerclub/pupils' club
Geschossfläche (SIA 416)/total floor area 4'257 m²
Nutzfläche (SIA 416)/net area 2'818 m²
Rauminhalt RI (SIA 116)/volume 19'353 m³
Gebäudevolumen (SIA 416)/net volume 15'941 m³
Anlagekosten (BKP 1–9 inkl. MWSt.)/overall costs incl. VAT 18'910'000 CHF
Gebäudekosten (BKP 2 inkl. MWSt.)/net construction costs incl. VAT 11'756'000 CHF
Gebäudekosten/m² GF/net construction costs per m² floor area 2'762 CHF/m²
Gebäudekosten/m³ RI (SIA 116)/construction costs per m³ volume 607 CHF/m³
Anmerkung/remark Kennzahlen beziehen sich auf Erweiterung/figures refer to extension

Erweiterung Schulanlage Bachtobel
Bachtobel School, extension
Zürich-Wiedikon, Switzerland
Marco Graber, Thomas Pulver, Bern/Zürich

Südwestansicht mit Durchblick/south-west elevation, with view through

Text: Daniel Kurz, Photo: Hannes Henz, Heinrich Helfenstein

## Durchblick

Im Gartenstadtquartier Friesenberg hatte Albert Heinrich Steiner 1947 im Bemühen um einen kindergerechten Massstab eine Pavillonschule aus Sandstein und Holz erbaut. Die dezentrale Lage ergab kurze Schulwege für die Unterstufenschüler. Statt eines Pausenplatzes umgibt ein Garten mit alten Obstbäumen die kleine Schule. Mit der sanften Instandsetzung des Schulpavillons ging 1999 bis 2003 eine Erweiterung um drei Klassen der Mittelstufe einher, die ein beachtliches Raumprogramm auslöste: Zu den drei Klassenzimmern kamen Gruppenräume, ein Werkraum, ein Handarbeitsraum, Schulleitungs- und Lehrerzimmer, eine Turnhalle und ein Hort-

## Vistas

In 1947, Albert Heinrich Steiner built a small pavilion school of sandstone and wood on a child-friendly scale in the garden city district of Friesenberg. The school is situated in the middle of the residential district so that the pupils only have to travel a short distance to school. The little school is surrounded by a garden that contained old fruit trees and serves as a playground. From 1999 to 2003, sensitive maintenance work on the school pavilion was accompanied by extension work to accommodate three more classes. This measure substantially

Klassenzimmer/classroom

Lehrerbereich/teachers' area

Ostansicht/east elevation

Halle/hallway

Halle im Erdgeschoss/hallway on the ground floor

bereich. Diese neuen Räumlichkeiten nehmen den Grossteil des Volumens im Neubau ein. Im renovierten Altbau wurde die Bibliothek und in der alten Turnhalle ein Mehrzwecksaal eingerichtet. Der Erweiterungsbau ist von der Idee geleitet, die landschaftlichen Vorzüge der Anlage zu erhalten. Seine zweiseitig orientierten Klassenzimmer erlauben den Blick durch das Gebäude hindurch über die Stadt. Die Beplankung aus kanadischer Zeder bestimmt die äussere Erscheinung des Neubaus, der auf einem unregelmässig geformten Grundriss aufbaut. Die innere Struktur der neuen Schule basiert auf einer Erschliessungstypologie, welche aus den topographischen Gegebenheiten des Ortes und aus (stadt-)räumlichen Überlegungen

increased the number of rooms: in addition to the three classrooms, the extension now accommodates a workshop, a handicrafts room, a room for the school head and a teachers' room, a gymnasium and a day-care area. These new rooms take up most of the space in the new building. A library has been set up in the renovated old building, and the old gymnasium was turned into a multifunctional hall. The design for the extension was inspired by the idea of preserving the fine landscaping of the complex. The classrooms, which have windows on two sides, offer a view through the building and out onto the city. The new building, which is clad externally in Canadian cedar panels, has an irregular plan. The internal structure of

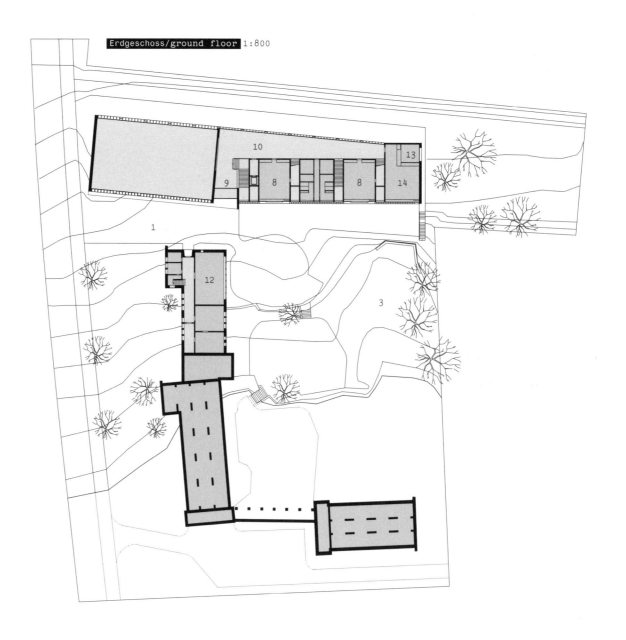

Erdgeschoss/ground floor 1:800

Ostfassade/east elevation 1:800

Südfassade/south elevation 1:800

hergeleitet wurde und vom traditionellen Korridortyp erheblich abweicht. Eine grosszügige, eineinhalbgeschossige Halle empfängt Kinder und Besucher. Sie wirkt repräsentativ und öffentlich. Die Schulzimmer im Obergeschoss gruppieren sich zu zweien um eine Vorzone mit Garderobe und Gruppenraum; sie sind zweiseitig belichtet und bieten Ausblicke auf die Stadt im Norden und die Gartenanlage im Süden. Das durchdachte Erschliessungssystem generiert eine Vielzahl von Verbindungswegen und räumlichen Erlebnissen. Das Farbkonzept unterstreicht diese Diversität. Wie im grossbürgerlichen Wohnungsbau entsteht eine subtile Abstufung von Öffentlichkeitsgraden innerhalb der verschiedenen Bereiche des Schulhauses.

the new school building is based on an access typology adapted to the topographical features of the location and spatial considerations. As such, it represents a radical departure from the traditional corridor-type structure. A spacious, one-and-a-half-storey hall welcomes the children and visitors. The classrooms on the upper floor are arranged in pairs around an intimate anteroom area accommodating a cloakroom and a group room. They receive daylight on both sides and offer a wonderful view of the city to the north and the gardens to the south. The carefully planned access system provides a variety of links and spatial experiences, which are emphasised by a subtle colour concept. As in a middle-class family house, the different areas within the school subtly differentiate between the more public and the more private areas.

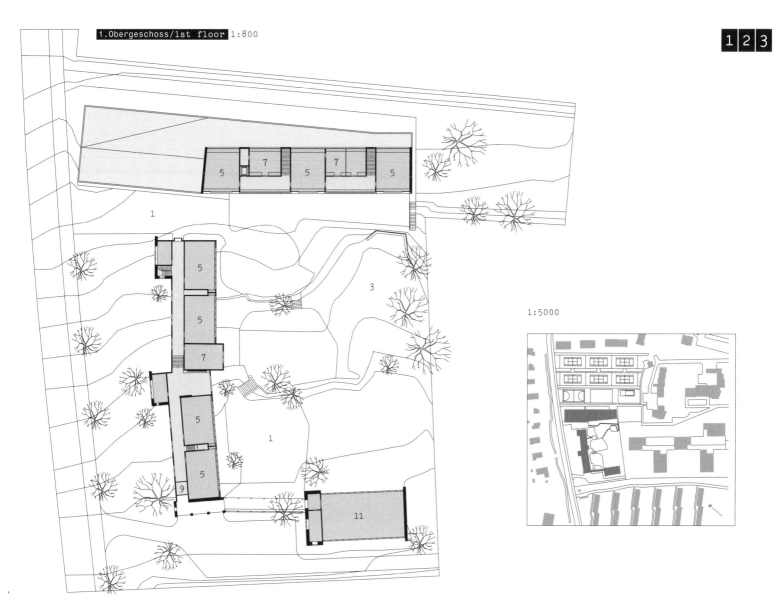

1:5000

Untergeschoss/basement 1:800

Querschnitt/section 1:800

Bachtobel

Primarschule/primary school

Architektur/architecture Marco Graber, Thomas Pulver Architekten ETH BSA SIA, Bern/Zürich

Landschaftsplanung/landscape architecture Guido Hager, Zürich

Wettbewerb/competition 1999

Bauzeit/construction period 2001–2002

SchülerInnen/students 60 Erweiterungsbau/extension (140 Gesamtanlage/overall complex) (Alter/age 7–12)

Klassen/classes 3 (7 Gesamtanlage/overall complex)

Spezialangebote/special features Hort, Turnhalle/day-care centre, sports hall

Geschossfläche (SIA 416)/total floor area 2'698m²

Nutzfläche (SIA 416)/net area 1'819m²

Rauminhalt RI (SIA 116)/volume 12'003m³

Gebäudevolumen (SIA 416)/net volume 10'805m³

Anlagekosten (BKP 1–9 inkl. MWSt.)/overall costs incl. VAT 9'090'000 CHF

Gebäudekosten (BKP 2 inkl. MWSt.)/net construction costs incl. VAT 7'115'000 CHF

Gebäudekosten/m² GF/net construction costs per m² floor area 2'637 CHF/m²

Gebäudekosten/m³ RI (SIA 116) construction costs per m³ volume 593 CHF/m³

Energiekennzahl Wärme/specific energy consumption 57.5 kWh/m²a

Anmerkung/remark Kennzahlen beziehen sich auf Erweiterung/figures refer to extension

Nordostansicht/north-east elevation

Text: Daniel Kurz, Photo: Theodor Stalder visus GmbH

Erweiterung Schulanlage Lachenzelg
Lachenzelg School, extension
Zürich-Höngg, Switzerland
ADP, Beat Jordi Caspar Angst, Zürich

Blick in den Innenhof/
view into the inner courtyard

## Erweiterte Bedürfnisse

Mit den Schulhäusern Lachenzelg (1953) und Imbisbühl (1957) konzipierte Roland Rohn auf dem gleichen Areal zwei grundlegend verschiedene Bauten: Das ältere Schulhaus ist eine solide und traditionelle Anlage mit einbündigen Korridoren, das vier Jahre später erbaute bietet dagegen ein faszinierendes Raumerlebnis. Es gruppiert sich im «split-level» um einen verglasten Innenhof; schwebende Treppen verbinden die zweiseitig belichteten Klassen. Der Einfluss der bahnbrechenden Zürcher Ausstellung «Das neue Schulhaus» von 1953 ist nicht zu verkennen. Bei der Erneuerung der Schulanlage war es das vorrangige Ziel, die mit 55 Quadratmetern sehr kleinen

## Growing Needs

With the schools in Lachenzelg (1953) and Imbisbühl (1957), Roland Rohn designed two very different buildings on the same site. The older of the two schools is a solid, traditional structure with single-depth corridors, whereas the more recent building offers a fascinating experience of space. The school is arranged on 'split levels' around a glazed quadrangle; floating stairs link the classrooms, which are lit on two sides. The influence of the path-breaking Zurich exhibition 'The New School' in 1953 is unmistakable. When the school was renovated, one

Altbau, erneuertes Klassenzimmer/
old building, renovated classroom

Altbau, neue Korridorfront/
old building, new corridor façade

Korridor Obergeschoss/access way, first floor

Erweiterungsbau, Terrasse/extension building, terrace

Klassenzimmer des älteren Baus durch Gruppenräume zu entlasten. Diese wurden im bestehenden Bau durch die Aufteilung
von Klassenzimmern geschaffen. Darüber hinaus sollte der
Schule ein gemeinschaftlicher Bereich mit Aula, Bibliothek
und Mensa angegliedert werden, der auch dem Quartier zur
Benutzung offen steht. Der zweigeschossige Erweiterungsbau im
Eingangsbereich der Schule hat zwei Gesichter: Die graue
Aussenseite wird durch die Holzlaibungen der Fenster warm ge-
tönt. Die Hauptfassade richtet sich jedoch zum Innenhof,
der mit seiner strengen Ordnung an ein Kloster des Cinquecento

of the prime goals was to enlarge the rather small classrooms (which occupied 55 square metres). This was done
by assigning to each classroom a group room, which was
created by dividing up a classroom. Furthermore, the
extension building was designed as a communal area that
now includes a school hall, a library and a canteen, which
can also be used by the local residents. The two-storey
extension standing next to the entrance area presents two
faces: the wooden reveals lend the grey exterior a warm
hue, whereas the stern structuring of the main façade
looking onto the quadrangle calls to mind a cinquecento
monastery. The corridor bordering the quadrangle links
three unequal wings: the two-storey hall in the north, the

1:5000

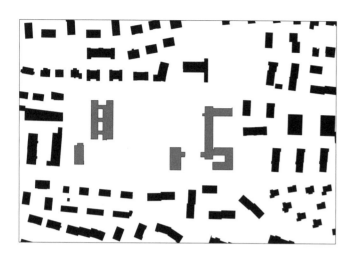

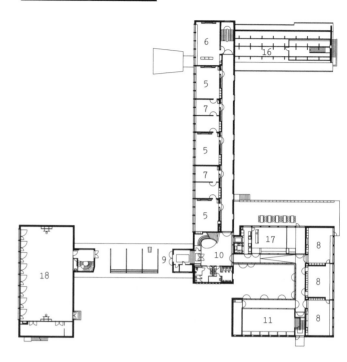

**Untergeschoss/basement** 1:1000

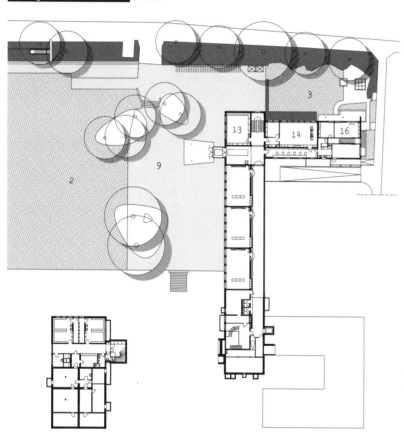

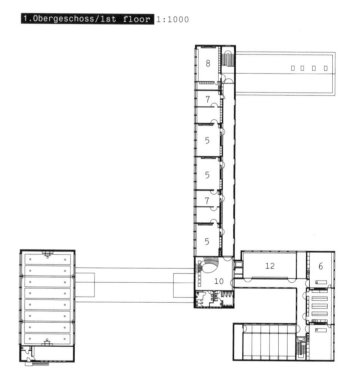

erinnert. Der umlaufende Erschliessungskorridor verbindet
drei ungleiche Gebäudeflügel: den zweigeschossigen Saal
im Norden, Mensa und Bibliothek im Süden sowie Schulzimmer für
Werken und Naturkunde im Westen. Eine grosse, holzbeplankte
Gartenterrasse lädt zum Aufenthalt im Freien ein. Robuste
Materialien, warme Farben und viel Licht charakterisieren den
Innenausbau. Die Nutzungen sind auf Wunsch der Nutzerseite
räumlich und funktional deutlich voneinander getrennt;
die Bibliothek verfügt gegenwärtig nur über begrenzte Öff-
nungszeiten, und das Angebot des Mittagstischs wird erst von
wenigen Schülerinnen und Schülern beansprucht.

canteen and library in the south, and special classrooms
for crafts and the natural sciences in the west. A large,
wood-panelled garden terrace invites users to linger.
The interior is characterised by robust materials, warm
colours and copious light. In compliance with users'
requests, the various functions have been separated
spatially. The library is only open for short periods at
a time. Although lunch is available, few pupils take
advantage of the offer at present.

Erdgeschoss, Erweiterungsbau/ground floor of extension building 1:250

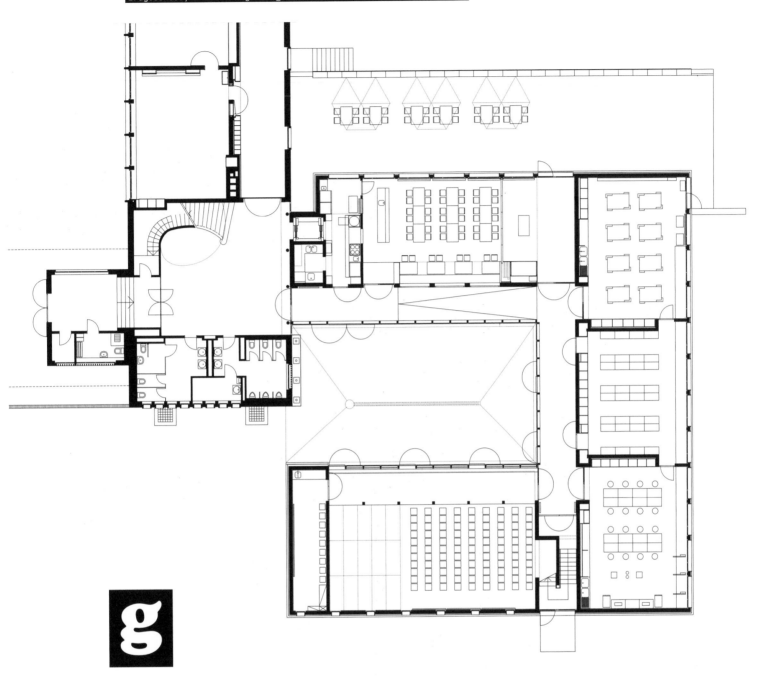

g

Lachenzelg

Sekundarschule/secondary school
Architektur/architecture ADP Architekten AG, Zürich Beat Jordi Caspar Angst
Landschaftsplanung/landscape architecture Vetsch Nipkow und Partner, Zürich
Studie/study 1998
Bauzeit/construction period 2001–2004
SchülerInnen/students 420 (Gesamtanlage/overall complex) (Alter/age 12–16)
Klassen/classes 21 (Gesamtanlage)
Spezialangebote/special features Mittagstisch, Quartiersaal/midday meals, community hall
Geschossfläche (SIA 416)/total floor area 1'175 m²
Nutzfläche (SIA 416)/net area 809 m²
Rauminhalt RI (SIA 116)/volume 5'900 m³
Gebäudevolumen (SIA 416)/net volume 4'600 m³
Anlagekosten (BKP 1–9 inkl. MWSt.)/overall costs incl. VAT 5'200'000 CHF
Gebäudekosten (BKP 2 inkl. MWSt.)/net construction costs incl. VAT 3'753'000 CHF
Gebäudekosten/m2 GF/net construction costs per m² floor area 3'194 CHF/m²
Gebäudekosten/m³ RI (SIA 116)/construction costs per m³ volume 636 CHF/m³
Anmerkung/remark Kennzahlen beziehen sich auf Erweiterung/figures refer to extension

Erweiterung Schulanlage Kügeliloo
Kügeliloo School, extension
Zürich-Oerlikon, Switzerland
Fosco Fosco-Oppenheim Vogt, Zürich

Südostansicht/south-east elevation

Text: Daniel Kurz, Photo: Theodor Stalder visus GmbH

### Kompakt

Die Schulanlage Kügeliloo entstand 1954 in einem reinen Wohnviertel in Zürich-Nord. 1999 erfolgte eine Instandsetzung, die mit der Erweiterung von 12 auf 21 Klassen verbunden wurde. Dringender Raumbedarf in der Schule verlangte nach einer schnellen und nachhaltigen Lösung. Der elegante Erweiterungsbau ist klar und flexibel strukturiert. Die Fassaden zum Pausenhof und zur Wehntalerstrasse sind wie die innere Tragstruktur in Ortsbeton ausgeführt, die Klassenzimmerfronten aus grossformatigen Fensterelementen gefügt. Die Bauweise erlaubte eine extrem kurze Bauzeit. Das Innere weist zwei

### Compact

Kügeliloo School was built in a purely residential suburb in Zürich-Nord in 1954. In 1999 repairs were carried out as part of a programme to extend the school's capacity from twelve to twenty-one classrooms. Urgent need for more space called for a quick and lasting solution. The elegant extension has a clear and flexible structure. Both the façades facing the schoolyard and Wehntalerstrasse, and the internal load-bearing structure are made of site-poured concrete; the classroom fronts feature prefabricated glazed façade panels. Thanks to this mode of construction, work was completed in a very short time. The interior has two parallel areas. The access area is

Nordwestansicht/north-west elevation

parallele Zonen auf: Die Erschliessungszone ist von der durchlaufenden Kaskadentreppe geprägt. Der Künstler Daniel Schibli setzte im Garderobenbereich gezielte Farbakzente. Die Klassen- und Gruppenräume liegen in einer Schicht und sind durch nicht tragende Wände getrennt, was spätere Veränderungen im Grundriss erleichtert. Wie die Erschliessungszone sind auch diese Räume von der Wirkung des sichtbar gelassenen Betons geprägt. Ihre schlichte Materialisierung lässt Raum für die Aneignung durch die Schule selber. Die Schulhauserweiterung setzt in ökologischer Hinsicht Massstäbe. Der Energiebedarf des Schulhauses liegt unter dem Minergie-Grenzwert von 144 MJ/m² im Jahr. Die

dominated by the continuous cascading stairs. Artist Daniel Schibli has used colour to create emphasis in the cloak-room area. The classrooms and group rooms are not separated by load-bearing walls — a feature designed to facilitate any plan changes in the future. As in the case of the access area, the appearance of these rooms is marked by the presence of the visible concrete. The simple realisation of this part of the complex allows the school to adapt the rooms to suit its needs. The extension sets ecological standards. The school's energy require-

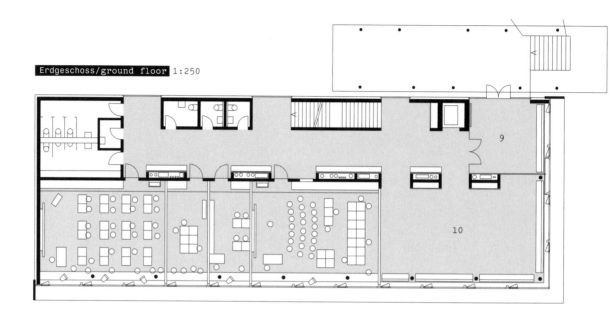

Erdgeschoss/ground floor 1:250

1:2000

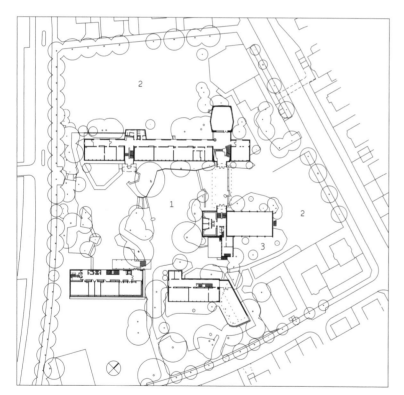

Heizenergie wird über eine Wärmepumpe mit Erdsonden gewonnen. Die Frischluft wird über Erdregister je nach Jahreszeit gekühlt oder vorgewärmt und sorgt das ganze Jahr über für ein angenehmes Raumklima. Bei der Instandsetzung des Altbaus verband sich der Respekt vor der wertvollen Substanz mit neuen farblichen Akzenten. Alt- und Neubau sind durch das künstlerische Projekt von Andres Lutz und Anders Guggisberg verbunden. 120 kleine Messingschilder berichten von Vorkommnissen, die sich entweder tatsächlich an dem betreffenden Ort ereignet haben oder sich – vielleicht – in Zukunft ereignen werden.

ment is below the so-called Minergie standard of 144 MJ/m$^2$ per annum. Heating is supplied by a heat pump with subterranean loops. Depending on the time of year, fresh air is cooled or prewarmed by the ground register to create a pleasant room temperature all the year round. The repairs done on the old building combined respect for its valuable structure and materials with a new colour concept, which added emphasis here and there. Andres Lutz and Anders Guggisberg's artistic project links the old and new buildings. 120 small brass plates record incidents that have actually occurred or will – perhaps – occur there in the future.

NW-Fassade/nw elevation 1:800

2.Obergeschoss/2nd floor 1:800

Längsschnitt/section 1:800

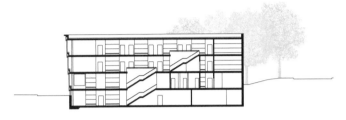

1.Obergeschoss/1st floor 1:800

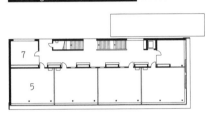

Querschnitt/section 1:800

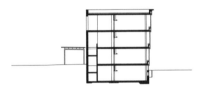

Untergeschoss/basement 1:800

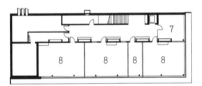

SO-Fassade/se elevation 1:800

Kügeliloo

Primarschule/primary school
Architektur/architecture Fosco Fosco-Oppenheim Vogt Architekten, Zürich
Landschaftsplanung/landscape architecture berchtold.lenzin, Landschaftsarchitekten, Zürich
Studie/study 1998
Bauzeit/construction period 2001–2001
SchülerInnen/students 120 Erweiterungsbau/extension (380 Gesamtanlage/overall complex) (Alter/age 7–12)
Klassen/classes 6 (19 Gesamtanlage/overall complex)
Spezialangebote/special features Hort/day-care centre
Geschossfläche (SIA 416)/total floor area 2'173 m²
Nutzfläche (SIA 416)/net area 1'312 m²
Rauminhalt RI (SIA 116)/volume 9'119 m³
Gebäudevolumen (SIA 416)/net volume 7'820 m³
Anlagekosten (BKP 1–9 inkl. MWSt.)/overall costs incl. VAT 6'862'000 CHF
Gebäudekosten (BKP 2 inkl. MWSt.)/net construction costs incl. VAT 5'616'000 CHF
Gebäudekosten/m² GF/net construction costs per m² floor area 2'584 CHF/m²
Gebäudekosten/m³ RI (SIA 116)/construction costs per m³ volume 616 CHF/m³
Minergiekennzahl/Minergie factor 23.9 kWh/m²a
Anmerkung/remark Kennzahlen beziehen sich auf Erweiterung/figures refer to extension

`Erweiterungsbau, Südansicht/extension building, south elevation`

**Erweiterung Schulanlage Mattenhof**
**Mattenhof School, extension**
Zürich-Schwamendingen, Switzerland
B.E.R.G. Architekten, Zürich

`Obergeschoss, Klassenzimmer/upper floor, classroom`

`Gesamtansicht/general view`

Text: Daniel Kurz, Photo: Reinhard Zimmermann

## Neues Raumprogramm

Wenn kleine Kinder Häuser zeichnen, steht der Kamin oft schief auf dem Dach, und die Fenster sind grösser als in Wirklichkeit. Einen ähnlichen Eindruck vermittelt auch der Erweiterungsbau des Schulhauses Mattenhof, der eine Anlage aus den fünfziger Jahren ergänzt. An diesem Bau wurden die heute gültigen Raumvorgaben der Stadt Zürich entwickelt und erstmals verwirklicht. Der neue Baukörper ist präzis und harmonisch in die bestehende, landschaftlich gestaltete Anlage an einem sanft geneigten Hang gefügt. Er steht im Dialog mit den bestehenden Bauten und ist durch eine gedeckte Pausenhalle mit ihnen verbunden. Volumen und Materialisierung des Neubaus orientieren sich an den bestehenden Bauten. Motive wie die vorstehenden Fenster und Dachoberlichter sowie

## New Building Standards

When small children draw houses, the chimney often stands crooked on the roof and the windows are too big. The extension to Mattenhof School, which dates from the 1950s, conveys a similar impression. It was with this project that the city of Zurich developed its present standards for school and classroom design. The new building is integrated harmoniously into the existing landscaped site. It enters into a dialogue with the existing buildings to which it is linked via a covered walkway. The volume and materials of the new building adhere closely to those of the old structure. Motifs such as projecting windows, rooflights and robust surfaces have

Obergeschoss, Klassenzimmer/upper floor, classroom

Obergeschoss, Klassenzimmer/upper floor, classroom

Erdgeschoss, Lehrerbereich/
ground floor, teachers' area

Treppe/stairway

Südostfassade/south-east façade

die robusten Oberflächen werden neu interpretiert, was
der Gesamtanlage einen einheitlichen, zurückhaltenden Ausdruck verleiht. Jedem der drei Schulhäuser sowie der Turnhalle
werden Unterrichts- und entsprechende Gemeinschaftsräume
zugewiesen. Durch das Angebot von Ganztagesstrukturen kommt
der Identität der Schule eine erweiterte Bedeutung zu,
die mit der Einführung der Grundstufe noch zunehmen wird.
Das Raumangebot der ganzen Schule muss daher flexibel nutzbar
und für künftige Anforderungen ausreichend sein. Der Neubau
schliesst mit dem mittleren Geschoss an den Pausenplatz
an. Hier liegen Foyer und Mehrzwecksaal, der Lehrerbereich und
ein Klassenzimmer. Ein zentraler Erschliessungsraum mit
geschwungenen Treppen und grossen Vorräumen durchdringt das
Gebäude. Die Schulräume sind von besonderer Grosszügigkeit
und integrieren auch die Fläche der Gruppenräume. Man betritt

been reinterpreted to give all parts of the complex a
common identity. Each of the three school buildings and
the gymnasium are assigned both classrooms and common
rooms. The provision of all-day facilities has enriched
the school's identity: the integration of a junior school
will broaden its scope still further. Flexible rooms
are essential in order to accommodate all these different
uses and to fulfil any new requirements the school may
have in the future. The three-storey new building borders
on the schoolyard and contains the foyer, the multifunctional hall, the teachers' area and a classroom.
A central corridor with curving stairs and large anterooms
extends right through the building. The large classrooms (80 square metres), which include the group room

Querschnitt/section 1:500

Erdgeschoss/ground floor 1:500

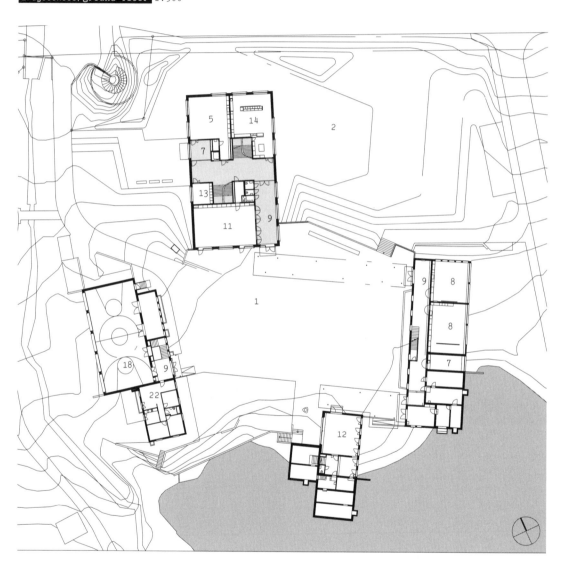

sie über einen eigenen Garderobenraum, der sich zu dem 80 Quadratmeter grossen Klassenzimmer hin öffnet. Die grossen Einheiten ermöglichen Team-Teaching und Lernen in Gruppen; sie können auch zukünftige Schulformen wie die Grundstufe aufnehmen. Besonders eindrücklich sind die Raumverhältnisse im Obergeschoss, in dem die leicht geneigten Decken von den Lichtkaminen der Lukarnen aufgeschnitten werden, so dass eine stark bewegte, helle Deckenlandschaft entsteht. In frischen Farben gehaltene Einbauschränke und Regale bieten viel Stauraum. Zusätzlich stehen zum Korridor hin verglaste Arbeitsnischen zur Verfügung. Im unteren, an den Garten anschliessenden Geschoss sind Kindergarten und Horträume mit Mittagsverpflegung sowie der Raum für die musikalische Früherziehung untergebracht.

areas, are entered through their own cloakrooms. These large units allow for team teaching and group work. They have been designed to accommodate other types of school, such as a junior school, in the future. The rooms on the top floor are particularly impressive. Their gently sloping ceilings are pierced by daylight tubes set in the rooflights to create a vibrantly lit ceiling. Lively coloured built-in cupboards and shelves provide plenty of storage space, whilst glazed niches facing the corridor provide additional work areas. The lower floor, which has direct access to the garden, contains a kindergarten and rooms providing midday care as well as a room for music classes.

Längsschnitt/section 1:500

Obergeschoss/1st floor 1:500

Untergeschoss/basement 1:500

1:5000

Obergeschoss/1st floor 1:250

**Mattenhof**
Primarschule/primary school
Architektur/architecture B.E.R.G. Architekten GmbH, Zürich
Landschaftsplanung/landscape architecture Kuhn Truninger, Zürich
Wettbewerb/competition 2000
Bauzeit/construction period 2002–2003
SchülerInnen/students 100 Erweiterungsbau/extension (240 Gesamtanlage/overall complex) (Alter/age 7–12)
Klassen/classes 5 (12 Gesamtanlage/overall complex)
Spezialangebote/special features Hort/day-care centre
Geschossfläche (SIA 416)/total floor area 1'855 m²
Nutzfläche (SIA 416)/net area 1'619 m²
Rauminhalt RI (SIA 116)/volume 8'823 m³
Gebäudevolumen (SIA 416)/net volume 7'592 m³
Anlagekosten (BKP 1–9 inkl. MWSt.)/overall costs incl. VAT 8'300'000 CHF
Gebäudekosten (BKP 2 inkl. MWSt.)/net construction costs incl. VAT 5'540'000 CHF
Gebäudekosten/m² GF/net construction costs per m² floor area 2'987 CHF/m²
Gebäudekosten/m³ RI (SIA 116) construction costs per m³ volume 628 CHF/m³
Minergiekennzahl/Minergie factor 38 kWh/m²a
Anmerkung/remark Kennzahlen beziehen sich auf Erweiterung/figures refer to extension

**Gesamtschule in der Höh**
**In der Höh Comprehensive School**
Volketswil (Zürich), Switzerland
Gafner & Horisberger, Zürich

Südansicht, Eingang/south elevation, entrance

Text: Daniel Kurz, Photo: Beat Bühler

## Schulkultur

Schon Jahre vor ihrer Erbauung beschäftigte diese Schule die Fachwelt, die Gemeindeöffentlichkeit und die Medien: In einem dreijährigen Prozess, an dem sich Vertretungen von Architektur, Lehrerschaft und Gemeinde beteiligten, erarbeitete die Schulgemeinde ein zukunftsweisendes pädagogisches Konzept und klärte anschliessend die spezifischen Raumbedürfnisse. Kinder aus allen Schulstufen werden hier in Klassen gemischten Alters unterrichtet. Je zwei Klassen teilen sich einen abtrennbaren Raum. Starre Stundenpläne gibt es nicht, der Ablauf des Unterrichts in Klassen, Halbklassen und Gruppen wird am Anfang der Woche gemeinsam besprochen. Der Unterricht in dieser Schule beruht auf ständiger Bewegung, und die

## School Culture

Years before it was built, this school preoccupied the specialists, local people and the media. For three years the municipal authorities, together with architects', teachers' and community representatives, worked out an innovative educational concept and clarified its specific room requirements. Children of all levels are taught in mixed-age classes. Each classroom is shared by two classes and can be partitioned. There are no rigid timetables. The weekly teaching plan, organised in classes, semi-classes and groups, is discussed collectively at the beginning of the week. Teaching at this school is based on constant movement, and the furniture has been designed accordingly. Fitted with castors, both the tables and the blackboards can be pushed to and fro. There is no 'back' or 'front' in these classrooms, which are subdivided into a number of

Kulturraum als Unterrichtsbereich/
cultural room as teaching area

Innenhof/inner courtyard

Kindergarten/kindergarten

Möblierung ist dieser Anforderung angepasst. Die Tische lassen sich — ebenso wie die Wandtafeln — auf Rollen bewegen. In den Schulzimmern gibt es kein vorne und hinten, dagegen zahlreiche, unterschiedlich eingerichtete Arbeitszonen: Pultgruppen, Computerarbeitsplätze, Lernbereiche auf Teppichen am Boden... und irgendwo dazwischen auch ein Lehrerpult. In der etwas zusammenhanglosen Umgebung seines Standorts in der Agglomeration liegt das kleine Schulhaus wie eine edle, flache Schatulle. Umlaufende Betonbänder fassen das Volumen; hohe Holzfenster und Fassadenplatten aus römischem Travertin geben ihm Wärme und Vornehmheit. Der jetzt erstellte quadratische Bau ist Teil einer wachsenden Anlage, die im Endausbau das ganze Baufeld bedecken wird. Viel Licht, warme Materialien und eine klare, modulare Raumstruktur charakterisieren das Innere. Ein begrünter Lichthof liegt im Kern des zweigeschossigen Gebäudes. Er wird von dem umlaufenden Korridor berührt, der

variously equipped working areas: groups of desks, computer workplaces, learning areas on the floor and — somewhere amongst all these — a teacher's desk. The little school lies there like a finely shaped, flat casket in its rather jumbled immediate surroundings in the middle of the vast agglomeration. Strips of concrete embrace the building, whilst high wooden windows and façade panels of Roman travertine lend it a warm and elegant appearance. The recently completed quadratic building is part of a growing complex that will cover the entire site when finished. Inside, one is struck by the plenteous light entering the building as well as by the warm materials and clearly defined modular structure. At the centre of

Schnitt NS/section ns 1:1000

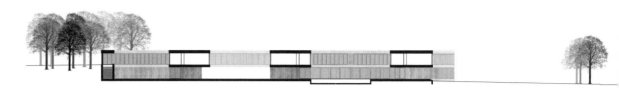

Erdgeschoss Gesamtprojekt/ground floor overall project 1:1000

Obergeschoss Gesamtprojekt/1st floor overall project 1:1000

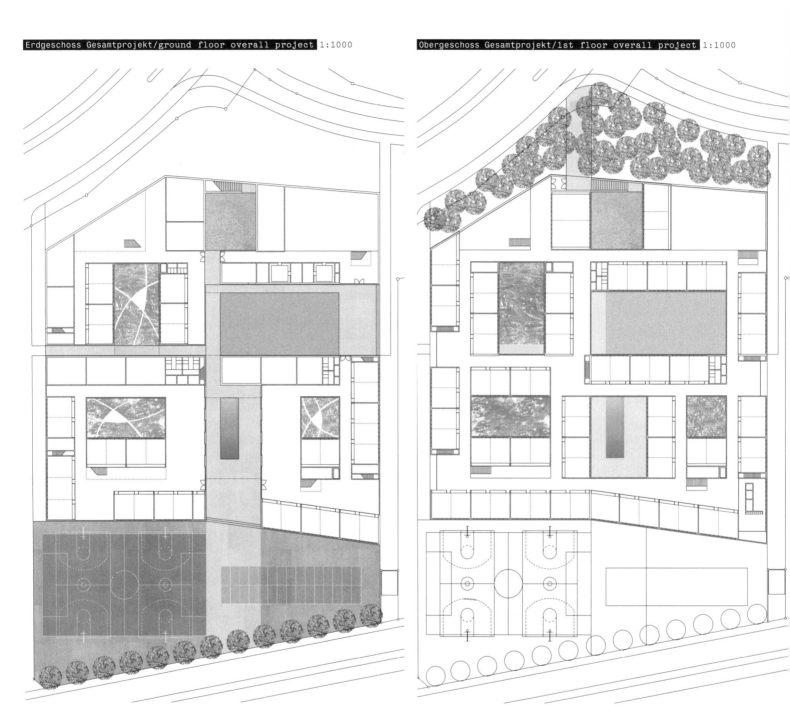

alle Räume verbindet. Die äussere Gebäudeschicht ist in gleichwertige, modular teil- und kombinierbare Räume aufgeteilt, die das Raumprogramm «Universalräume» nennt. Das quadratische Grundmodul ergibt einen Büro- oder Gruppenraum, zwei solcher Einheiten ein Klassenzimmer, von denen wiederum je zwei mit Faltwänden zu einer Suite verbunden sind (die Faltwände stehen gegenwärtig überall offen). Im Erdgeschoss befinden sich der Kindergarten, die Unterstufe, spezialisierte Unterrichtsräume, die Küche und der Kulturraum, der für Veranstaltungen und für den täglichen Mittagstisch zur Verfügung steht. Im Obergeschoss liegen der Lehrerbereich und weitere Klassensuiten. Die grosszügigen Erschliessungsräume lassen sich bereichsweise für Gruppen- und Projektarbeit bespielen.

the building, is a planted light well, which is touched on by the surrounding corridor linking the rooms. The building's shell is subdivided to create a system of equally sized modular rooms — known as 'universal rooms' — which can be combined fully or in part. The quadratic basic module creates a single office or group room; two of these modules create a classroom, of which two can, in turn, be linked with folding walls to form a suite. (At present, all the folding walls are open.) On the ground floor there are specialised classrooms, a kindergarten, the primary school, the kitchen and the culture room, where various events are held and the midday meals are taken. The top floor accommodates the teachers' area and additional class suites. The spacious access areas can be used for group and project work.

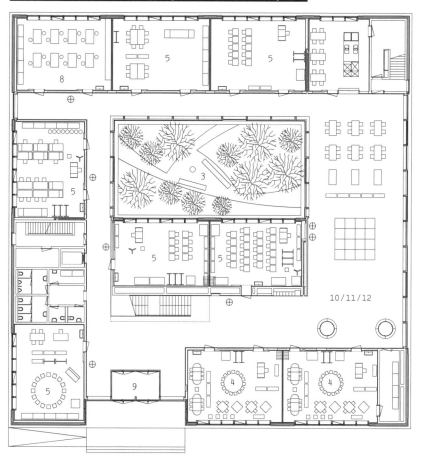

1:5000

Schnitt OW/section ew 1:1000

Südfassade/south elevation 1:1000

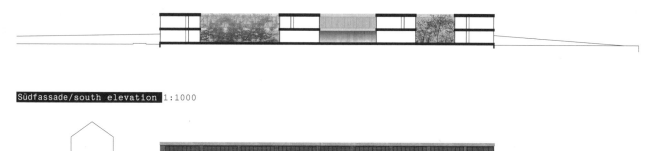

In der Höh
Gesamtschule/comprehensive school
Architektur/architecture Gafner & Horisberger Architekten GmbH, Zürich
Landschaftsplanung/landscape architecture Guido Hager, Zürich
Wettbewerb/competition 2000
Bauzeit/construction period 2002–2003
SchülerInnen/students 160 (Alter/age 5–15)
Klassen/classes 7 + 1 Kindergarten
Spezialangebote/special features Mittagstisch/midday meals
Geschossfläche (SIA 416)/total floor area 4'430 m²
Geschossfläche pro SchülerIn/floor area per student 28 m²
Nutzfläche (SIA 416)/net area 2'945 m²
Rauminhalt RI (SIA 116)/volume 17'715 m³
Gebäudevolumen (SIA 416)/net volume 15'635 m³
Anlagekosten (BKP 1–9 inkl. MWSt.)/overall costs incl. VAT 13'235'000 CHF
Gebäudekosten (BKP 2 inkl. MWSt.)/net construction costs incl. VAT 10'520'000 CHF
Gebäudekosten/m² GF/net construction costs per m² floor area 2'375 CHF/m²
Gebäudekosten/m³ RI (SIA 116)/construction costs per m³ volume 594 CHF/m³
Minergiekennzahl/Minergie factor 31.7 kWh/m²a
Anmerkung/remark Angaben beziehen sich auf den bereits realisierten Teil/figures refer to built section

Zurich International School
Zurich International School
Wädenswil (Zürich), Switzerland
Galli & Rudolf, Zürich

Nordansicht/north elevation

Text: Daniel Kurz, Photo: Hannes Henz, Naas & Bisig

## Die Schulgemeinschaft

Die rund 400 Schülerinnen und Schüler dieser englisch-
sprachigen Privatschule stammen aus über 30 Nationen. Ihre
Eltern sind in der Mehrzahl Angestellte internationaler
Firmen, die nur wenige Jahre im Raum Zürich verbringen. Für
Kinder und Eltern ist die Schule ein wichtiger sozialer
Treffpunkt. Die Schule liegt gleichsam exterritorial zwischen
Industriezone und Golfplatz, fern vom Siedlungsgebiet
und nahe der Autobahn. Das kompakte Volumen ragt mit seinen
schräg verlaufenden Fassaden, den versetzt angeordneten
Fensterbändern und grellen Farben aus der industriellen Umge-
bung heraus. Es gliedert sich in zwei Klassentrakte und
einen niedrigeren Zentralbereich. Die Planung erfolgte unter
hohem Zeit- und Kostendruck nach einem kurzen, zweistufigen
Wettbewerbsverfahren. Die Schule lieferte nicht nur das

## A School Community

The approximately 400 boys and girls attending this
private English-language school come from more than 30
different countries. Most of their par-ents are employed
by international companies and only spend a few years
in the Zurich area. Hence, the school is an important
meeting place for parents and children alike. The school
is located extraterritorially, as it were, between
an industrial zone and a golf course, well away from the
residential area and near to the motorway. The towering
compact volume with its irregular façades, offset
strip windows and bright colours stands out against the
school's industrial surroundings. The building is subdivided into two classroom wings and a lower central area.

Klassenzimmer, Primarschule/
classroom, primary school

Treppe und Bibliothek/stairway and library

Mehrzwecksaal und Halle/multi-purpose hall and hallway

Raumprogramm, sondern formulierte auch pädagogisch motivierte Grundsätze: Sichtbeton war ebenso zu vermeiden wie rechte Winkel, die Verwendung von Primärfarben war Pflicht. Die räumlichen Qualitäten der Schule erschliessen sich in ihrem offenen, an Durchblicken reichen Inneren. Die zentrale Halle bildet zusammen mit dem zweigeschossigen Mehrzweckraum im Zentrum der Schule einen lichterfüllten öffentlichen Bereich, an dem Empfangsschalter, Bibliothek und der Raum des Elternvereins liegen. Die Halle dient zugleich als Speisesaal – die einfachen Esstische können zusammengeklappt und weggestellt werden. Kurze Verbindungswege führen in die Klassentrakte. Die Schulzimmer sind in Gruppen rund um einen gemeinsamen Vorraum angeordnet, der auch für den Unterricht benützt wird. Ihre teilweise verglasten Wände er-

Planning was carried out under extreme pressure to keep cost and time to a minimum following a brief, two-phase competition. The school itself not only came up with the room arrangement but also formulated pedagogically motivated principles regarding materials and interior design: fair-faced concrete was as much to be avoided as right angles, whilst primary colours were obligatory. The school's spatial qualities are apparent in its open interior, which offers a wealth of views through the complex. In combination with the two-storey multifunctional room at the centre of the building, the central hall creates a light-filled area where the reception desk, the library and the parents' association room are located. The hall also serves as a canteen. The simple dining tables can be folded up and stored. There are short walkways leading to the classroom wings. The classrooms are arranged in groups around a common anteroom,

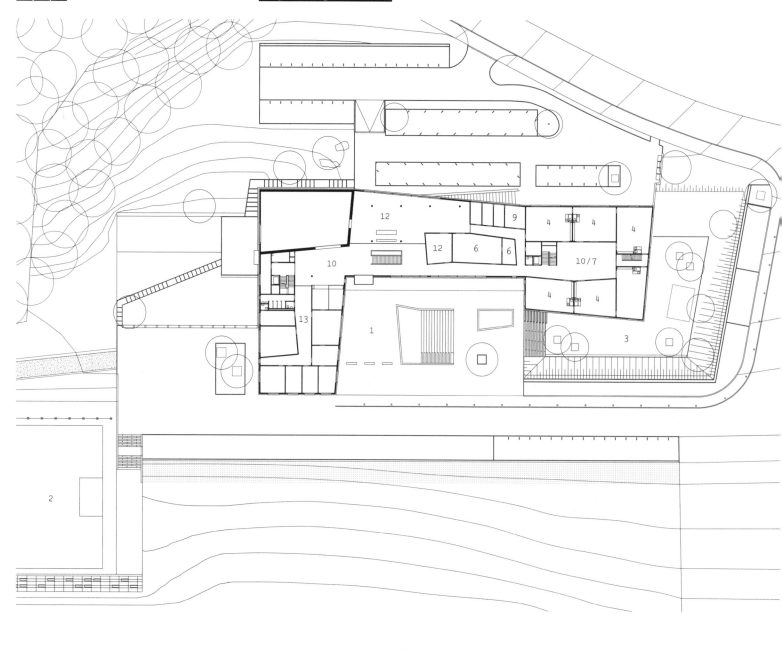

**Längsschnitt/section** 1:800

**Querschnitt/section** 1:800

lauben Ein- und Durchblicke. Die feuerpolizeilichen An-forderungen zur Nutzung des gemeinsamen Vorraums wurden mit Hilfe von Verbindungstüren zwischen den Klassen erfüllt, die jedem Zimmer zwei Fluchtwege offen lassen. Der Schulbe-trieb wirkt lebhaft und informell. Die Möbel, von den Lehrern individuell zusammengestellt, sind einfach, leicht und beweglich, jedoch nicht höhenverstellbar. Die Kinder sind oft in Bewegung, sie arbeiten in kleinen Gruppen an Tischen, manchmal auch am Boden. Die konsequente und schlichte Materialisierung der Räume (graue Schieferböden und Parkett, weisse Wände und Akustikdecken, runde Deckenleuchten) bringt Ruhe in das bunte Treiben.

which is also used for teaching. Their partly glazed walls provide two-way views. The fire-safety requirements regulating the use of the anteroom are satisfied by the doors linking the classrooms, which provide two escape routes per room. The school has a lively, informal feel. The furniture, put together individually by the teachers, is simple, light and mobile, although not of ad-justable height. The children are frequently on the move. They work in small groups at tables, or sometimes on the floor. The simple materials used for the rooms (grey slate and parquet for the floors, white walls, acoustic ceilings and round ceiling lamps) introduce an element of order into this colourful school.

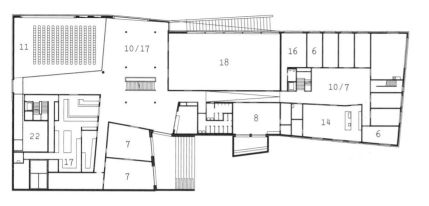

1:10000

1.Obergeschoss/1st floor 1:800

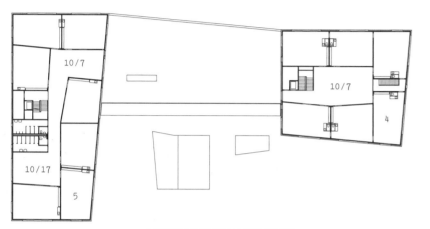

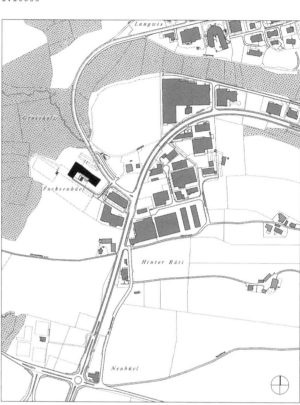

Klassenbereich Primarschule/
classroom area, primary school 1:400

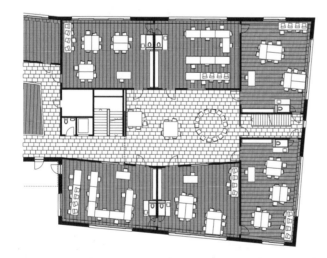

Zurich International School
Englischsprachige Privatschule/International School English-speaking private school
Architektur/architecture Galli & Rudolf Architekten ETH SIA, Zürich
Landschaftsplanung/landscape architecture Rotzler Krebs Partner, Winterthur
Wettbewerb/competition 1999
Bauzeit/construction period 2000–2002
SchülerInnen/students 450 (Alter/age 5–11)
Klassen/classes 22 + 6 Kindergarten
Spezialangebote/special features Rezeption, Elternclub, Tagesbetreuung/reception, parents' club, day-care
Geschossfläche (SIA 416)/total floor area 6'759m²
Geschossfläche pro SchülerIn/floor area per student 15m²
Nutzfläche (SIA 416)/net area 6'216m²
Rauminhalt RI (SIA 116)/volume 33'788m³
Gebäudevolumen (SIA 416)/net volume 29'508m³
Anlagekosten (BKP 1–9 inkl. MWSt.)/overall costs incl. VAT 17'952'000 CHF
Gebäudekosten (BKP 2 inkl. MWSt.)/net construction costs incl. VAT 15'528'000 CHF
Gebäudekosten/m² GF/net construction costs per m² floor area 2'297 CHF/m²
Gebäudekosten/m³ RI (SIA 116)/construction costs per m³ volume 460 CHF/m³
Energiekennzahl Wärme/specific energy consumption 48.9 kWh/m²a
Anmerkung/remark z.T. Mehrfachnutzungen/multiple usage

Südostansicht, Erweiterungsmöglichkeit/
south-east elevation with extension possibility

Erdgeschoss, Halle/ground floor, hallway

Südostansicht, Erweiterungsmöglichkeit/
south-east elevation with extension possibility

Klassenzimmer/classroom

## Primarschulhaus Linden
## Linden Primary School

Niederhasli (Zürich), Switzerland
Bünzli & Courvoisier, Zürich

**1**

Text: Alan Wakefield, Photo: Hannes Henz, Alan Wakefield

## Modular

Trotz oder vielmehr dank der Nähe zum Flughafen Zürich ist die Gemeinde Niederhasli in den letzten Jahren stark gewachsen. Der Anstieg der Schülerzahlen, verbunden mit dem vermehrten Unterricht in Kleinklassen, machte den Bau eines neuen Primarschulhauses notwendig. Das realisierte Raumprogramm basiert auf den Richtlinien des Kantons Zürich. Als Besonderheit war bei der Ausschreibung des Wettbewerbs eine schrittweise Erweiterung von sechs auf zwölf Klassenzimmer mit den entsprechenden Spezial- und Nebenräumen gefordert. Diese Vorgabe führte zu einem linearen Gebäudekörper, der, ausgehend von der Turnhalle mit Garderoben und Lehrerbereich, drei identische Module aneinander reiht. Diese bestehen aus zwei Klassenzimmern plus Gruppenraum

## The Modular School

Despite, or rather because of, its proximity to Zurich Airport, the community of Niederhasli has grown considerably over the past few years. An increasing number of pupils, along with the trend towards small classes, made a new primary school necessary. The room arrangement of the completed building was based on the canton of Zurich's guidelines. A special competition requirement was to gradually increase the number of classrooms from six to twelve, and also to provide needed special-use and adjacent rooms. The result was a linear building which, starting at the gymnasium with its cloakrooms and

Turnhalle/gymnasium

Nordostfassade/north-east façade

Eingangsbereich/entrance

im Obergeschoss und einem Spezialzimmer mit Nebenräumen im Erdgeschoss. Durch diese Disposition und die «Haus-im-Haus»-Konzeption können später weitere Module angefügt werden. Bei der Annäherung an das Gebäude fällt zuerst die grosse Gebäudetiefe und die beachtliche Auskragung zum Pausenplatz hin auf. Beides zeichnet sich an der geschlossenen Gebäudestirn ab, welche das — vorläufig — letzte «Glied der Kette» abschliesst. Die «Betonschale» kontrastiert zum Lärchenholz, das im Bereich der Fenster nach aussen tritt. Die grossen Fensterflächen mit den tiefen Brüstungen beziehen die Umgebung in das Schulzimmer ein. Die Aussenräume des Schulareals sorgen für den erwünschten Abstand zur Nachbarschaft. Die allseitig in Holz ausgekleideten Unterrichtsräume vermitteln eine warme, geborgene Atmosphäre. Die Intimität der Räumlichkeiten im Obergeschoss wird durch das einfallende Licht

teachers' area, comprises three identical modules joined in a row. Each of these modules consists of two classrooms and a group room on the upper floor plus a special room with adjacent rooms on the ground floor. Thanks to this arrangement and the 'house-in-house' conception, further modules can be added later. Approaching the building, one is initially struck by its great depth and the long cantilevered section facing the schoolyard. Both are identifiable on the building's end wall, which forms the — provisional — final link in the chain. The concrete 'shell' contrasts strikingly with the larch, which is visible outside around the windows of the classroom façade. The large windows, with their low breasts, invite the world outside into the classrooms. The open space

`Querschnitt/section` 1:800      `Längsschnitt/section` 1:800

`Erdgeschoss/ground floor` 1:800

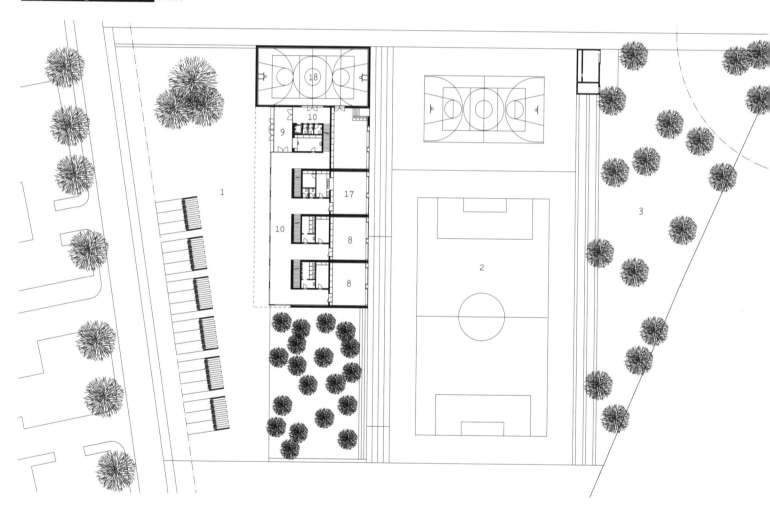

und den Verzicht auf Ein- und Ausblicke im Korridorbereich betont. Die Differenzierung zwischen Lernen in der Schulstube und Spielen auf dem Pausenhof wird bewusst als Wechselspiel zweier sehr unterschiedlicher Erlebniswelten inszeniert. Dieses traditionelle Schulhausverständnis ist auch akustisch im Kontrast zwischen der gedämpften Unterrichtsatmosphäre und der lärmigen Pausenhalle erfahrbar, welche im Erdgeschoss die Räume zusammenbindet. Die Klarheit der Struktur, die Geborgenheit der Klassenräume, verbunden mit der Robustheit des Gebäudes, und die flexibel zu handhabenden Erweiterungsmöglichkeiten sind eine adäquate Antwort auf das heterogene und sich schnell wandelnde Umfeld.

around the school establishes the desired distance to the neighbourhood. The classrooms, completely clad in wood, create a warm atmosphere with a homely feel. The distinction between classroom learning and playing in the yard is consciously staged as the interplay between two very different worlds of experience. This traditional conception of a school building is also noticeable aurally in the contrast between the subdued classroom atmosphere and the noisy break hall that links the rooms on the ground floor. The clarity of the structure, the intimacy provided by the classrooms, the building's robustness and the option of flexible extension are a satisfying response to the school's heterogeneous and rapidly changing surroundings.

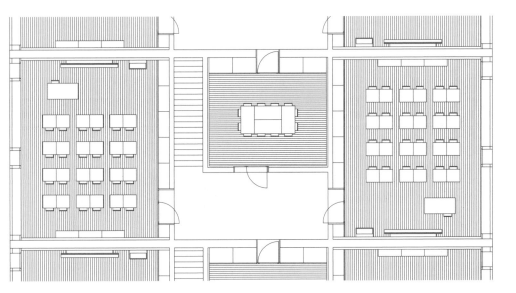

1

Obergeschoss/1st floor 1:800 1:5000

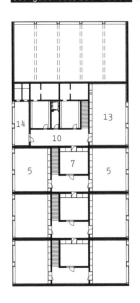

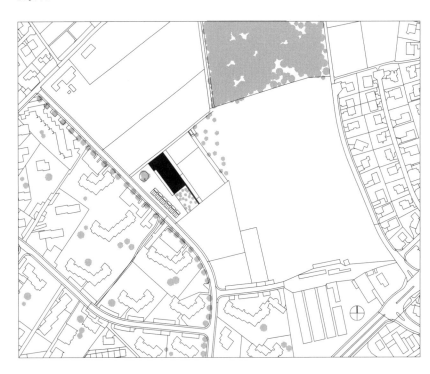

Linden
Primarschule/primary school
Architektur/architecture Bünzli & Courvoisier Architekten ETH SIA, Zürich
Landschaftsplanung/landscape architecture Vogt, Landschaftsarchitekten AG, Zürich
Wettbewerb/competition 1999
Bauzeit/construction period 2001–2003
SchülerInnen/students 120 (Alter/age 7–12)
Klassen/classes 6
Spezialangebote/special features Mittagstisch/midday meals
Geschossfläche (SIA 416)/total floor area 2'700 m²
Geschossfläche pro SchülerIn/floor area per student 23 m²
Nutzfläche (SIA 416)/net area 1'700 m²
Rauminhalt RI (SIA 116)/volume 13'444 m³
Anlagekosten (BKP 1–9 inkl. MWSt.)/overall costs incl. VAT 12'496'000 CHF
Gebäudekosten (BKP 2 inkl. MWSt.)/net construction costs incl. VAT 8'530'000 CHF
Gebäudekosten/m² GF/net construction costs per m² floor area 3'159 CHF/m²
Gebäudekosten/m³ RI (SIA 116)/construction costs per m³ volume 634 CHF/m³

Aula mit offener Faltwand/aula with folding partition open

Obergeschoss, Gruppenraum/upper floor, group room

Oberstufenzentrum Thurzelg
Thurzelg Secondary School
Oberbüren (St. Gallen), Switzerland
Staufer & Hasler, Frauenfeld/Zürich

Text: Daniel Kurz, Photo: Fredy Bühler, Heinrich Helfenstein

## Die Gemeindeschule

Das Oberstufenzentrum bildet einen markanten öffentlichen Ort in der ländlichen Gemeinde. Zwei grosse, ruhige Baukörper, übereck gestellt, spannen zwei unterschiedliche Aussenräume auf. Das zum Pausenplatz hin auskragende Obergeschoss aus Holz lagert auf dem massiven Erdgeschoss und formt eine gedeckte Pausenhalle als prägnanten Zugang zur Schule. Im Innern öffnet sich der Raum zu einer zweigeteilten, zentralen Halle, die über Oberlichter natürliches Licht erhält. Lehrerbereiche, Schulleitung, Bibliothek, Aula und spezialisierte Unterrichtsräume besetzen das in Sichtbeton erstellte Erdgeschoss; die Aula kann für grössere Veranstaltungen mit der Halle verbunden werden. Im Obergeschoss liegen die Klassen- und Gruppenräume an der umlaufenden Galerie. Hier ist

## A Community Building

The secondary school constitutes a public landmark in this rural community. Two large staggered buildings with a calm air occupy two very different outside spaces. The cantilevered wooden upper storey, which rests on the solid ground floor, creates a covered recreation hall beneath it which forms a compact school entrance facing the schoolyard Inside, the space forms a central hall, divided in two, which receives natural light from skylights. The ground floor, executed in fair-faced concrete, accommodates teachers' areas, the school management offices, the library, the assembly hall and classrooms for special subjects. The assembly hall can be used in conjunction with the central hall for staging major events. On the top floor, the classrooms and group rooms line the gallery

Halle/hall

Obergeschoss, Galerie/1st floor, gallery

Halle/hall

Schule und Mehrzweckhalle/
school and multi-purpose hall

Holz das charakteristische Material. Klasse und Gruppenraum
sind zu einer flexibel kombinierbaren Unterrichtseinheit
gruppiert. Ihre klare gegenseitige Zuordnung hat eine sichtbar intensive Nutzung zur Folge. Oberlichter geben dem
Gruppenraum ein weiches Licht. Durch sorgfältige Materialisierung erhalten der Gruppen- und Klassenraum den Charakter
einer Werkstatt. Die Turnhalle dient auch als kommunale
Mehrzweckhalle. Sie öffnet sich mit der Breitseite zum
Schulplatz; ihre hohe, kupferverkleidete Fassade ist über
eine Vorhalle aus Holz an den Platz angebunden. Trennvorhänge
ermöglichen die Unterteilung in drei Hallen; der federnd
verlegte Parkettboden, ein Bühnenhaus und seitliche Zuschauer-

that runs round the hall. The prominent material here
is wood. Single classrooms and group rooms are arranged to
form a variously combinable teaching unit. Their clearly
defined arrangement clearly encourages intensive use.
The group room is filled with soft light from the skylights. The gymnasium also serves the community as
a multifunctional hall. Its long side opens out onto the
schoolyard. Its high, copper-clad façade is linked to
the square via a wooden entrance hall. Curtains serve to
partition the hall, creating three separate areas;

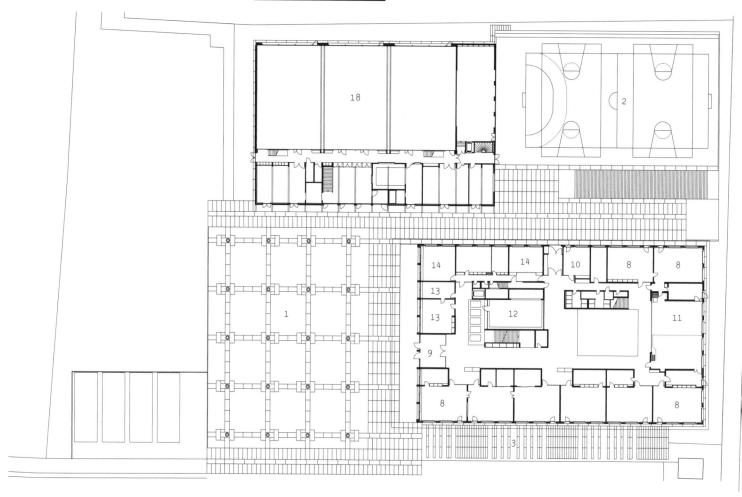

Obergeschoss/1st floor 1:400

galerien erlauben vielseitige Nutzungen. Den Bau dieser Schulanlage erforderte das St. Galler Schulgesetz von 1983, das die Zusammenführung von Real- und Sekundarschulen verlangt. Es dauerte indessen 15 Jahre, bis sich die drei am Bau beteiligten Gemeinden zu einem gemeinsamen Bauprojekt entschliessen konnten. Das Resultat ist ein Bau, der kommunales Selbstbewusstsein repräsentiert und sich in hohem Mass für öffentliche Nutzungen öffnet. Die heutige Schulleitung war an der Projektentwicklung intensiv beteiligt und machte sich vor der Wettbewerbsausschreibung durch Studienaufenthalte mit bestehenden Oberstufenzentren vertraut, um an der Planung kompetent zu partizipieren.

the parquet flooring laid with elastic bearing material, a theatre, and spectators' galleries at the sides allow for a variety of uses. This school was a product of school legislation passed in St. Gallen in 1983, stating that the *Real- and Sekundarschule* (two different types of secondary school) had to be combined. It took fifteen years for the communes involved in the building to reach a decision on the joint construction project. The result was a building that reflects the community's self-awareness and is designed to encourage public use. The present school management was heavily involved in the project's development and, before inviting architects to participate in the competition, contributed to the planning by making study visits to existing secondary schools.

`Obergeschoss/1st floor` 1:800

`Obergeschoss/1st floor` 1:800

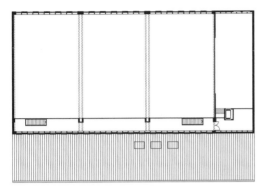

1:10000

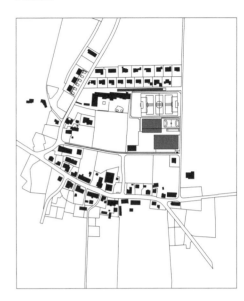

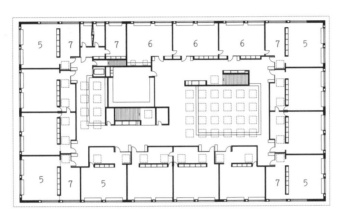

`Längsschnitt/section ew` 1:800

`Thurzelg`
Integratives Sekundarstufenzentrum/integrated secondary school
Architektur/architecture `Staufer & Hasler Architekten BSA SIA, Frauenfeld und Zürich`
Landschaftsplanung/landscape architecture `Ursula Weber, Oberbüren`
Wettbewerb/competition `1999–2000`
Bauzeit/construction period `2001–2002`
SchülerInnen/students `270 (Alter/age 13–16)`
Klassen/classes `12`
Spezialangebote/special features `Mehrzweck- und Doppelturnhalle/multiple usage hall`
Geschossfläche (SIA 416)/total floor area `8'182 m²`
Geschossfläche pro SchülerIn/floor area per student `27 m²`
Nutzfläche (SIA 416)/net area `5'100 m²`
Rauminhalt RI (SIA 116)/volume `40'606 m³`
Gebäudevolumen (SIA 416)/net volume `33'358 m³`
Anlagekosten (BKP 1–9 inkl. MWSt.)/overall costs incl. VAT `24'798'000 CHF`
Gebäudekosten (BKP 2 inkl. MWSt.)/net construction costs incl. VAT `17'940'000 CHF`
Gebäudekosten/m² GF/net construction costs per m² floor area `2'193 CHF/m²`
Gebäudekosten/m³ RI (SIA 116)/construction costs per m³ volume `442 CHF/m³`
Minergiekennzahl/Minergie factor `65.3 kWh/m²a`
Anmerkung/remark `Schüler mit speziellen Lernvoraussetzungen werden in Regelklasse integriert/students with special learning requirements are integrated into regular classes`

Erschliessungsbereich, Obergeschoss/access area, upper floor

n

Ostansicht mit Tanklager/
east elevation, with oil storage

Klassenzimmer und Gruppenraum/classroom and group room

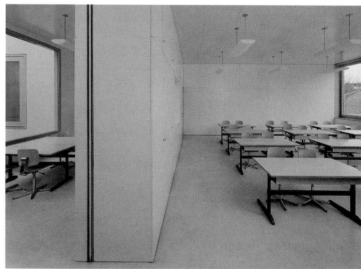

Text: Alan Wakefield, Photo: Ruedi Walti

## Eine Welt nach Innen

Die besondere Aufgabenstellung führte zu einer Lösung, die
mit verschiedenen Konventionen des Schulbaus gebrochen hat.
Im St.Johann-Quartier, einem traditionellen Arbeiterquartier
mit hohem Ausländeranteil, suchte die Stadt Basel nach
Raum für ein neues Schulhaus. In dem bereits sehr dicht bebauten Gebiet fand sie ein geeignetes Gelände durch den Teil-
abbruch eines nicht mehr benötigten Schweröllagers. Dieser
aussergewöhnliche Perimeter grenzt an die unterschiedlichsten
Bebauungsmuster und verfügt nur über minimale Umgebungs-
flächen. Obwohl die Architekten zunächst Vorbehalte gegen den
vorgeschlagenen Standort hatten, fanden sie durch Übernahme
der Volumetrie des abgebrochenen Gebäudeteils und die damit

## A World within a World

Responding to an unusual brief, the architects came up
with a solution that broke with a variety of conventions
on how schools are supposed to be built. The city of Basel
decided to erect a new school in the St.Johann Quarter, a
traditional working-class neighbourhood with a large share
of foreign residents. The city created a suitable yet
rather remarkable site in this densely built-up area by
partly demolishing an unused heavy oil storage facility.
This extraordinary perimeter, which disposes of very
little space, borders on the most heterogeneous urban patterns. At first, the architects had reservations about

Westansicht/west elevation

Westansicht/west elevation

Durchblick/vista

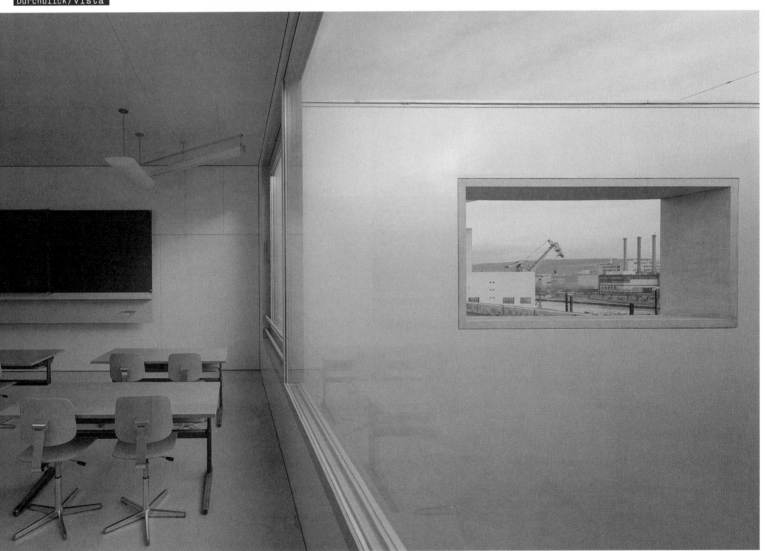

verbundene Gebäudetiefe eine bestechende Grundrisslösung. Die Turnhalle wurde in die vorhandene Abbruchgrube gesenkt, und das Schulhaus wurde auf ihr aufgebaut. Vier Lichthöfe führen im Inneren zu überraschenden Sichtbezügen zwischen allen Geschossen und nach aussen. Alle Klassenzimmer stossen mit der Schmalseite an die Aussenfassade; die mit Hilfe von Einbauschränken abgetrennten Gruppenräume sowie die Nebenräume erhalten Licht über die Innenhöfe. Zusammen mit den zwischen engen Gängen und kleinen Plätzen variierenden Erschliessungs- bereichen entsteht ein reiches Innenleben, das in starkem Kontrast zur sachlich-nüchternen äusseren Erscheinung des Ge-

the proposed location, but once they decided to work with the proportions and depth of the demolished building, they soon came up with a captivating solution for the ground plan. They sank the gymnasium into the existing demolition pit and erected the school building on top of it. Inside the complex, four light wells create amazing visual links between all the floors and to the outside. On their narrow side, the classrooms extend right up to the façade wall. The group rooms — which are partitioned off by built- in cupboards — and the adjoining rooms receive light from the light wells. These, together with the varied char- acter of the access areas — narrow corridors and small 'squares' — create a building whose rich inner life

West-Ansicht/west elevation 1:800

Erdgeschoss/ground floor 1:800

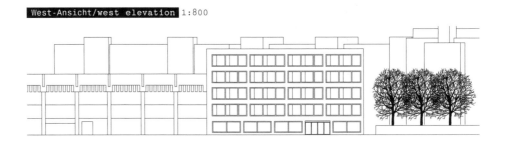

bäudes steht. Der auf Fotografien kühl wirkende Erschliessungsbereich besitzt eine grosse Erlebnisdichte und bietet
zumindest teilweise Ersatz für den knappen Aussenraum.
Die Schule bildet als Ergänzung des sperrigen Lagergebäudes
ein Bindeglied zwischen den Industrie- und den Wohnbauten
des Quartiers. Diese vermittelnde Funktion ist durch
die gezielten Ausblicke in die Umgebung auch im Schulalltag
spürbar. Die teilweise raue Aussenwelt wird auf Distanz
gehalten — aber nicht ausgeschlossen.

provides a marked contrast with the rational, sober
appearance it presents to the world outside. The entrance
area is designed for multifunctional use, a feature
that enriches users' experience of the building and makes
up for the lack of space around the building. The school,
which complements the massive warehouse building,
establishes a visual link between the industrial and the
residential buildings in the area. School-users are
repeatedly reminded of this mediating function by the
carefully created views of the surroundings. The outside
world — harsh in places — is kept at a distance, but
not shut out.

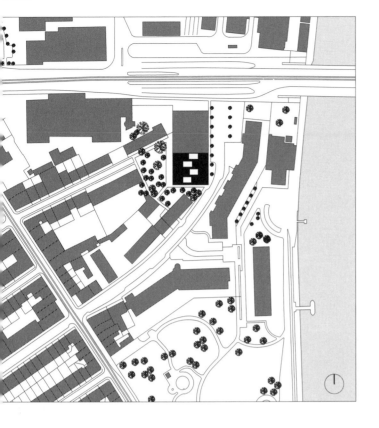

Schnitt NS/section ns 1:800

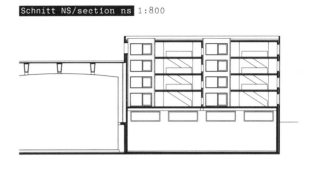

Schnitt OW/section ew 1:800

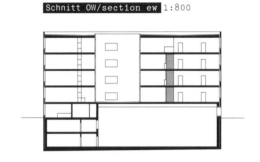

Untergeschoss/basement 1:800

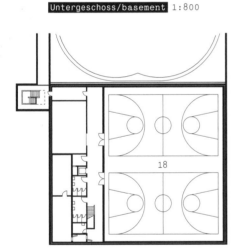

1.Obergeschoss/1st floor 1:800

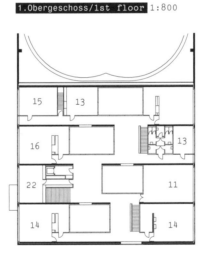

4.Obergeschoss/4th floor 1:800

Volta
Primarschule, Schulmodell St. Johann/primary school, scheme St. Johann
Architektur/architecture Miller & Maranta Architekten ETH BSA SIA, Basel
Landschaftsplanung/landscape architecture August Künzel, Binningen
Wettbewerb/competition 1996
Bauzeit/construction period 1998-2000
SchülerInnen/students 240 (Alter/age 7-11)
Klassen/classes 12
Spezialangebote/special features Doppelturnhalle, Hort/double sports hall, day-care centre
Geschossfläche (SIA 416)/total floor area 6'848 m²
Geschossfläche pro SchülerIn/floor area per student 29 m²
Nutzfläche (SIA 416)/net area 4'004 m²
Rauminhalt RI (SIA 116)/volume 30'517 m³
Gebäudevolumen (SIA 416)/net volume 27'055 m³
Anlagekosten (BKP 1-9 inkl. MWSt.)/overall costs incl. VAT 18'521'000 CHF
Gebäudekosten (BKP 2 inkl. MWSt.)/net construction costs incl. VAT 13'633'000 CHF
Gebäudekosten/m² GF/net construction costs per m² floor area 1'991 CHF/m²
Gebäudekosten/m³ RI (SIA 116)/construction costs per m³ volume 447 CHF/m³

**156**

Umnutzung Turnhalle, Schulanlage Bündtli
Conversion of a Gymnasium, Buendtli School
Maienfeld, Switzerland
Pablo Horváth, Chur

Südwestansicht/south-west elevation

Text: Alan Wakefield, Photo: Ralf Feiner

### Haus im Haus

In einer aus den siebziger Jahren stammenden Schulanlage
in Maienfeld wurden zusätzliche Klassenzimmer für die Oberstufe und Räumlichkeiten für einen Dreifach-Kindergarten
gesucht. Gleichzeitig sollte für Vereins- und Schulsportzwecke
eine grössere Sporthalle erstellt werden, wodurch die bestehende Turnhalle zur Disposition stand. Die Gemeinde schlug
die Umnutzung der Turnhalle in kleinteilige Nutzungsbereiche
vor. Der Architekt setzte diese Vorgaben in ein spannendes
räumliches Gefüge um, welches das Potenzial der Aufgabe
geschickt nutzt. Ein in die Halle gestellter Körper beinhaltet
die neuen Räumlichkeiten. Er bleibt durch seine Konstruktion

### A House in a House

A school built in Maienfeld during the 1970s required
additional classrooms for the secondary school as well
as rooms for a kindergarten divided into three groups.
Meanwhile, a larger sports hall was needed for clubs and
school sports, which opened the prospect of converting
the existing gymnasium. The community suggested subdividing
it to create distinct areas that could be put to different
uses. With this brief, the architect proceeded, with
great skill, to design an exciting complex. A structure
encompassing the new rooms has been erected in the former
gymnasium. The nature of this structure, and the materials used, ensure that it is readily identifiable as an
installation and that it harmonises with its immediate

Klassenzimmer/classroom

Kindergarten/kindergarten

Erschliessungszone, Kindergärten/access zones, kindergartens

Klassenzimmer/classroom

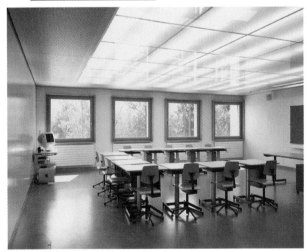

und das verwendete Material als Einbau erkennbar und fügt sich doch harmonisch ein. Durch die rückseitige Loslösung von der Hülle entsteht ein sehr hoher Luftraum, der den Zugang zu den Klassenzimmern im Obergeschoss und die Vorbereiche der Kindergärten im Erdgeschoss aufnimmt und durch das hoch liegende Fensterband über einen interessanten Lichteinfall verfügt. Beim Betreten der Verbindungsstege können die älteren Schüler die Kleinsten beim Spielen beobachten – ohne Risiko der gegenseitigen Störung. Die ursprünglichen Dimensionen der Turnhalle werden hier deutlich spürbar. Auf der anderen Fassadenseite sorgen schmale Glas- und Spiegelstreifen

surroundings. At the rear, the structure is separated from the shell, creating a very high void into which the entrance to the classrooms on the upper floor and the anteroom areas of the kindergartens on the ground floor have been integrated. The light entering through the high strip windows in the void creates an interesting impression. As they enter the walkways, the older pupils can watch the small ones playing without disturbing them, or being disturbed by them. The original dimensions of the gymnasium are much in evidence here. At the other end of the building, thin strips of glass and mirror form a fine partition between the installed structure and the façade, making the classrooms appear larger. From the

Erdgeschoss/ground floor 1:500

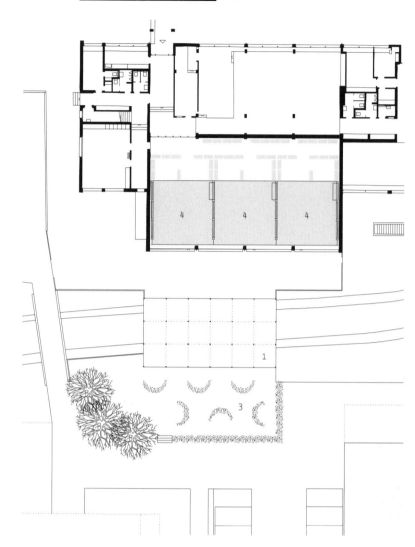

Südwestfassade/south-west elevation 1:500

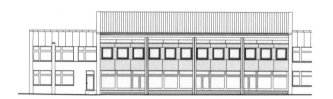

Längsschnitt/section 1:500   Querschnitt/section 1:500

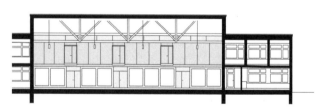

für eine feine Trennung zwischen Einbau und Fassade und vergrössern optisch die Unterrichtsräume. Von aussen lässt sich die ehemalige Turnhalle nur noch erahnen. Die Hauptfassade nach Südwesten weist bei den Kindergärten grosszügige Glasflächen auf, während die darüber liegenden Räume mit einer dichten Reihe von Lochfenstern versehen sind. Die mit einer Pergola ausgestattete Brückenterrasse über den vorbeifliessenden Bach löst das Problem des knappen Aussenraums für die Kindergärten. Ist die filigrane Stahlkonstruktion, welche die Holzkonstruktion überdeckt, einmal eingewachsen, bildet sie einen Raumkörper, der zum Verweilen einlädt. Der auf der anderen Seite liegende Heckengarten, die bestehende Baumgruppe, Kies- und Hartplatz bieten den Kindern erlebnisreiche Freiräume.

outside, one can only conjecture what the old gymnasium used to look like. The main façade facing south-west comprises large sheets of glass fronting the kindergartens; the rooms above, in contrast, display a dense row of single-wing windows. A bridge terrace straddles the stream flowing past the school and creates much needed additional outdoor space for the kindergarten. The filigree steel frame covering the wooden structure is expected to become overgrown and transform into an inviting three-dimensional structure. The hedges on the other side, alongside a clump of trees, the gravel area and the hard playground offer the children something of an adventure area.

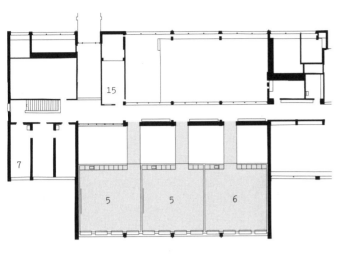

1:5000

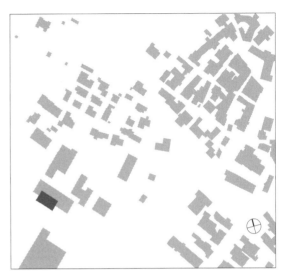

Obergeschoss/1st floor 1:250

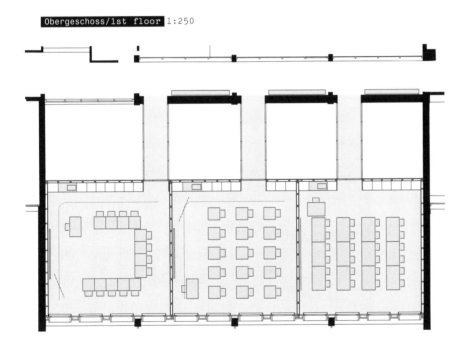

Bündtli
Kindergarten und Sekundarstufe/kindergarten and secondary school
Architektur/architecture Pablo Horváth Architekt SIA SWB, Chur
Landschaftsplanung/landscape architecture Lieni Wegelin, Malans
Wettbewerb/competition 2002
Bauzeit/construction period 2003
SchülerInnen/students 90 (Alter/age 5–6/13–15)
Klassen/classes 3 + 3 Kindergarten
Geschossfläche (SIA 416)/total floor area 840 m²
Nutzfläche (SIA 416)/net area 698 m²
Rauminhalt RI (SIA 116)/volume 2'978 m³
Gebäudevolumen (SIA 416)/net volume 2'528 m³
Anlagekosten (BKP 1–9 inkl. MWSt.)/overall costs incl. VAT 2'416'461 CHF
Gebäudekosten (BKP 2 inkl. MWSt.)/net construction costs incl. VAT 1'785'507 CHF
Gebäudekosten/m² GF/net construction costs per m2 floor area 2'126 CHF/m²
Gebäudekosten/m³ RI (SIA 116)/construction costs per m3 volume 600 CHF/m³
Anmerkung/remark Angaben umfassen nur Umbau Turnhalle/data refers to sports conversion hall only

Südwestansicht/south-west elevation

Südwestansicht/south-west elevation

Schule und Dorf/school and village

Gesamtschule Flims

**Flims Comprehensive School**

Flims, Switzerland

Ph. Wieting, M. Blätter — Werknetz Architektur, Zürich

Text: Alan Wakefield, Photo: Philipp Wieting, Ralf Feiner

### Magic Cube

Selbstbewusst überragt der Kubus des neuen Schulhauses
die Baumwipfel und die locker gestreuten Wohnbauten der
näheren Umgebung. Das Schulhaus gibt dem entlang der Haupt-
strasse gebauten Dorf und dem abseits des alten Kerns gelegenen Wohnquartier einen von weitem sichtbaren Schwerpunkt.
Die Verdichtung des Raumprogramms in einem zeichenhaften,
kompakten Gebäudekörper dient der Landschaft und dem Dorf,
aber auch der Schule und nicht zuletzt der Projektökonomie.
Im Zentrum der Entwurfsidee stand die Gesamtschule, die
ein gemeinsames Haus für Ober- und Unterstufe, ein Ort des
Miteinanders sein sollte. Die beiden Schulhäuser werden
zusammengerückt und mit einer Turnhalle zu einem komplexen
Ganzen gefügt. Alle drei betrieblichen Einheiten haben je
eine eigene Erschliessung, über die sie wiederum miteinander

### Magic Cube

The cubic new school rises confidently above the
treetops and the loose scattering of residential buildings
nearby. It gives both the village, which stretches along
the main road, and the residential district, located
outside the old centre, a focal point visible from afar.
The concentration of the various rooms in a compact structure has had a positive impact on the landscape, the
village, the school and, last but not least, the financing
of the project. The main idea behind the design was to
create a comprehensive school in a single structure shared
by the lower and upper schools in order to foster a
sense of community. The two parts of the school have been

Werken/handicraft

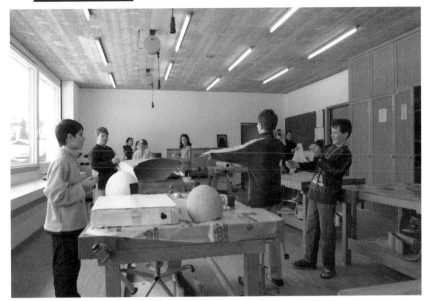

Treppe/stairway

Vorraum/anteroom

Turnhalle/gymnasium

verbunden sind. Die innere Transparenz lässt das Leben der anderen Bereiche spüren. Beeindruckend ist der Stimmungswechsel im Schulhaus bei Ertönen des Pausengongs. In allen Geschossen öffnen sich Türen, und die Treppenhäuser füllen sich mit Farben und Geräuschen. Die Mattglasscheiben werden zu Projektionsflächen von Licht, Konturen und Bewegung. Das Gebäude öffnet sich in drei Aussenbereiche: Der Aussenraum der Primarschule erhält durch das hangseitige Oberlicht mit Pausendach einen hofartigen Charakter, der offene Pausenbereich der Oberstufe erstreckt sich bis zum nahe gelegenen Bach, und über der Garage liegt der ebenfalls unmittelbar ans Gebäude angrenzende Sportplatz, der über einen separaten Eingang zur Sporthalle erreicht werden kann. Flexibilität wird bei diesem «Lernwürfel» nicht als Veränderung von Raum-

brought together and joined by a gymnasium to create a complex whole. All three operative units of this complex have their own entrances by which they are also connected to one another. The building's inner transparency allows those in one area to be clearly aware of life going on in the other areas. What is impressive is the change in atmosphere in the school when the break-time bell rings. Doors fly open on all floors and the stairs fill with colours and noise. The matt glass windowpanes transform into projection surfaces reproducing light, contours and movement. The building opens up onto three outside areas: with their slope-side skylight and covered area, the outside primary-school grounds have a courtly character; the open grounds of the upper school extend to the nearby brook; the sports ground, which can be reached via a separate entrance to the sports hall, lies above the

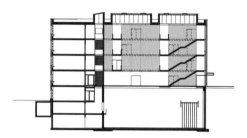

Querschnitt/section 1:800

Längsschnitt/section 1:800

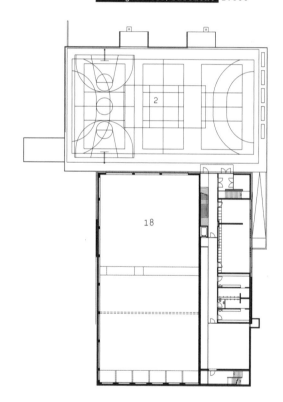

Untergeschoss/basement 1:800

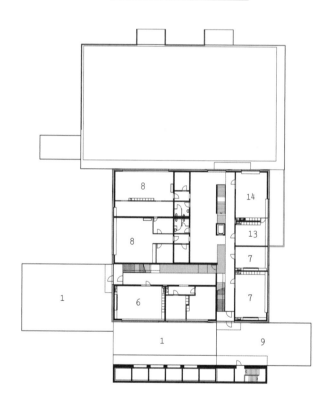

Erdgeschoss/ground floor 1:800

einteilungen, sondern als variable Verbindung von funktionellen Einheiten verstanden. Die räumliche Nähe wird zum betrieblichen Potenzial, die vielen Geschosse führen zu Erlebnisreichtum und ermöglichen die notwendige Entflechtung. Der Bezug zum Massstab der Kinder wird nicht über die Grösse des Gebäudes gesucht, sondern eher indirekt durch das Spiel mit Grössenverhältnissen, Raster, Konstruktion und Erscheinungsbild der Fassade hergestellt. Die Gebäudehülle aus Mattglas spiegelt, je nach Tages- und Jahreszeit, die Atmosphäre der Witterung.

garage. In this 'instruction cube', flexibility has been conceived not in terms of altering partitions but of creating a variable link between functional units. Spatial proximity is transformed into potential productive capacity and the many floors enrich users' experience and allow for much-needed spatial de-concentration. No attempt has been made to address the size of the children via the scale of the building; this has only been attempted indirectly, by playing with proportions, grids, the construction, and the appearance of the façade. The matt-glass building envelope reflects changes in the sky at all times of the day and year.

1:5000

1.Obergeschoss/1st floor 1:500

3.Obergeschoss/3rd floor 1:800

Flims
Gesamtschule/comprehensive school
Architektur/architecture Philipp Wieting, Martin Blättler — Werknetz Architektur Zürich
Wettbewerb/competition 1999
Bauzeit/construction period 2001—2003
SchülerInnen/students 320 (Alter/age 7—15)
Klassen/classes 16
Spezialangebote/special features Mehrfachsporthalle/multiple/sports hall, day-care centre
Geschossfläche (SIA 416)/total floor area 8'014m²
Geschossfläche pro SchülerIn/floor area per student 25m²
Nutzfläche (SIA 416)/net area 5'497m²
Rauminhalt RI (SIA 116)/volume 37'672m³
Gebäudevolumen (SIA 416)/net volume 34'048m³
Anlagekosten (BKP 1—9 inkl. MWSt.)/overall costs incl. VAT 18'330'987 CHF
Gebäudekosten (BKP 2 inkl. MWSt.)/net construction costs incl. VAT 15'512'063 CHF
Gebäudekosten/m² GF/net construction costs per m² floor area 1'936 CHF/m²
Gebäudekosten/m³ RI (SIA 116)/construction costs per m³ volume 412 CHF/m³

Schnitt durch das Modell/cross-section of the model

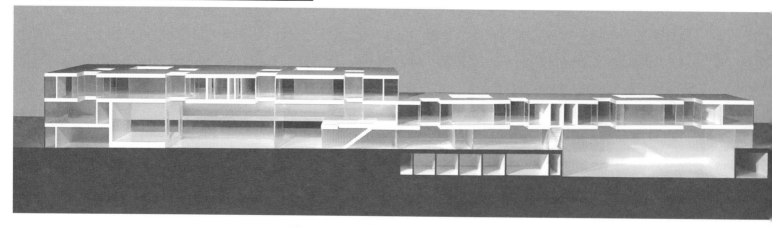

Lage im Quartier/site in the district

Schulanlage Herti
Herti School
Zug, Switzerland
Enzmann + Fischer, Zürich

Jahrgangseinheit: offen/'year-unit': open

Text: Alan Wakefield, Photo: Enzmann + Fischer

## Die Jahrgangseinheit

Da in dem Quartier Herti in den nächsten Jahren Wohnungen für bis zu 2'000 Personen erstellt werden sollen, hat die Stadt Zug im Frühling 2002 einen Wettbewerb für ein neues Oberstufenzentrum durchgeführt. Das siegreiche Projekt überzeugt durch die Anbindung an das Quartier und stellt ein Raumangebot zur Verfügung, das auf die neuen Unterrichtsformen und den integrativen Anspruch einer modernen Oberstufe reagiert. Die flache Grossform des neuen Schulhauses bildet den Abschluss der Schulanlage neben den mehrgeschossigen Wohnbauten. Eine eigentliche Erfindung stellt die «Jahrgangs-

## The 'Year-Unit'

As the construction of housing units accommodating up to 2,000 people is planned for the Herti district over the next few years, the town of Zug decided to run a competition for a secondary school in spring 2002. The convincing feature of the winning project was the way it established a close relationship between the school and the neighbourhood on the one hand, and its spatial design, which catered for new forms of teaching and the integrative demands of a modern secondary school, on the other. The large flat building forms a boundary between the school premises and the neighbouring multi-storey residential buildings. The school's 'year-unit' is a very innovative feature: groups of four classrooms and the same number

Jahrgangseinheit: Gruppenraum abgetrennt/
'year-unit': group room partitioned off

einheit» dar, eine Anordnung von jeweils vier Klassenzimmern und ebenso vielen Gruppenräumen um einen gemeinsamen Jahrgangsraum, der zum zentralen Ort der Kommunikation wird. Innerhalb dieser Einheit können durch mobile Trennwände verschiedenste räumliche Anordnungen nach den Erfordernissen der jeweils gewünschten Unterrichtsmodelle rasch und einfach realisiert werden. Durch die bis zur Decke reichenden Oberlichter und die zwischen jeweils zwei Klassenzimmern liegenden Aussenterrassen erhalten die Unterrichts- und Gruppenräume sowie der Jahrgangsraum Licht von mehreren Seiten. Die Anordnung in eine Klassenzimmereinheit und eine Jahrgangseinheit fördern das selbstständige Arbeiten in Gruppen und klassenübergreifende Modelle in Bezug auf Alters-

of group rooms are arranged around a common 'year-room', which serves as a communication centre. Mobile partition-walls make it possible to create a wide variety of room arrangements quickly and simply in this unit and thus meet the requirements of the desired teaching model. High windows reaching up to the ceiling and outside terraces situated between pairs of classrooms ensure that the classrooms, group rooms and 'year-room' receive light from several sides. The classroom/year unit arrangement fosters not only independent group work but also inter-class models on the basis of age groups, achievement levels and teaching approaches. The design of the classroom clusters alluded to in the competition programme met with great interest at the school. The teaching levels with their external terraces display the qualities and features

**Erdgeschoss/ground floor** 1:800

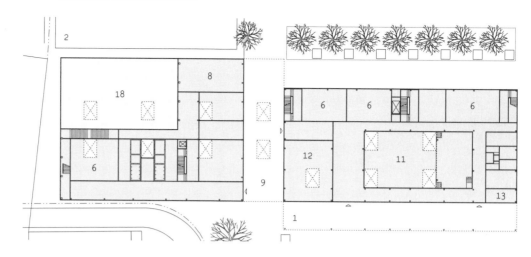

**1.Obergeschoss/1st floor** 1:800

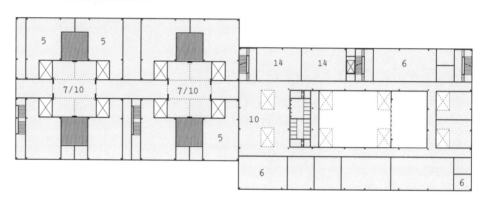

**2.Obergeschoss/2nd floor** 1:800

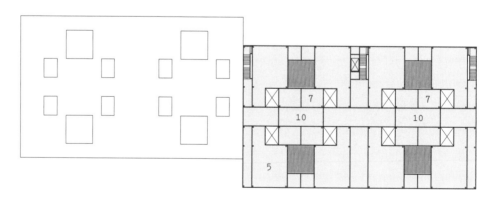

stufen, Leistungsniveaus oder Schularten. Diese architektonische und pädagogische Umsetzung einer im Wettbewerbsprogramm angedeuteten Clusterbildung stösst bei der Schule auf grosses Interesse. Die Unterrichtsgeschosse mit den Aussenterrassen weisen Qualitäten und Merkmale einer Pavillonschule auf. Sie werden jedoch durch die darunter liegenden Gemeinschafts- und Spezialräume mit den Vorzügen einer kompakteren Schulanlage kombiniert. Im Erdgeschoss sind vor allem die quartierbezogenen Nutzungen angeordnet. Neben der Bibliothek und den Räumen für die Schulleitung befinden sich hier auch das Foyer und der Zugang zur Mehrzweckhalle mit Bühne. Durch die Lichthöfe, welche die Klassentrakte durchdringen, erhalten die um ein Geschoss versenkte Turnhalle und der zweigeschossige Mehrzwecksaal Tageslicht. Zusätzlich werden interessante Blickbezüge in andere Geschosse und Nutzungen möglich.

of a so-called pavilion school. Here, however, they can be combined — thanks to the common rooms and special rooms situated beneath them — with the advantages of a more compact school. The ground floor is primarily devoted to district-related uses. This is where the library, the rooms for the school management, the foyer and the entrance to the multifunctional hall with the school stage are located. The gymnasium and two-storey multifunctional hall, sunk an entire level, receive the light from the patios that penetrate the classroom wings. Users can enjoy interesting visual perspectives onto different levels and functions.

Längsschnitt/section 1:800

Querschnitt/section 1:800

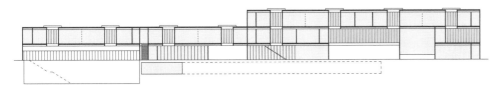

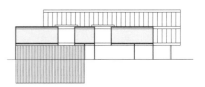

1.Obergeschoss, «Jahrgangseinheit»/
1st floor, 'year unit' 1:250

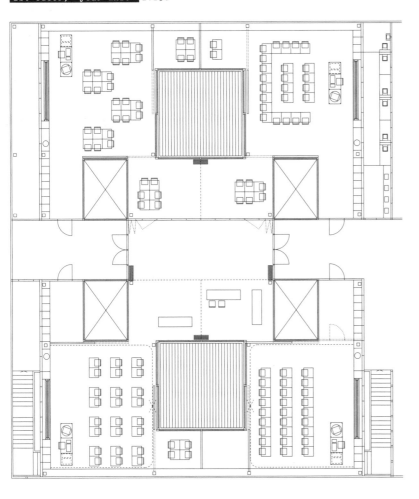

1:5000

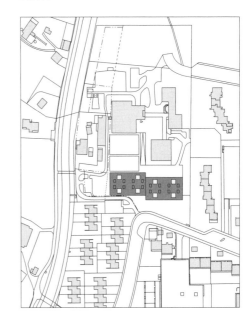

Herti
Sekundarschule/secondary school
Architektur/architecture Enzmann + Fischer AG Architekt/innen BSA SIA, Zürich
Wettbewerb/competition 2002
Bauzeit/construction period offen/open
SchülerInnen/students 360 (Alter/age 12–16)
Klassen/classes 18
Spezialangebote/special features Mehrfachsporthalle, Mittagstisch/midday meals, multiple sports hall
Geschossfläche (SIA 416)/total floor area 7'548 m²
Geschossfläche pro SchülerIn/floor area per student 21 m²
Nutzfläche (SIA 416)/net area 4'988 m²
Rauminhalt RI (SIA 116)/volume 34'000 m³
Anlagekosten (BKP 1–9 inkl. MWSt.)/overall costs incl. VAT 25'950'000 CHF
Gebäudekosten (BKP 2 inkl. MWSt.)/net construction costs incl. VAT 20'015'000 CHF
Gebäudekosten/m² GF/net construction costs per m² floor area 2'652 CHF/m²
Gebäudekosten/m³ RI (SIA 116)/construction costs per m³ volume 589 CHF/m³

Nordwestansicht/north-west elevation

Primarschule Riedmatt
Riedmatt Primary School
Zug, Switzerland
Reinhard Nägele, Adrian Twerenbold, Zürich

Turnhalle und Schule/gymnasium and school

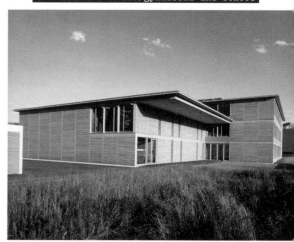

Korridor als Unterrichtsbereich/corridor as learning area

Text: Alan Wakefield, Photo: Guido Baselgia

## Schulhaus im Quartierpark

Durch die Nähe zum See und die ruhige Lage am westlichen
Stadtrand wurde das Siedlungsgebiet an der alten Lorze
ein beliebtes Wohnquartier für Familien. Diese Entwicklung
führte zu einem Mangel an Schulraum, verbunden mit dem Bedürfnis nach einer öffentlichen Freizeitinfrastruktur. Auf die
Nutzung von Sporthalle und Schule durch Vereine und Quartier
wurde grossen Wert gelegt. Neue Bedürfnisse wie Computer-
schulung, Mittagstisch, Arbeiten im Team, individuelles Lernen
und ein Mittagstisch sollten in dem Projekt ebenfalls ihren
Niederschlag finden. Das neue Schulhaus übernimmt die Aus-

## School, Sports Centre and Park

Its proximity to the lake and its tranquil location on
the western outskirts of the town made the settlement on
the old Lorze an attractive residential area for families.
As a result, not only did school places become necessary,
but the desire for public leisure facilities also grew.
Local residents and clubs attached great value to having
access to a sports hall and school facilities. New functions, among them computer training, lunch facilities,
team work and individual learning, were also envisaged by
the project. The new school takes up the alignment of

Erschliessungsbereich/access area

Dienstzone im Klassenzimmer/
service zone in the classroom

richtung der vorhandenen Sportplätze und bindet diese in die Gesamtanlage ein. Die Gestaltung der Umgebung orientiert sich am Charakter des ehemaligen Riedgebiets und verzichtet auf unnötig versiegelte Flächen. Schulhausumgebung, Sport- anlage und Freizeitflächen werden zu einer grosszügigen Parklandschaft verknüpft und stehen der Quartierbevölkerung zur Verfügung. Eine zentrale Eingangshalle im Erdgeschoss verbindet Aussenräume, Turnhalle und Schule miteinander. Die separate Erschliessung des Sportbereichs und bewegliche Bühnenelemente sorgen für eine hohe Nutzungsflexibilität. Der doppelgeschossige Singsaal wird als Aula, Mittagstisch, Versammlungs- und Musikraum multifunktional genutzt. Ein Office kann für grössere Anlässe, aber auch als Küche für den

the existing sports grounds, which it integrates into the overall complex. The design of the surrounding area found inspiration in the character of the old marshes, and sought to avoid sealed surfaces wherever possible. The open spaces around the school building, the sports centre and the leisure areas are linked to create a large parkscape open to local residents. A central entrance hall on the ground floor connects the outside spaces, the gymnasium and the school. The separate entrance to the sports area and the mobile-stage components ensure highly flexible use. The two-storey choral hall is designed for multifunctional use as a great hall, a canteen, as well as an assembly

Erdgeschoss/ground floor 1:500

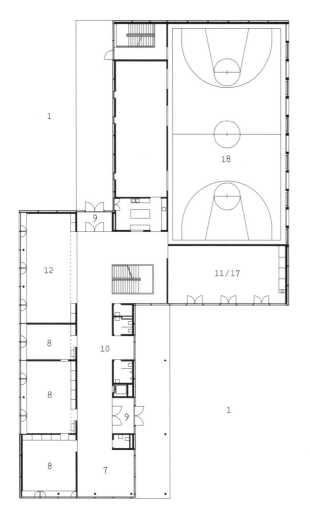

1.Obergeschoss/1st floor 1:500

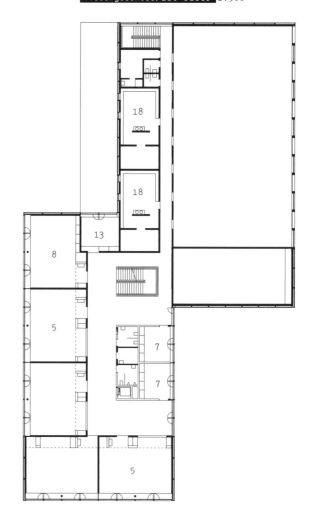

Schnitt/section 1:500

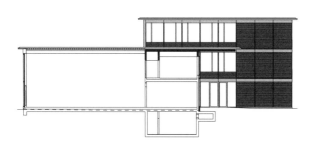

Schnitt/section 1:500

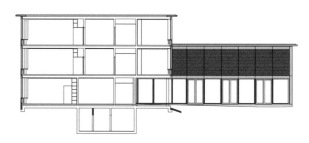

Mittagstisch eingesetzt werden. Die Klassenzimmer haben auf der Seite zum Korridor eine 140 Zentimeter tiefe Dienstzone, welche neben dem Eingangsbereich mit Schulwandbrunnen und allen Schrank- und Abstellflächen eine Nische für die Computerarbeitsplätze aufnimmt. Letztere kann auch für Bastel- oder Kleingruppenarbeit verwendet werden. Die eingesetzten Materialien Holz und Beton schaffen eine starke sinnliche Verbindung mit der naturnahen Umgebung. Die Vorfabrikation der Fassadenelemente, Versickerungsanlagen für Meteorwasser und Sonnenkollektoren für die Brauchwassererwärmung sind weitere interessante Aspekte eines erstaunlich kostenbewussten Projektes.

hall and music room. There is also kitchen, which can be used for midday meals and on special occasions. Along the corridor side, the classrooms have a 140-cm-wide ser-vice zone which not only accommodates the entrance area (with its wall washstands, cupboards and work surfaces), but also provides a niche for computer workstations. The niche can also be used for handicrafts and working in small groups. Wood and concrete - the materials employed here - provide a powerful, sensuous link with the natural surroundings. Other interesting features of this astonishingly cost-conscious project are the prefabricated façade elements, the rainwater drainage, and the solar collectors for warming water.

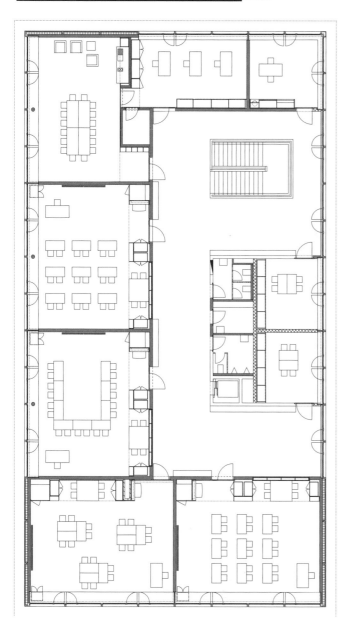

1:5000

Riedmatt

Geleitete Primarschule mit integrativer Schulung/primary school with integrated teaching

Architektur/architecture Reinhard Nägele und Adrian Twerenbold, Dipl. Architekten ETH SIA, Zürich

Landschaftsplanung/landscape architecture Rotzler Krebs Partner, Winterthur

Wettbewerb/competition 1995

Bauzeit/construction period 2000–2001

SchülerInnen/students 120 (Alter/age 7–12)

Klassen/classes 6 + Kleinklasse/small unit class

Spezialangebote/special features Mittagstisch/midday meals

Geschossfläche (SIA 416)/total floor area 3'900 m²

Geschossfläche pro SchülerIn/floor area per student 33 m²

Nutzfläche (SIA 416)/net area 2'300 m²

Rauminhalt RI (SIA 116)/volume 20'646 m³

Gebäudevolumen (SIA 416)/net volume 18'405 m³

Anlagekosten (BKP 1–9 inkl. MWSt.)/overall costs incl. VAT 12'675'000 CHF

Gebäudekosten (BKP 2 inkl. MWSt.)/net construction costs incl. VAT 9'445'000 CHF

Gebäudekosten/m² GF/net construction costs per m² floor area 2'422 CHF/m²

Gebäudekosten/m³ RI (SIA 116)/construction costs per m³ volume 457 CHF/m³

Anmerkung/remark Unterrichtsräume werden z.T. vom Quartier benutzt/classrooms are partly used by the local community

Centre Scolaire des Ouches
Les Ouches School
Quartier des Ouches, Genève, Switzerland
Andrea Bassi, Genève

Obergeschoss, verglaste Klassenzimmer/
upper floor, glass-walled classrooms

Text: Daniel Kurz, Image: Andrea Bassi

## Die Schule als Quartierzentrum

Den Teilnehmern des Architekturwettbewerbs war eine doppelte Aufgabe gestellt. Einerseits sollte der Neubau, so das Wettbewerbsprogramm, «das Quartierleben dynamisieren und den Austausch zwischen den künftigen Nutzerinnen und Nutzern anregen: Kleinkinder und Eltern, Schülerinnen und Lehrerschaft, Vereine und städtische Dienste». Andererseits war eine schwierige städtebauliche Ausgangslage zu meistern: Die Umgebung des Bauplatzes weist die unterschiedlichsten Bauformen, Massstäbe und städtebaulichen Muster auf. Turm- und Scheibenhäuser der sechziger Jahre stehen neben dem Torso der international bekannten Gartenstadtsiedlung Cité d'Aïre

## A Neighbourhood Centre

According to the brief, competition participants had to fulfil two objectives: to 'enliven the neighbourhood and to stimulate an exchange between future users of both genders, small children and parents, pupils and teachers, clubs and municipal services.' And they had to come up with a design that would hold its own in a complex urban setting. The site lies in an area with a rich diversity of buildings, structures of varying scale, and manifold urban patterns. Towers and slab buildings dating from the 1960s stand alongside the torso of the internationally famous garden city settlement of Cité d'Aïre (Camille Martin, Arnold Hoechel, 1920—1926). Andrea Bassi fulfilled the two objectives with a building that unites all functions under one roof and — despite its compact basic form —

(Camille Martin, Arnold Hoechel, 1920–1926). Andrea Bassi löste diese doppelte Aufgabe mit einem Bau, der alle Nutzungen unter einem Dach vereint und der sich, trotz seiner kompakten Grundform, mit Gartenhöfen zum Quartier öffnet. Die Verteilung von Masse und Leerraum vermittelt zwischen den unterschiedlichen Massstäben der Nachbarschaft und regelt die Unterbringung der verschiedenen Nutzungen im Gebäude. Eine gedeckte Hauptachse durchläuft die Schule im Erdgeschoss und bildet von Strasse zu Strasse eine öffentliche Verbindung. Die Anlage verteilt sich auf drei Geschosse, tritt aber nach aussen nur zweigeschossig in Erscheinung. Halb in den Boden versenkt sind die öffentlichen Nutzungen: Mehrzwecksaal, Turnhalle, Vereinsräume und städtische Dienste. Auf Stras-

opens out onto the neighbourhood through its garden courtyards. The distribution of masses and voids mediates between the varying scales that characterise the neighbourhood and determines the location of the various functions within the building. A covered central axis runs through the school on the ground floor, forming a public access route between the streets. The school occupies three floors, even though it looks like a two-storey building from the outside. The public facilities are partly sunk into the ground: the multifunctional hall, the gymnasium, the clubrooms and the municipal services. The main entrance with the covered central axis and the teachers'

**Obergeschoss/1st floor** 1:250

**Erdgeschoss/ground floor** 1:800

**Untergeschoss/basement** 1:800

senniveau liegt das Eingangsgeschoss mit der gedeckten Haupt-achse. Hier befinden sich der Haupteingang und der Lehrer-bereich. In je eigenen Gebäudeflügeln sind Kindergarten und Hort untergebracht, das Obergeschoss steht ganz der Primar-schule zur Verfügung. Die Klassen sind konsequent nach Osten und Westen ausgerichtet. Kurze Korridore münden in die zentralen Räume der Bibliothek und einer weiten Vorhalle, die dank zusätzlicher Fluchttreppen für klassenübergreifenden Unterricht nutzbar ist. Grosse Öffnungen zwischen Klassen-zimmern und Gängen fördern den visuellen Kontakt. Das Schul- und Quartierszentrum ist wie eine Stadt im Kleinen konzipiert. Die Erschliessungswege sind von unterschiedlichem Öffent-lichkeitsgrad. Sie laufen in belebten Plätzen zusammen, bilden ruhige Abschnitte und definieren Nutzungsbereiche, die wie Stadtquartiere in sich geschlossen und doch miteinander ver-bunden sind.

area are on street level. The kindergartens and a day home for children are each assigned a distinct wing, whilst the upper floor is reserved for the primary school. The classes face east and west. Short corridors open out into the central rooms of the library and a large anteroom that can be used for inter-class lessons thanks to the additional emergency stairs. Large openings between the classrooms and corridors foster visual contact. The school and neighbourhood centre is designed as a miniature town, and the circulation routes permit varying degrees of public access. They converge at bustling centres, or create peaceful sections and clearly defined functional areas, which, like city neighbourhoods, are hermetic yet inter-linked.

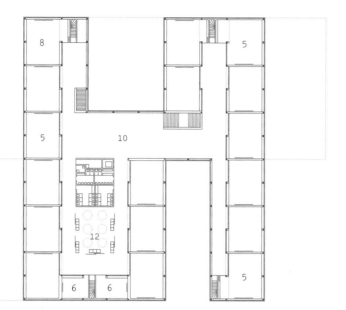

1:5000

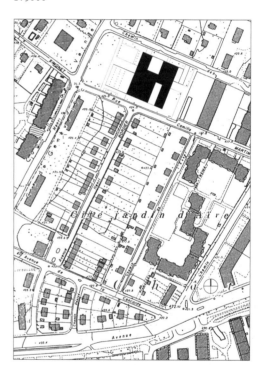

Schnitt OW/section ew 1:800

Schnitt NS/section ns 1:800

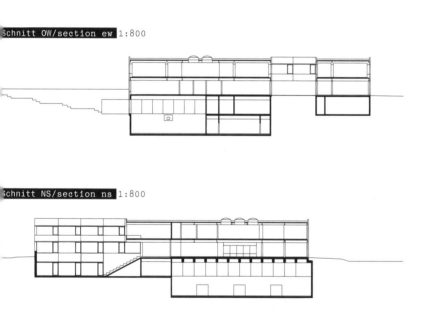

Les Ouches

Primarschule mit Kleinkinder- und Vorschulbereich/primary school with infant and preschool area
Architektur/architecture Andrea Bassi, Architecte EAUG/FAS/SIA, Genève
Landschaftsplanung/landscape architecture La Touche Verte, Genève
Wettbewerb/competition 2001
Bauzeit/construction period 2003–2005
SchülerInnen/students 320 (Alter/age 7–11) + 80 Krippenplätze/crèche places (Alter/age 0–6)
Klassen/classes 16
Spezialangebote/special features Kleinkinderkrippe, Quartier- und Vereinräume, Mehrzweckhalle/nursery, community and club rooms, multipurpose hall
Geschossfläche (SIA 416)/total floor area 7'096 m²
Geschossfläche pro SchülerIn/floor area per student 22 m²
Nutzfläche (SIA 416)/net area 4'443 m²
Rauminhalt RI (SIA 116)/volume 35'212 m³
Gebäudevolumen (SIA 416)/net volume 30'716 m³
Anlagekosten (BKP 1–9 inkl. MWSt.)/overall costs incl. VAT 27'100'000 CHF
Gebäudekosten (BKP 2 inkl. MWSt.)/net construction costs incl. VAT 21'980'000 CHF
Gebäudekosten/m² GF/net construction costs per m² floor area 3'098 CHF/m²
Gebäudekosten/m³ RI (SIA 116)/construction costs per m³ volume 624 CHF/m³
Energiekennzahl Wärme/specific energy consumption 47.5 kWh/m²a

Evangelische Gesamtschule EGG
EGG Evangelical Comprehensive School
Gelsenkirchen-Bismarck, Deutschland/Germany
Plus+ Bauplanung, Neckartenzlingen

Gedeckter Erschliessungsgang/
covered passageway

Bibliothek/library

Klassentrakt mit Aufbauten/
classroom wing with upper storeys

Text: Alan Wakefield, Photo: Plus+ Bauplanung

## Partizipativer Schulbau

Die durch die evangelische Kirche von Westfalen neu erstellte fünfzügige Gesamtschule ist im Rahmen einer umfassenden Wohngebietsentwicklung der Stadt Gelsenkirchen-Bismarck
entstanden. Die Schulanlage ist mit ihren Grünflächen in
das neue städtische Wohnumfeld und dessen soziales Leben integriert. Durch das Konzept «Familien-, Erziehungs-, Lebens-
und Stadtteilschule (FELS)» werden pädagogische Ansätze verwirklicht, die direkt an der Lebenssituation der Kinder
und Jugendlichen anknüpfen. Sowohl die Schule wie auch die
in der Nähe erstellte Einfamilienhaussiedlung waren Projekte
der Internationalen Bauausstellung Emscher Park. Der Einbezug
der späteren Nutzer bei der Planung der Schulanlage war ein
zentrales Anliegen der Architekten. Im Sinne partizipativen
Planens wurden im Rahmen von zwei Projektwochen Lehrer, Eltern
und insbesondere Schülerinnen und Schüler aufgefordert,

## Participatory School Planning

The new comprehensive school, which was erected by
the Protestant Church of Westphalia, is part of an extensive residential development scheme planned by the
town of Gelsenkirchen-Bismarck. Through its green areas,
the school is integrated into the new urban residential
environment and its social life. Within the framework
of a concept entitled 'Familien-, Erziehungs-, Lebens- und
Stadtteilschule (FELS)' [school for the family, education,
life and the district], educational goals are being
implemented which relate directly to the experiences and
living situation of the children and young people. Both
the school and the nearby residential estate of detached

Südansicht mit Bibliothek (rechts)/
south elevation with library (right)

Klassenzimmer, zweigeschossig/
classroom on two storeys

Mensa («Wirtshaus»)/canteen('Wirtshaus')

ihre Ideen und Vorstellungen in Architekturmodellen im Massstab
von 1:10 darzulegen und sich so am Bauprozess zu beteiligen.
Die relativ lange Planungszeit, eine einfache Baustruktur und
die heterogene Architektursprache waren notwendige Voraussetzungen, um ein solches Projekt zu realisieren, das auf die
Identifikation seiner Nutzerinnen und Nutzer mit dem Gebäude
setzt. Um theoretisches, praktisches und soziales Lernen miteinander zu verbinden, ist ein Raumprogramm entwickelt worden,
das neben den eigentlichen Unterrichtsräumen auch ausserschulische Aktivitäten mit einbezieht. Entlang einer internen
Verbindungsachse mit vielen Nischen und Ausbuchtungen, welche
eine Art «Lernstrasse» bildet, sind Räume mit doppelten

houses are projects of the 'Emscher Park' International
Building Exhibition. From the start, the architects
attached great importance to involving future users in
planning the future school. Following the principles
of participatory planning, they invited teachers, parents
and, above all, pupils to participate in the building
process by presenting ideas and concepts in the form
of 1:10 architectural scale models over a period of
two weeks. The relatively long planning period, the simple
building structure and the heterogeneous architectural
language were preconditions for realising a project of this
nature. Current school performance reveals, furthermore,
that involving the school's future neighbours in its
planning has fostered identification with the school and
reduced vandalism. In order to combine theoretical,
practical and social learning, a spatial programme was

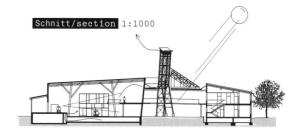

Schnitt/section 1:1000

Erdgeschoss/ground floor 1:1000

Schnitt/section 1:1000

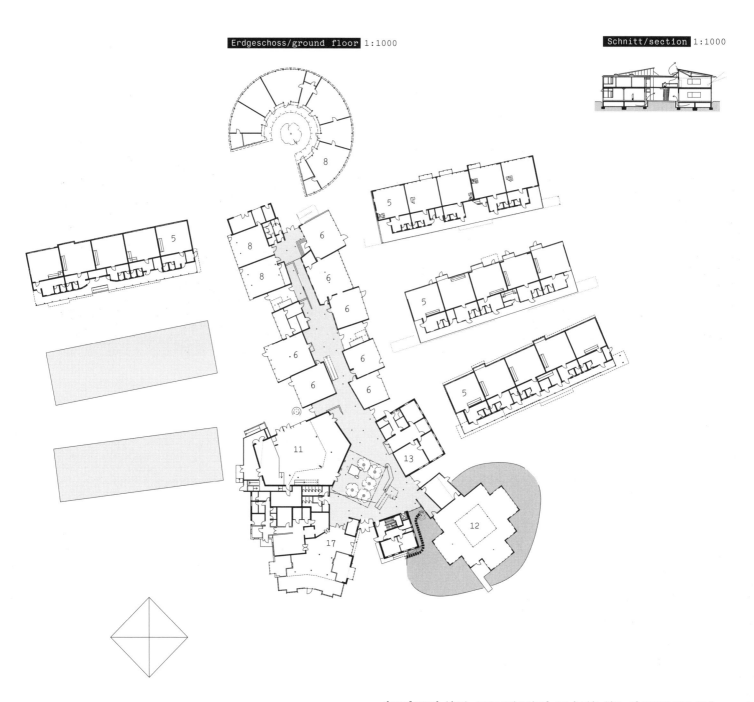

Nutzungsmöglichkeiten wie Theater, Bibliothek, Ateliers etc. angesiedelt. Die Namensgebung nach der Funktion der Räume (wie Apotheke, Stadthaus, Kino etc.) spiegelt die Idee der «Community School» wider – eine selbst verwaltete Stadt im Kleinen. Die eigentlichen Klassentrakte, welche in Etappen realisiert wurden, sind von diesem Bereich leicht abgesetzt. Durch die Konstruktion in Holz und die unterschiedliche Autorenschaft der verschiedenen Anlageteile entstand ein improvisiert wirkender Gebäudeausdruck. Besonders viel Wert wurde auf ein gutes Raumklima gelegt, das durch die Verwendung von baubiologischen Materialien, wärmespeicherfähiger Konstruktionen und eines natürlichen Lüftungskonzeptes gewährleistet ist.

developed that concentrated on both the classrooms and extra-curricular activities. An internal axis lined with recesses and projections, serving as a kind of 'educational road', links dual-use rooms (theatre, library, studios, etc.) located on either side. The rooms, named after their respective functions (e.g. chemist's, town hall, cinema, etc.), reflect the idea of a community school as a miniature self-managed town. The wings housing the classrooms proper were built in stages, and are slightly offset from this area. Its wooden structure and the mixed authorship of the various parts of the school give the building an extremely dynamic appearance. Great importance was attached to creating a good room climate. This has been ensured by using biological building materials, a heat-storing construction and natural ventilation.

1:5000

Obergeschoss/1st floor 1:1000

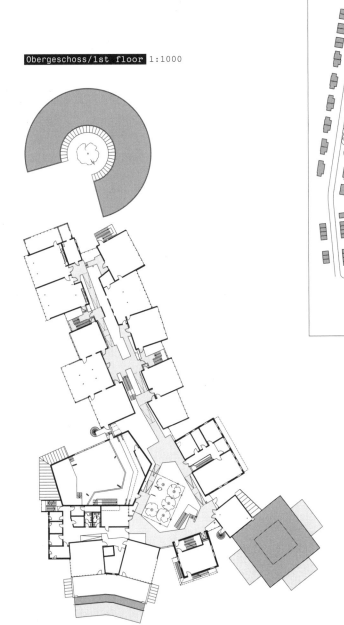

Evangelische Gesamtschule EGG
Integrative Gesamtschule/integrated secondary school
Architektur/architecture Plus+ Bauplanung GmbH, Peter Hübner, Neckartenzlingen
Landschaftsplanung/landscape architecture Christoph Harms
Wettbewerb/competition 1993
Bauzeit/construction period 1997–2004
SchülerInnen/students 900 (geplant/planned 1100, Alter/age 11–19)
Klassen/classes 30 (geplant/planned 40)
Spezialangebote/special features diverse Quartiernutzungen/community usages
Geschossfläche/total floor area 16'500 m$^2$
Geschossfläche pro SchülerIn/floor area per student 18 m$^2$
Nutzfläche/net area 13'650 m$^2$
Gebäudevolumen/volume 76'080 m$^3$
Anlagekosten (inkl. MWSt.)/overall costs incl. VAT 23'008'000 EUR
Gebäudekosten (inkl. MWSt.)/net construction costs incl. VAT 18'132'000 EUR
Anlagekosten/m$^2$ GF/cost of building/m$^2$ floor area 1'394 EUR/m$^2$
Anlagekosten/m$^3$ GV/cost of building/m$^3$ volume 302 EUR/m$^3$

S

Primarschule De Eilanden
**De Eilanden Primary School**
Amsterdam, Niederlande/Netherlands
Architectuurstudio Herman Hertzberger, Amsterdam

Westseite/west façade

Aktionshalle/activity hallway

Galerie/gallery

Text: Daniel Kurz, Photo: Herman Hertzberger,
Margreet van der Woude, Kees Rutten

## Huckepack

Im holländischen Schulbau spielt Herman Hertzberger seit Jahrzehnten eine herausragende Rolle. Die Schulen dieses Landes werden in der Regel nicht vom Staat, sondern mit staatlichen Mitteln zumeist von konfessionellen Trägerschaften oder Montessori-Vereinigungen geführt. Für diese errichtete Herman Hertzberger eine ganze Reihe von Schulen, die als gemeinsames Thema stets eine zentrale Halle aufweisen, welche der Schulgemeinschaft als gemeinsamer Begegnungs- und Aktionsraum dient. Die Primarschule De Eilanden im Zentrum

## Piggyback

Herman Hertzberger has played an outstanding role in school construction in Holland for decades now. The schools there are generally not built by the state, but by denominational organisations or Montessori associations assisted by state funds. Herman Hertzberger has designed a whole series of schools for them. The prominent feature of all his buildings is the central hall intended to serve the school community as a place for encounters and activities. De Eilanden Primary School, located in the centre of Amsterdam, is a poetically fashioned exemplar of this school construction philosophy. Although the waterside site

Erdgeschoss, Aktionshalle/ground floor, activity hallway

Erdgeschoss, Aktionshalle/ground floor, activity hallway

Vorraum und Klassenzimmer/anteroom and class

Schule und Wohnen am Wasser/school and residences on the water

von Amsterdam ist ein poetisch gestimmtes Muster dieser Schulbauphilosophie. Der vorhandene Bauplatz am Wasser war reizvoll, aber knapp und kostspielig. Aus der Not machte die Bauherrschaft eine Tugend, indem sie über die Schule eine kleine Wohnbebauung stapelte. Die Schule mit zehn Klassen belegt die zwei unteren Geschosse des Gebäudekomplexes. Zwei im rechten Winkel angeordnete Schlitze durchschneiden den Bau längs und quer und bringen Tageslicht bis ins Erdgeschoss.

was very appealing, it was also very confined and expensive, so the clients made a virtue out of necessity and placed eight residential units on top of the school. The school, comprising ten classes, occupies the two bottom floors of the building complex. Two slits set at right angles cut through the building lengthways and widthways and allow daylight to reach even the ground floor. The entrance, which is at the side of the building and has a portico shape like a canal lock, leads into the central hall, which is extended at one side to create an activities

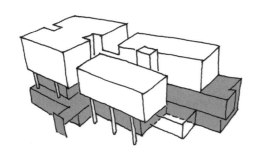

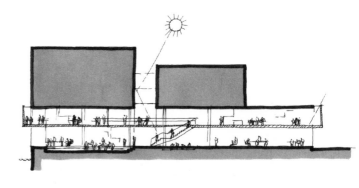

**Erdgeschoss/ground floor** 1:250

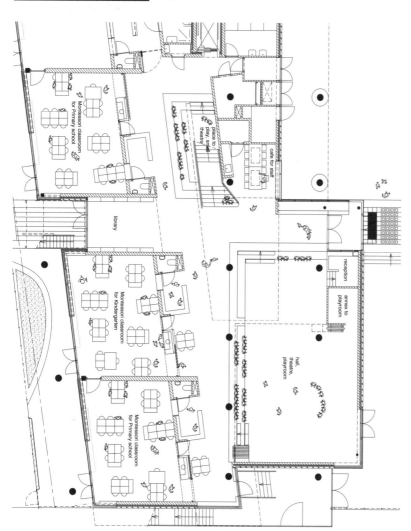

**Obergeschoss/1st floor** 1:500

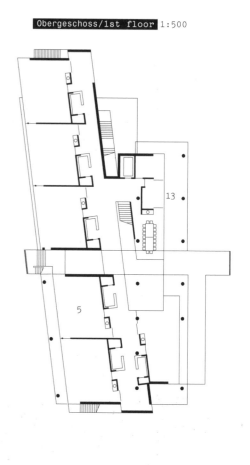

Der seitlich gelegene Eingang mit Portikus in Form eines Schleusentors führt in die zentrale Halle, die sich seitlich zum Aktionsraum erweitert. Treppe, Sitzstufen und Arbeitsnischen machen aus diesem zweigeschossigen Raum einen vielfältig nutzbaren Bereich. Glaswände und Arbeitsnischen im Korridor sorgen für Transparenz und ermöglichen vielfältige Lernarrangements. Die Wohnüberbauung über der Schule ruht auf hohen Säulen, weitgehend von der Schule abgelöst. Sie besteht aus acht exklusiven Einheiten, die von einem anderen Architekturbüro (Herenmarkt Architecten) entworfen wurden.

room. Stairs, rising tiers of seats and work niches transform this room into a multifunctional space. Glass walls and work niches in the corridor provide transparency and create a variety of learning arrangements. The residential structure on top of the school rests on high columns, which stand more or less detached from the school. The residential building comprises eight exclusive units designed by a different architect's office (Herenmarkt Achitecten).

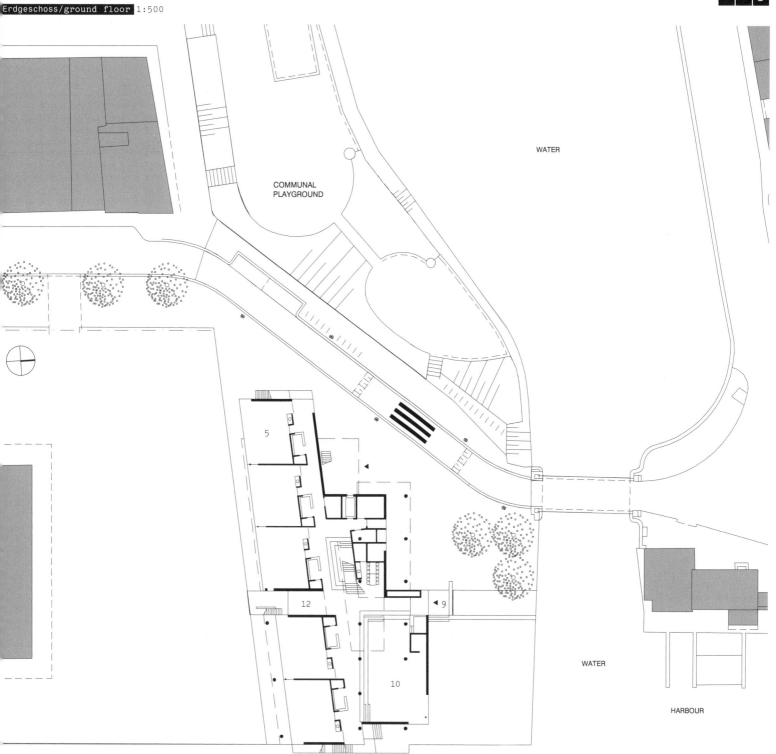

WATER

COMMUNAL
PLAYGROUND

5

12

9

10

WATER

HARBOUR

De Eilanden
Montessori-Primarschule/Montessori Primary School
Architektur/architecture Architectuurstudio Herman Hertzberger, Amsterdam
Landschaftsplanung/landscape architecture Dienst Binnenstad, Amsterdam
Bauzeit/construction period 2001–2002
SchülerInnen/students 300 (Alter/age 4–12)
Klassen/classes 11
Spezialangebote/special features Mehrzweckhalle/multi-purpose hall
Geschossfläche/total floor area 1'333 m²
Geschossfläche pro SchülerIn/floor area per student 4 m²
Nutzfläche/net area 810 m²
Gebäudevolumen/volume 4'746 m³
Anlagekosten (inkl. MWSt.)/overall costs incl. VAT 1'134'450 EUR
Anlagekosten/m² GF/cost of building/m² floor area 851 EUR/m²
Anlagekosten/m³ GV/cost of building/m³ volume 239 EUR/m³
Anmerkung/remark Schulhaus ist Teil einer Wohnüberbauung/the school is part of a building complex

Kindercluster Voorn
Voorn Children's Cluster
Leidsche Rijn, Utrecht, Niederlande/Netherlands
Frencken Scholl Architecten, Maastricht

Vorraum und Klassenzimmer/foyer and classroom

Eingangshalle, «Forum»/entry hall 'Forum'

Text: Daniel Kurz, Photo: Arjen Schmitz

## Breite Schule

Für das neu geplante Stadtviertel Leidsche Rijn (Utrecht)
wurde 1998 eine Schulanlage mit dem Angebot und der Aus-
strahlung eines Quartierzentrums benötigt. Im städtebaulichen
Konzept waren fünf Einzelnutzungen rund um ein gemeinsames
Forum vorgesehen: zwei Volksschulen, ein Freizeitzentrum,
eine Sportanlage, eine Kindertagesstätte und ein Hort. Der
Entwurf von Frencken Scholl fasst diese Nutzungen in einem
einzigen Gebäudekomplex zusammen und schafft Mehrwert durch
die gemeinsame Nutzung von Räumen. Das eröffnet jeder Institution mehr Möglichkeiten, als sie sich alleine leisten
könnte. Die zwei Schulen bilden einen langen Gebäuderiegel mit

## Community School

In 1998, it was apparent that the newly planned
district of Leidsche Rijn in Utrecht needed a school with
all the appeal and facilities of a neighbourhood centre.
The urban-development concept envisaged five different uses
centred on a common forum: two primary schools, a leisure
centre, a sports centre, and a crèche and children's
day-care centre. Frencken Scholl's design combines these
different functions in a single building complex. This
has the advantage of giving all the different institutions shared access to the space available, giving them
greater choice than they would have if each were to
use the rooms alone. The two schools form a long slab with
a joint entrance area, the forum, to which the other

Freizeitzentrum (links)/leisure centre (left)

Freizeitzentrum (links)/leisure centre (left)

Verbindungstrakt, Schule und Tageshort/
connecting wing, school and day-care centre

Turnhalle und Verbindungstrakt/gymnasium and connecting wing

Klassenzimmer und Vorraum/classroom and foyer

einem grossen gemeinsamen Eingangsbereich, dem Forum. An diesen sind weitere Nutzungen angedockt. Das so entstandene Kindercluster ist ein Pionierwerk für die Bewegung der «breiten Schulen» in den Niederlanden. Trotz der Grösse der Anlage, die für 750 bis 800 Kinder geplant ist, ist keine «Lernfabrik» entstanden, sondern eine klug gegliederte Anlage, die den Kindern überschaubare Einheiten bietet. Die Schulen sind aus separat erschlossenen Raumgruppen (Cluster) von jeweils vier Klassen aufgebaut. Diese teilen sich jeweils einen gemeinsamen Arbeitsbereich, der für Gruppenarbeit, Projekt- und Werkstattunterricht genutzt werden kann. Flexibilität und Anpassungsfähigkeit an zukünftige, veränderte

functions are also linked. The children's cluster that has thus come into being is a pioneering work for the Dutch movement for 'community schools'. Despite the size of the complex, which is designed to handle 750 to 800 children, it has not turned out to be a 'teaching factory', but a cleverly laid-out development providing the children with distinct, compact units. The schools are made up of groups of rooms (clusters), with separate entrances, serving four classes each. Each cluster is assigned a common work area that can be used for group work or for project and workshop classes. Flexibility and adaptability to changing future needs were the prime design goals. With this in mind, hardly any of the inside walls are load-

Erdgeschoss/ground floor 1:800

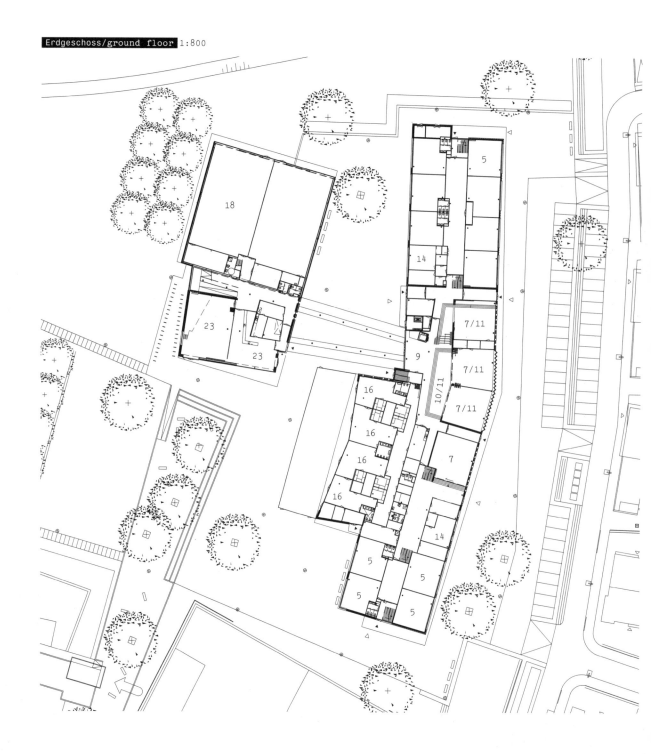

Längsschnitt/section 1:800

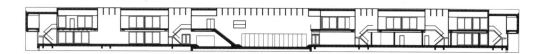

Bedürfnisse sind wichtige Entwurfsziele. So sind fast alle inneren Trennwände nicht tragend ausgeführt. Sollte die Schule in Zukunft zu gross sein, können einzelne Module problemlos abgespalten und einer anderen Nutzung zugeführt werden. Im Sinn umfassender Nachhaltigkeit wurde ein energetisch sparsames Gebäude konzipiert. Die kontrollierte Raumlüftung ist regelungstechnisch optimiert; die Wärme der Abluft wird über eine Wärmepumpe zurückgewonnen. Die Materialisierung der Schule ist einfach und solide, die Farbgebung zurückhaltend: Die Kinder bringen die Farbe in die Schule. Es sollte kein «kindliches» Gebäude entstehen, sondern eine Anlage, in der die Kinder nach ihrer eigenen Art leben können.

bearing. Should the school prove to be too large in the future, individual modules can be hived off with no trouble at all and assigned a different use. An energy-saving building was designed to meet the goals of all-round sustainability. The rooms have an optimised ventilation control system. The warm waste air is recycled by a heat pump. The school complex is simple and solid and has an unobtrusive colour scheme — the children themselves may be relied on to bring colour into the school. The aim was not to create a 'kiddies'' building, but a space where children could live as they choose.

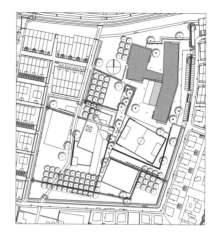
Obergeschoss/1st floor 1:800

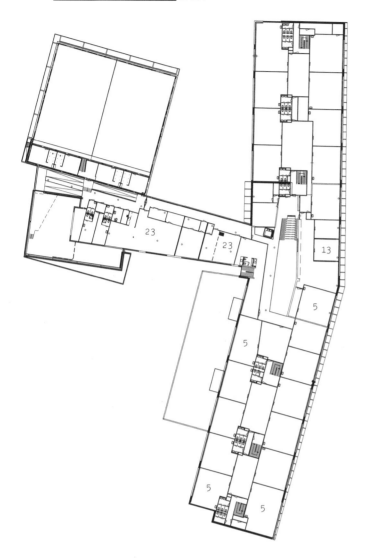

1.Obergeschoss, Klassenbereich
1st floor, group of classrooms 1:250

**Kindercluster Voorn**

Primarschule/primary school
Architektur/architecture Frencken Scholl Architecten, Maastricht
Landschaftsplanung/landscape architecture Ingenieursbureau, Utrecht
Bauzeit/construction period 2000-2001
SchülerInnen/students 900 (Alter/age 0-12)
Klassen/classes 32
Spezialangebote/special features «Breite Schule» Kinderkrippe, Hort, Freizeitanlage/crèche, day-care centre, leisure centre
Geschossfläche/total floor area 6'710 m²
Geschossfläche pro SchülerIn/floor area per student 7 m²
Nutzfläche/net area 4'740 m²
Gebäudevolumen/volume 29'054 m³
Anlagekosten (inkl. MWSt.)/overall costs incl. VAT 5'761'416 EUR
Gebäudekosten (inkl. MWSt.)/net construction costs incl. VAT 4'084'022 EUR
Anlagekosten/m² GF cost of building/m² floor area 859 EUR/m²
Anlagekosten/m³ GV cost of building/m³ volume 198 EUR/m³
Energiekennzahl Wärme/specific energy consumption 125.0 kWh/m²a

Heimdalsgade Sekundarschule
Heimdalsgade Secondary School
Copenhagen, Dänemark/Denmark
Kant Arkitekter, Copenhagen

Themenbereich Naturwissenschaft/
theme area: natural science

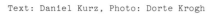

Text: Daniel Kurz, Photo: Dorte Krogh

### Schule in der Fabrik

Im Zentrum von Kopenhagen lag eine über 100 Jahre alte, vielfach umgebaute Brotfabrik, die 2001 zu einer Sekundarschule umgenutzt wurde. Das relativ kleine Grundstück und die besonderen Raumverhältnisse der Fabrik wurden zum Ausgangspunkt des Entwurfs für eine ungewöhnlich gegliederte Schule. Der Entwurf beruht auf einer Matrix-Organisation. Nicht Klassenzimmer, sondern fünf Themenbereiche sind die räumlichen Einheiten: Musik und Tanz, Naturwissenschaft und Experiment, Internationales und Kultur, Werken und Ästhetik. Organisa-

### A School in a Factory

In the centre of Copenhagen stands a century-old bakery that has undergone frequent conversion. In 2001, it was transformed into a secondary school. The relatively small premises and the building's interior spatial relations provided the point of departure for designing a school with an unusual room plan. The design is based on a matrix with theme areas — and not classrooms — as the basic spatial units. The theme headings are music/dance, natural science/experiment, international/culture, aesthetics/practical. The 300 pupils are divided into five major classes. For the lessons, which take place in the

Das «pädagogische Servicecenter»/
the 'Pedagogical Service Centre'

Südansicht, Treppenhaus/south elevation, stairwell

Empfang und Garderobe/reception area and lockers

torisch sind die 300 Schülerinnen und Schüler in fünf grosse Klassen eingeteilt. Für den Unterricht, der in den Themenbereichen stattfindet, teilen sie sich in kleinere Gruppen wechselnder Grösse. Um das Raumgewirr der alten Fabrik zu ordnen, legten die Architekten eine Querachse durch den Gebäudekomplex, die den Blick auf den geplanten, gegenüberliegenden Stadtpark lenkt. An dieser Achse liegen Eingang, Empfang und Gebäudeerschliessung. Von hier aus sind die Themenbereiche und die Schulkantine direkt erreichbar. Beim Empfang im Erdgeschoss liegt das «pädagogische Servicecenter» – der wichtigste Raum der Schule: Hier finden sich Computer, Bücher und Besprechungstische. Jeder Themenbereich ist durch feste Kerne der Länge nach gegliedert und teilt sich so in

theme areas, classes are subdivided into smaller groups of varying size. To introduce order into the chaotic room arrangement in the old bakery, the architects introduced an axis that runs transversely through the entire complex and directs one's glance onto the projected city park opposite. The entrance, reception and access system are situated along this axis, from where one has direct access to the theme-areas and the canteen. The 'pedagogical service centre' (the most important room in the school) is located next to the reception on the ground floor and contains computers, books and conference tables. Structured by the fixed core areas, each theme-area is divided into a quiet

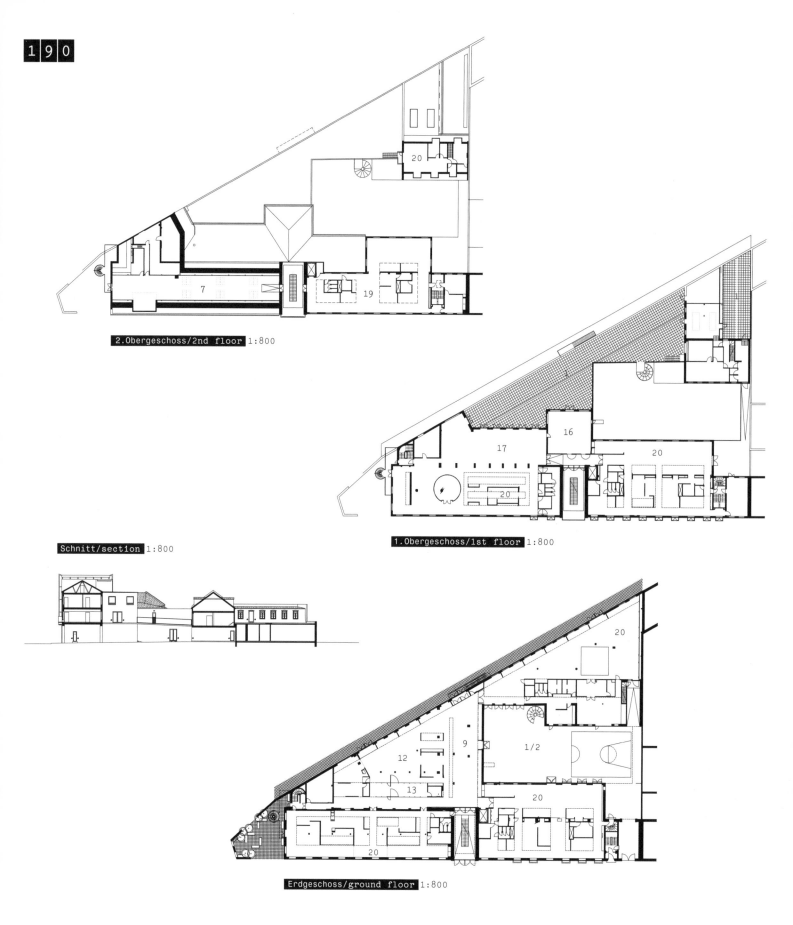

2.Obergeschoss/2nd floor 1:800

1.Obergeschoss/1st floor 1:800

Schnitt/section 1:800

Erdgeschoss/ground floor 1:800

einen ruhigen Studienbereich und eine lebhaftere Werkstatt-
zone. Schiebetüren erlauben es, quer zu dieser Längsgliederung
vier bis sechs kleinere Einheiten für Gruppenarbeit ab-
zutrennen. Die Aussenwände sind konsequent freigespielt, um
eine freie Zirkulation zu ermöglichen. Zum Themenbereich
gehören Räume für die Fachlehrenden und zugeordnete Nassräume.
Die Sekundarschule Heimdalsgade liess für ihren Bedarf
auch besonderes Mobiliar entwickeln. Die Tisch sind auf Rollen
gelagert, um sie beweglich zu machen. Eine Firma, die auf
Mobiliar für Airlines spezialisiert ist, lieferte die fahr-
baren Caddies für Schülerinnen und Schüler.

study area and a livelier workshop area. Sliding doors
make it possible to partition off four to six smaller units
for group work. A gap has been left between the external
and the partition walls to allow free circulation. The
theme-area also contains workspace for the teachers as well
as wet rooms. Heimdalsgade Secondary School had special
furniture custom built to suit its requirements. The tables
are mounted on castors to permit easy movement. A company
specialised in airline furniture supplied the portable
caddies for use by the pupils.

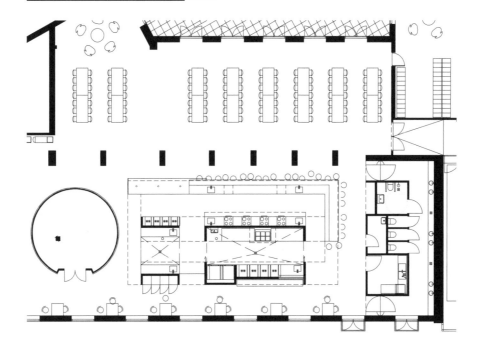

1:2500

Erdgeschoss, Thema «Praktisch-Ästhetisch»/
ground floor, 'practical-aesthetic' 1:250

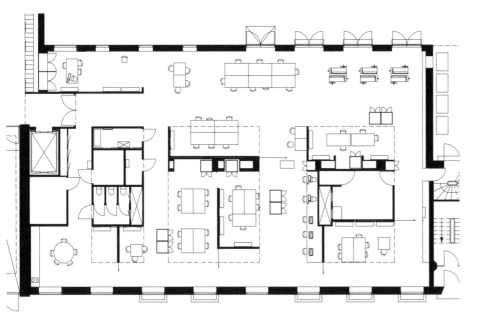

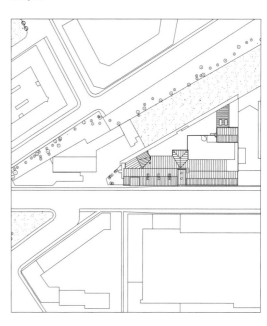

Heimdalsgade
Sekundarschule/secondary school
Architektur/architecture Kant Arkitekter A/S, Copenhagen
Bauzeit/construction period 2000–2001
SchülerInnen/students 300 (Alter/age 13–16)
Klassen/classes 5
Spezialangebote/special features Grossgruppen und Themenbereiche statt Klassen/large groups, theme areas. no classes
Geschossfläche/total floor area 4'672 m²
Geschossfläche pro SchülerIn/floor area per student 16 m²
Nutzfläche/net area 4'000 m²
Gebäudevolumen/volume 16'350 m³
Anlagekosten (inkl. MWSt.)/overall costs incl. VAT 7'916'000 EUR
Anlagekosten/m² GF cost of building/m² floor area 1'694 EUR/m²
Anlagekosten/m³ GV cost of building/m³ volume 484 EUR/m³

Gesamtansicht/general view

Offener Lernbereich, «Home Area»/
open teaching area ('Home Area')

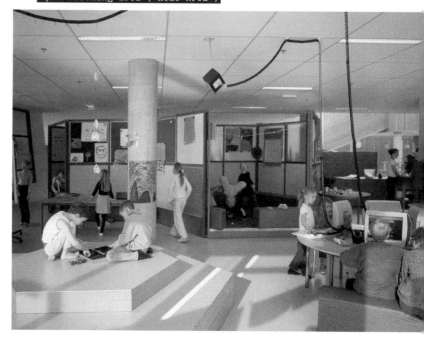

Hellerup Primarschule
Hellerup Primary School
Gentofte (Copenhagen), Dänemark/Denmark
Arkitema, Århus

Text: Daniel Kurz, Photo: Torben Eskerod, David Trood

Open Space

Die dänische Stadtgemeinde Gentofte — ein wohlhabender
Vorort von Kopenhagen — hat den Ehrgeiz, das «beste Schulwesen»
im Land aufzubauen. Um dieses ambitiöse Ziel zu erreichen,
arbeiten seit 1998 Fachleute der Gemeinde im Projekt SKUB
(Schulentwicklung und -ausbau) mit BürgervertreterInnen
zusammen (www.skub.dk). Dabei wird insbesondere Wert darauf
gelegt, die Kinder in ihren kognitiven, sozialen und per-
sönlichen Fähigkeiten zu fördern. Die Hellerup-Schule ist das
spektakulärste Projekt in diesem Entwicklungsprozess. Das
kompakte, dreigeschossige Gebäude erhebt sich auf einem
annähernd quadratischen Grundriss von 60 Metern Seitenlänge.
Die Aluminiumfassade erinnert an die industrielle Vergangenheit des Quartiers, das auf einem Teil des Tuborg-Areals
entsteht. Das Innere der Schule ist von grösstmöglicher

Open Space

The Danish municipality of Gentofte, a wealthy Copenhagen suburb, aims to establish the 'best school system'
in the country. Municipal experts in the SKUB (school
planning and construction) project have been working
together with residents' representatives (www.skub.dk)
since 1998 to achieve this ambitious goal. Great importance is attached to promoting the children's cognitive,
social and personal skills. The Hellerup School is the
most spectacular project in this development scheme. The
compact three-storey building stands on an almost square
ground plan with a side length of sixty metres. The
aluminium façade is a reminder of the industrial past of
this district, which is being developed on a part of the

**Schulgarten/school garden**

**Aussichtspunkt/view point**

**Treppenhalle/stairwell**

**Zentrale Treppenhalle/central staircase**

Offenheit. Die offene Treppenhalle, «Kolosseum» genannt, bildet den Kern der Anlage. Sie erhält Tageslicht von oben und dient bei grossen Anlässen auch als Versammlungssaal. Gleichzeitig bildet sie den Verbindungsweg zur Turnhalle, zur Schulverwaltung, zum «Kulinarium» genannten Raum für Hauswirtschaftsunterricht, zum «Kulturium», das für den schöpferischen und musikalischen Unterricht gedacht ist, zum «Naturium» und auch zum «Universum», einer Bibliothek mit Leseraum und Computerarbeitsplätzen. In einem intensiven Planungsprozess von Pädagoginnen und Architektinnen gemeinsam entwickelt, ist die Schule darüber hinaus Ausdruck eines völlig neuen Raumverständnisses: Als offene Lernlandschaft kennt sie keine Klassenzimmer mehr. Vielmehr erschliesst die zentrale Treppenhalle auf drei Geschossen Arbeitsflächen,

former Tuborg premises. Inside, the school displays a maximum degree of openness. The open staircase hall, which is called the Colosseum, is the core of the complex. It receives daylight from above and also serves as an assembly hall on important occasions. From the hall, one has access to the gymnasium, the school management offices, the Kulinarium (domestic science and home economics), the Kulturium (creative activities and music), the Naturium, and the Universum, a library with a reading room and computer workplaces. The school, a product of educators and architects co-operating closely in an intensive planning process, also embodies a completely new understanding of space as an open learning landscape,

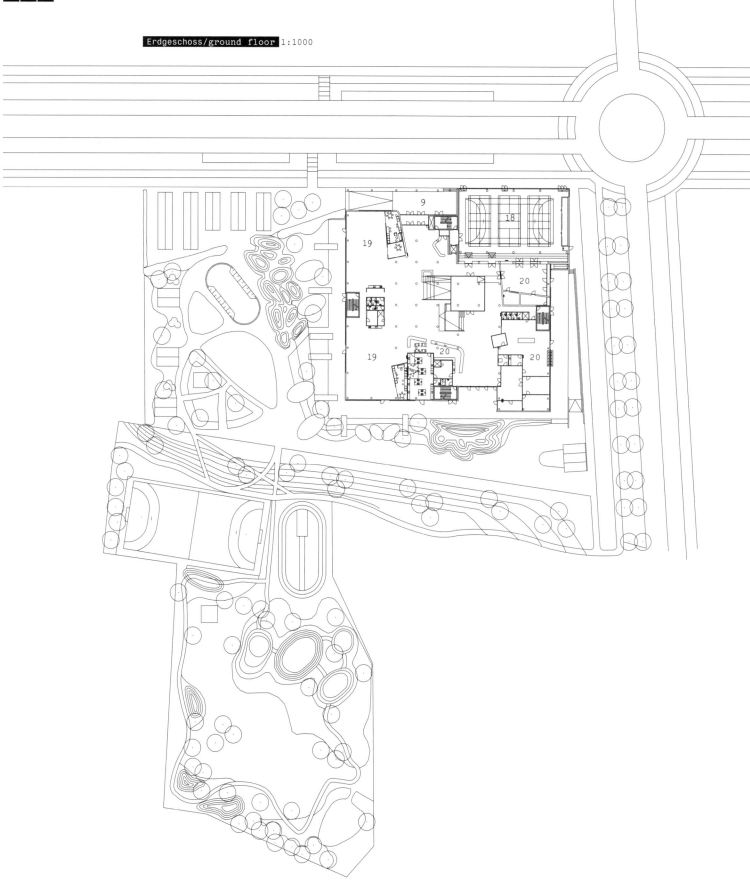

die im Grundriss stark an ein Grossraumbüro erinnern. Diese so genannten Home Areas von 330 bis 400 Quadratmetern sind in kleinere und grössere Teilflächen aufgeteilt. Das ganze Haus ist von einer Atmosphäre der Interaktion und Zusammenarbeit geprägt. Kleine, mit Matratzen ausgestattete Iglus dienen als Rückzugsort für kontaktmüde Kinder und als ruhige Besprechungsräume. In den offenen Geschossflächen finden sich nur wenige abgeschlossene Räume: einerseits die WCs und andererseits die Teambüros der Lehrkräfte.

with no classrooms. The central staircase provides direct access to three storeys of workspaces arranged like an open-plan office. These so-called home areas of between 330 and 400 square metres are partitioned, creating small and large sub-areas. Interaction and co-operation generate an exciting atmosphere throughout the building. Small igloos, equipped with mattresses, provide a retreat for children who wish to be alone. They can also be used as quiet areas for meetings. Apart from the toilets and the teachers' team offices, there are very few closed rooms on the open floors.

**1.Obergeschoss/1st floor** 1:800

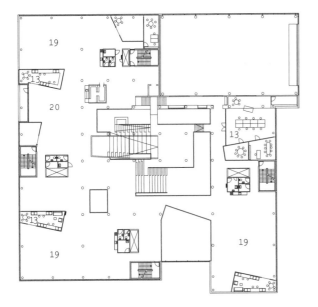

**2.Obergeschoss/2nd floor** 1:800

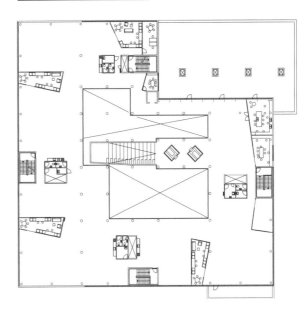

**Schnitt/section** 1:800

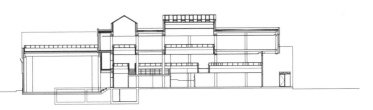

**Hellerup**
Gesamtschule mit Team Teaching/comprehensive school with team teaching
Architektur/architecture **Arkitema A/S, Århus**
Landschaftsplanung/landscape architecture **Arkitema A/S, Århus**
Wettbewerb/competition **2000 (Konzept/concept)**
Bauzeit/construction period **2000–2002**
SchülerInnen/students **750 (Alter/age 6–16)**
Klassen/classes **30**
Spezialangebote/special features **Kombinierte Mehrzweck-Turnhalle/multiple hall combined with sports hall**
Geschossfläche/total floor area **8'200m²**
Geschossfläche pro SchülerIn/floor area per student **11m²**
Nutzfläche/net area **7'035m²**
Gebäudevolumen/total volume **35'000m³**
Anlagekosten (inkl. MWSt.)/overall costs incl. VAT **11'800'000 EUR**
Anlagekosten/m² GF/cost of building/m² floor area **1'439 EUR/m²**
Anlagekosten/m³ GV/cost of building/m³ volume **337 EUR/m³**
Anmerkung/remark **Offene Raumeinteilung/flexible floor plans**

Modell der Anlage/model

## Bakkeløkka Sekundarschule
## Bakkeløkka Secondary School
Nesodden (Oslo), Norwegen/Norway
NAV Arkitekter, Oslo

Südfassade/south façade

Park/park

Text: Daniel Kurz, Photo: Kim Müller

## Lernlandschaft

Die Bakkeløkka-Schule kennt keine Klassen oder Lehrer.
Stattdessen sind die 270 Schülerinnen und Schüler in drei
grosse Niveaugruppen (levels) eingeteilt, die je einen Unterrichtsbereich zugeteilt bekommen. Kleinere Gruppen von
rund 15 Kindern werden von einem Mentor oder einer Mentorin
betreut, mit der sie täglich ihren Lern-Fahrplan besprechen,
der sich aus Einzelstudium, Gruppenarbeit und Frontal-
unterricht zusammensetzt. An der Ostseite eines Hügels gelegen, ist die Bakkeløkka-Schule in ein Waldstück gebaut,
dessen verbliebene Bäume rund um den Bau einen schattigen Park
bilden. Der fliessende Landschaftsraum der Umgebung setzt

## The Learning Landscape

The Bakkeløkka Secondary School knows neither classes
nor teachers. Instead, the 270 pupils are assigned to
one or other of three main levels, each of which is allocated an instruction area. Smaller groups of around fifteen
children are monitored by a mentor, with whom they come
together each day to discuss their learning schedules that
comprise individual study, group work and traditional
teaching. Bakkeløkka school stands on the eastern side of a
hill in a forested area; trees create a shady park around
the building. The flowing, open landscape is echoed by the
building's open learning environment. A solid bastion —
as the architects call it — with a brick façade stands at
the foot of the hill. Communal offices, conference rooms,

Westansicht/west elevation

Mediathek/media library

Gruppenarbeit/group work

sich im Inneren als offene Lernlandschaft fort. Ein massiver Sockelbau mit Sichtbacksteinfassade, den die Architekten als «Bastion» bezeichnen, besetzt die Hügelkante. Kommunale Büros, Sitzungsräume, Spezial-Unterrichtszimmer, die Mensa und eine offene Treppenhalle kommen in diesem Gebäudeteil unter, der auch ausserhalb der Unterrichtszeit öffentlich zugänglich ist. Der eigentliche Unterrichtsbereich liegt in einem zweiten Baukörper, der sich als holzverkleideter Querbalken hell und leicht über die Bastion legt. Unter der weiten Auskragung des Obergeschosses bildet er einen gedeckten Aussenbereich, der in die Eingangshalle und zum Informationszentrum mit Bibliothek und Computerbereich führt. Die zwei Unterrichtsgeschosse öffnen sich mit grossen, flächenbündigen

special classrooms, a canteen and an unenclosed staircase are all accommodated in this part of the building, which is open to the public. The teaching area proper is contained in the second building: a cantilevered beam-like structure clad in light-coloured wood that rests softly on the bastion. A covered outside area leads into the entrance hall and to the information centre, which contains a library and a computer zone. The two storeys accommodating the classrooms have large windows set flush with the façade, and open out onto the wooded surroundings. Each of the three different levels has been assigned an area of its own. The

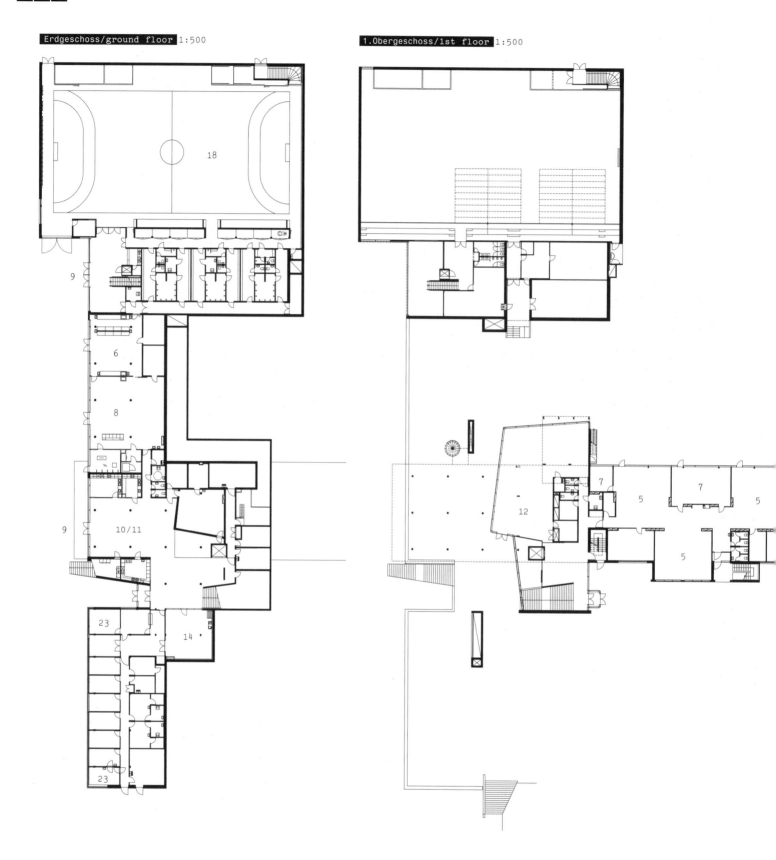

Fenstern in die waldige Umgebung. Jeder der drei Niveaugruppen ist ein eigener Bereich zugeteilt. Die traditionelle Unterteilung in Korridor und Unterrichtszimmer entfällt; nur die Gruppenräume sind mit Türen abgeschlossen. Statt Klassenzimmern gibt es Zonen für kognitives Lernen, Gruppenarbeit und stilles Arbeiten. Der Bezug zur Natur war in diesem Projekt von besonderer Bedeutung. Er kommt in der intensiven Anlehnung an die Landschaft und ebenso in der Materialwahl für die Umgebung zum Ausdruck, die auf einheimischem Holz und Granit aufbaut. Im Gebäudeinneren sind robuste und umweltfreundliche Materialien verarbeitet worden.

traditional subdivision into corridor and classroom has been abandoned. Only the group rooms are closed with doors. In the place of classrooms, there are zones for cognitive learning, group work and quiet study. A harmonious relationship to nature was of particular importance in this project, and this is reflected not only in the architecture's strong reliance on the landscape but also in the choice of materials for the outside, where local wood and granite predominate. Robust and environmentally friendly materials have been used inside the building. A ventilation system operating on natural ventilation principles has been installed here to regulate the temperature and humidity.

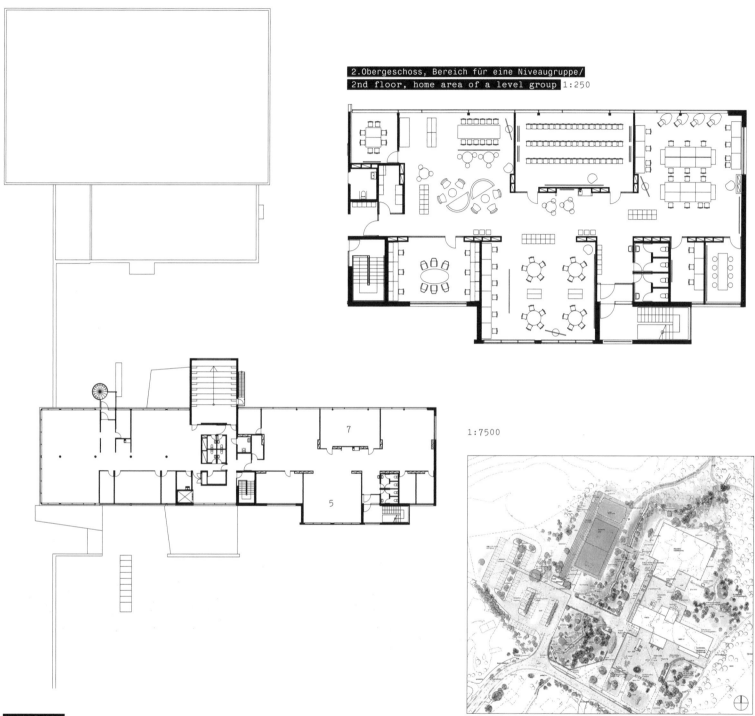

2.Obergeschoss/2nd floor 1:500

2.Obergeschoss, Bereich für eine Niveaugruppe/
2nd floor, home area of a level group 1:250

1:7500

Bakkeløkka

Sekundarschule mit Team Teaching/secondary school with team teaching

Architektur/architecture NAV AS Arkitekter, Oslo

Landschaftsplanung/landscape architecture Østengen & Bergo AS

Wettbewerb/competition 2000

Bauzeit/construction period 2001–2002

SchülerInnen/students 270 (Alter/age 13–16)

Klassen/classes 9

Spezialangebote/special features Niveaugruppen statt Klassen, Räume für Gemeinde/level groups instead of classes, rooms for community

Geschossfläche/total floor area 6'330 m²

Geschossfläche pro SchülerIn/floor area per student 23 m²

Nutzfläche/net area 4'270 m²

Gebäudevolumen/volume 27'900 m³

Anlagekosten (inkl. MWSt.)/overall costs incl. VAT 12'125'000 EUR

Gebäudekosten (inkl. MWSt.)/net construction costs incl. VAT 10'425'000 EUR

Anlagekosten/m² GF cost of building/m² floor area 1'915 EUR/m²

Anlagekosten/m³ GV cost of building/m³ volume 435 EUR/m³

Anmerkung/remark Unterricht immer in Teams/teaching always in teams

Öko-Hauptschule Mäder
**Mäder Eco-School**
Mäder, Österreich/Austria
Baumschlager & Eberle, Lochau

Südansicht/south elevation

Text: Wolfgang Jean Stock (München), Photo: Eduard Hueber

## Vielschichtig

Mäder, ein ursprünglich armes Dorf an der Landesgrenze
zur Schweiz, bemüht sich seit einigen Jahren um den Status einer «Öko-Gemeinde». Das ortsplanerische Konzept schliesst
auch eine Folge von öffentlichen Wegen und Plätzen ein. Dieses
fussgängerfreundliche Netz verdichtet sich im Bereich der
«neuen Mitte», wo alle schulischen und kulturellen Einrichtungen liegen, unter anderem der von Baumschlager & Eberle
entworfene Gemeindesaal (1995). Der Neubau der Öko-Hauptschule
hat das Ortszentrum erheblich aufgewertet. Durch die Stellung

## Multi-layered

Mäder, once a poor village on the border to Switzerland, has been striving to gain the status of an 'eco-com-
munity' for several years now. The village planning concept
consequently includes a number of public footpaths and
squares. This pedestrian-friendly network is concentrated
on the 'new centre', where all the school and cultural
facilities are located, among them the community hall designed by Baumschlager & Eberle, which was completed
in 1995. Their new eco-school has considerably upgraded the
new village centre. The position of the two buildings
units, which are separate above ground level, has created
not only two outside areas (a public square and a school-

Turnhalle/gymnasium

Schule und Turnhalle/school and gymnasium

Klassenzimmer/classroom

Oberlichter, Erschliessungszone/skylights, access zone

Klassenzimmer/classroom

der beiden oberirdisch getrennten Baukörper sind nicht nur zwei neue Aussenräume entstanden (öffentlicher Platz und Schulhof), sondern auch klare Raumkanten. Das über Niveau viergeschossige Schulhaus wie auch die flache, weil zu einem Drittel ins Erdreich abgesenkte Doppelturnhalle sind kompakte Baukörper mit einem möglichst geringen Flächen- und Energieverbrauch. Der Entwurf orientiert sich an den engen Zusammenhängen zwischen Form, Funktion, Ökonomie und Ökologie. Die rundum zweischichtige Fassade des Schulhauses besteht aus einer Holz-Glas-Konstruktion, die von einem hinterlüfteten Mantel aus geschuppten Glaslamellen umhüllt wird. Durch die

yard) but also clear spatial boundaries. The school building, which rises four storeys above the ground, as well as the flat double gymnasium, a third of which is sunk into the ground, are compact structures with a minimal spatial and energy requirement. The design proceeds from the assumption that form, function, economy and ecology are closely interrelated. The two-layer façade, which circles the entire school building, is made of wood and glass and has a ventilated envelope of imbricated glass slats. The building's appearance changes as the sun moves, its

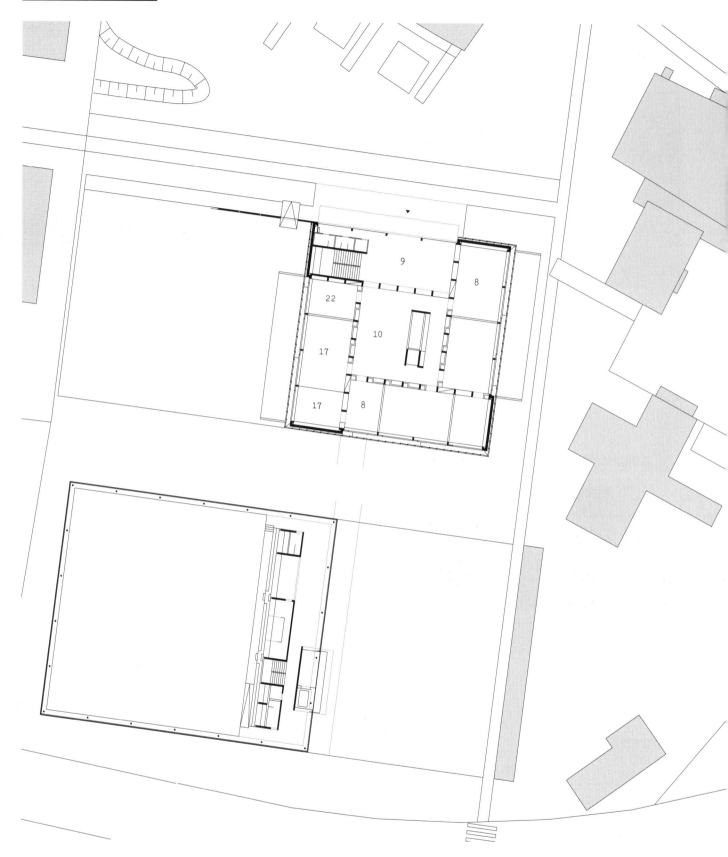

je nach Sonnenstand wechselnden Zustände von Transparenz ändert sich die Erscheinung des Baukörpers: von seiner Ent-materialisierung im Streiflicht bis hin zum Spiegel der Umgebung. Die weitgehende Verglasung der Fassaden ermöglicht zusammen mit einem zentralen Lichtschacht und Oberlichtbändern in den Kastenwänden aus Holz eine natürliche Durchbelichtung der Geschosse, trotz ihrer Grundfläche von 27 mal 27 Metern. Auf den Normalgeschossen gruppieren sich jeweils sieben aussenliegende Klassenzimmer um einen grosszügigen Pausen-bereich. Ökologischer Ansatz, Raumökonomie und Raumqualität sind in diesem Gebäude eine Synthese eingegangen.

level of transparency ranging from a dematerialized aspect when highlighted to a simple reflection of the surround-ings. The largely glazed façade, the central light shaft, and the overhead strip windows in the wooden box walls along the classrooms, provide extensive natural lighting of all floors, despite their having an area of 27x27 metres. On each standard floor, seven classrooms are grouped around a spacious break area. The building is a synthesis of an ecological approach, an economic use of space and excellent room quality.

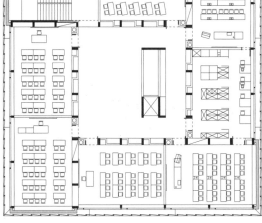

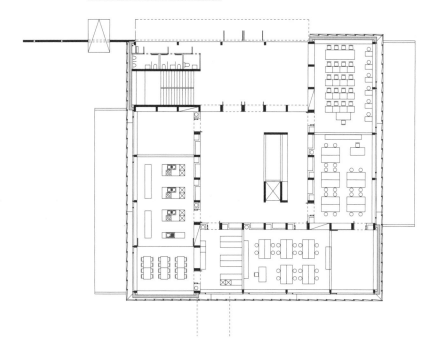

1:8000

Schnitt/section 1:500

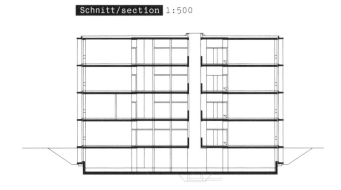

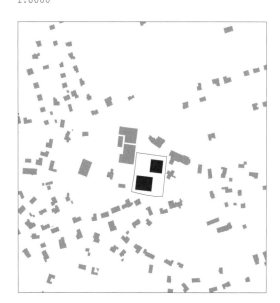

Öko-Hauptschule Mäder
Sekundarschule/secondary school
Architektur/architecture Baumschlager & Eberle, Lochau
Landschaftsplanung/landscape architecture Vogt, Landschaftsarchitekten AG, Zürich
Wettbewerb/competition 1992
Bauzeit/construction period 1996–1998
SchülerInnen/students 200 (Alter/age 11–15)
Klassen/classes 8
Spezialangebote/special features Mensa, Mehrfachsporthalle/canteen, multiple sports hall
Geschossfläche/total floor area 5'940m²
Geschossfläche pro SchülerIn/floor area per student 30m²
Nutzfläche/net area 3'728m²
Gebäudevolumen/volume 23'171m³
Anlagekosten (inkl. MWSt.)/overall costs incl. VAT 6'400'000 EUR
Gebäudekosten (inkl. MWSt.)/net construction costs incl. VAT 4'900'000 EUR
Anlagekosten/m² GF/cost of building/m² floor area 1'077 EUR/m²
Anlagekosten/m³ GV/cost of building/m³ volume 276 EUR/m³
Energiekennzahl Wärme/specific energy consumption 18.0 kWh/m²a
Anmerkung/remark Nachhaltigkeit ist wichtiger Teil des Projektes und des Unterrichts/sustainability
is an important part of the project and of the lessons

Altbau und Erweiterung/old building and annexe

Nordseite/north side

Erweiterung Karviaistie Schule
Karviaistie Special School, extension
Malmi, Helsinki, Finnland/Finland
Kirsti Sivén & Asko Takala, Helsinki

Text: Kirsti Sivén, Asko Takala, Photo: Kirsti Sivén, Michael Klöpfer

## Wandelhalle und Theater

   1998 wurde ein Architekturwettbewerb für die Instandsetzung der beiden bestehenden Schulgebäude aus Holz sowie eine umfassende Erweiterung ausgeschrieben. In der Schule befindet sich seit Herbst 1970 eine Sonderschule mit speziellen Förderprogrammen. Insgesamt 70 Kinder werden in unterschiedlich kombinierten Gruppen von je 10 Lernenden unterrichtet. Alle Schüler haben einen individuellen Lernplan, der es ihnen ermöglicht, die Gesamtschule in ihrem eigenen Tempo zu absolvieren und dabei die jeweils festgelegten Ausbildungsziele zu erreichen. Diese Ziele sind auf die Fähigkeiten der Kinder abgestimmt. Zu den Höhepunkten in jedem

## A Comprehensive Extension

   The invited architectural competition was arranged 1998 to repair the two old wooden school buildings on the site and build new premises for the school. Since the autumn of 1970, the school has served as a special school for adapted education. A total of 70 children study in groups of 10 in combined classes. All pupils have an individual study plan that will help them to complete the comprehensive school in their own terms while achieving the goals set for their education. These are tailored to the children's capabilities. One of the highlights of each school year is the production and performance of a musical. All the pupils and staff members are involved in the production either on the stage or otherwise. For about two months, the school is just like a big workshop with the

Werken/handicraft

Theatersaal/theatre

Mensa/canteen

Laubengang/covered walkway

Schuljahr gehört die Produktion und Aufführung eines Musicals.
An dieser Aufführung sind alle Kinder und Lehrkräfte auf
der Bühne oder an anderer Stelle beteiligt. Über einen
Zeitraum von etwa zwei Monaten ähnelt die Schule einem grossen
Workshop, in dem Lehrer und Kinder für die Aufführung
proben, zeichnen, malen, sägen, nageln, nähen und singen.
Die Architektur des Erweiterungsprojekts soll eine warme und
offene Atmosphäre für das individuelle Lernen unterstützen.
Der neue Schultrakt umfasst den nach Südwesten ausgerichteten
Schulhof mit einer schützenden Geste. Der lang gestreckte
Verbindungskorridor bildet eine Wandelhalle zwischen den ein-
zelnen Gebäudeabschnitten, in der auch die Cafeteria unter-

children and teachers rehearsing scenes, drawing, painting,
sawing, nailing, sewing and singing. The architectural
idea was to help create a supportive, warm and open
atmosphere for intimate learning. Physically that meant
saving the existing buildings from strong technical
alternations by placing all special facilities to the connecting section. The school building resembles protective
embracing arms that surround the courtyard, which faces
south west. Each of the three buildings dominate one corner
of the courtyard. The corridor running along the side
of the building is a pathway interconnecting the individual
building sections that house the cafeteria and the
workshops. When used for preparing the musical, the music
classroom serves as the stage, while sets and costumes
are made in the manual skills workshop. The renovation of

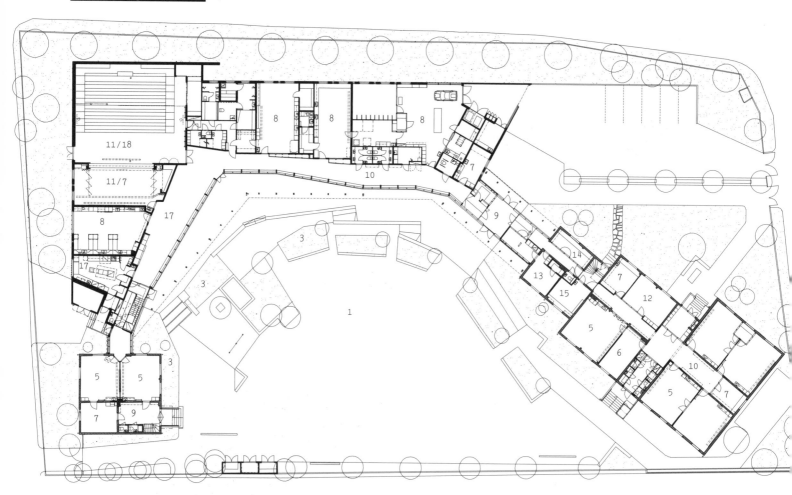

`Erdgeschoss/ground floor` 1:500

`Werken/handycraft` 1:250

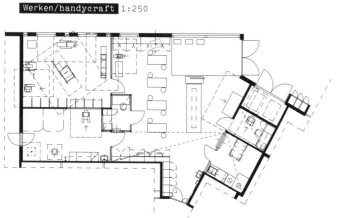

`Unterschiedliche Klassenzimmer/`
`individually shaped classrooms` 1:250

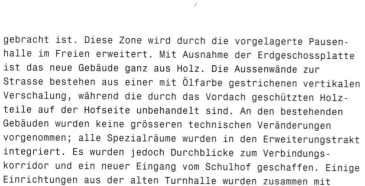

gebracht ist. Diese Zone wird durch die vorgelagerte Pausen-halle im Freien erweitert. Mit Ausnahme der Erdgeschossplatte ist das neue Gebäude ganz aus Holz. Die Aussenwände zur Strasse bestehen aus einer mit Ölfarbe gestrichenen vertikalen Verschalung, während die durch das Vordach geschützten Holz-teile auf der Hofseite unbehandelt sind. An den bestehenden Gebäuden wurden keine grösseren technischen Veränderungen vorgenommen; alle Spezialräume wurden in den Erweiterungstrakt integriert. Es wurden jedoch Durchblicke zum Verbindungs-korridor und ein neuer Eingang vom Schulhof geschaffen. Einige Einrichtungen aus der alten Turnhalle wurden zusammen mit neuem Mobiliar in die Klassenzimmer eingebracht.

the old buildings was limited indoors, old spaces were rearranged following the program and the nature of the buildings. Corridor-views through buildings and a new entrance to the courtyard were opened. Some old gym-equipment were located to class-rooms with new fur-niture. Except for the ground floor slab, the new building is made entirely of wood. The external walls facing the street consist of oil-painted vertical boarding. The wood components in the glass wall of the courtyard corridor and the canopy columns are made of natural-finish wood and the board components of plywood.

`Nordfassade, Hof/north elevation with yard` 1:500

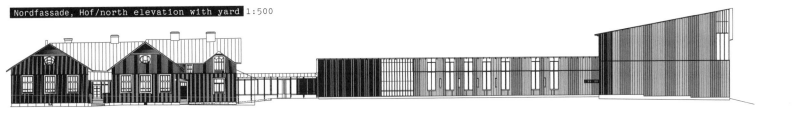

`Südwestfassade/south-west elevation` 1:500

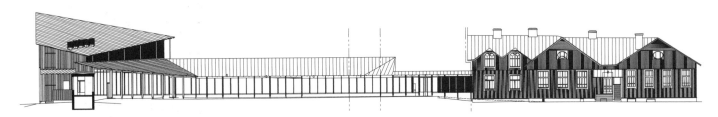

1:5000

`Schnitt/section` 1:500

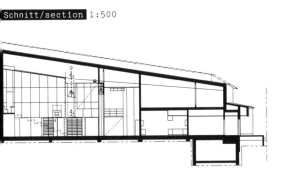

`Karviaistie`
Gesamtschule mit indiviueller Lernförderung/comprehensive school with individual tutoring
Architektur/architecture `Kirsti Sivén & Asko Takala Arkkitehdit Oy Helsinki`
Landschaftsplanung/landscape architecture `Architects + Maisema-arkkitehdit Byman & Ruokonen Oy`
Wettbewerb/competition `1998`
Bauzeit/construction period `2000–2001`
SchülerInnen/students `70` (Alter/age 7–16)
Klassen/classes `7`
Spezialangebote/special features `Kombinierte Mehrzweck-Turnhalle/multiple hall combined with sports hall`
Geschossfläche/total floor area `2'136 m²`
Geschossfläche pro SchülerIn/floor area per student `31 m²`
Nutzfläche/net area `1'336 m²`
Gebäudevolumen/volume `10'700 m³`
Anlagekosten (inkl. MWSt.)/overall costs incl. VAT `4'390'000 EUR`
Anlagekosten/m² GF/cost of building/m² floor area `2'055 EUR/m²`
Anlagekosten/m³ GV cost of building/m³ volume `410 EUR/m³`
Anmerkung/remark `Jährliche Musicalproduktion als prägendes Element des Schuljahres/annual musical production is a highlight of the school year`

**Aurinkolahti Gesamtschule**
**Aurinkolahti Comprehensive School**
Vuosaari, Helsinki, Finnland/Finland
Jeskanen-Repo-Teränne & Leena Yli-Lonttinen, Helsinki

Observatorium/observatory

Modell: Halle und «Zellen»/
model: central hall and 'cells'

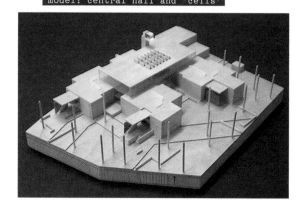

Text: Daniel Kurz,
Photo: Jussi Tiainen, Mikko Auerniitty, Viotto Niemelä

## Atriumschule

Die Stadt Helsinki organisierte den Wettbewerb für
diese auf 540 Schülerinnen und Schüler ausgelegte Anlage zusammen mit dem Verband der finnischen Stahlindustrie – mit
Folgen für die Gestaltung des Schulhauses, das mit seinem Zen-
tralraum und den offenen Unterrichtsbereichen die heute
geltenden Grundsätze des finnischen Schulhausbaus verkörpert.
Denn Stahlstützen und Betonträger bilden die Tragkonstruktion,
Stahl und Glas sind – neben Birkenholz – die dominierenden
Materialien im Innenausbau, und aus Aluminiumblech sind die

## The Atrium School

The city of Helsinki held the competition for this
mixed-school complex, which is designed to accommodate 540
pupils, in co-operation with the Finnish steel industry
association. This had consequences for the design of
the school, which, with its central room and open teaching
areas, embodies the prevailing principles behind Finnish
school construction. Steel columns and concrete girders
form the load-bearing structure, steel and glass (together
with light birch) are the dominant materials on the
interior, whilst the façades are of hot galvanised, tinted
aluminium sheet. The school's landmark, visible from afar,

Halle/the hall

Halle und Galerien/
central hall with galleries

Zelle und Halle/cell and hallway

feuerverzinkten, eingefärbten Fassaden. Als weithin sichtbares Kennzeichen überragt der frei stehende Aussichtsturm die ganze Anlage. Die dreigeschossig aufragende, lichte Halle bildet das lebhafte funktionale und gesellschaftliche Zentrum der Schule. An die Halle sind die niedrigeren farbigen Baukörper der «Zellen» genannten Unterrichtseinheiten und der Turnhalle angegliedert. Die rundum verglaste Halle wird von acht schmalen Stahlsäulen getragen. Treppen und Galerien schieben sich in den Hallenraum hinein und verbinden die verschiedenen Teile des Gebäudes. Die Halle dient als Schul-cafeteria und als Mehrzwecksaal. Der angrenzende, zwei-geschossige Kunst- und Werkraum kann gegebenenfalls auch als

is its freely standing observatory, which dominates the entire complex. The well-lit three-storey-high hall is the school's lively functional and social centre. Smaller buildings — or 'cells' — containing the classrooms and the gymnasium are joined to the four sides of the hall. The hall, which is glazed on all sides, is supported by eight slender steel columns. The stairs and the galleries linking the various parts of the building penetrate the hall, which also serves as a school cafeteria and multifunctional area. An art studio and workshop adjoining the hall can, if necessary, also be opened up to it to

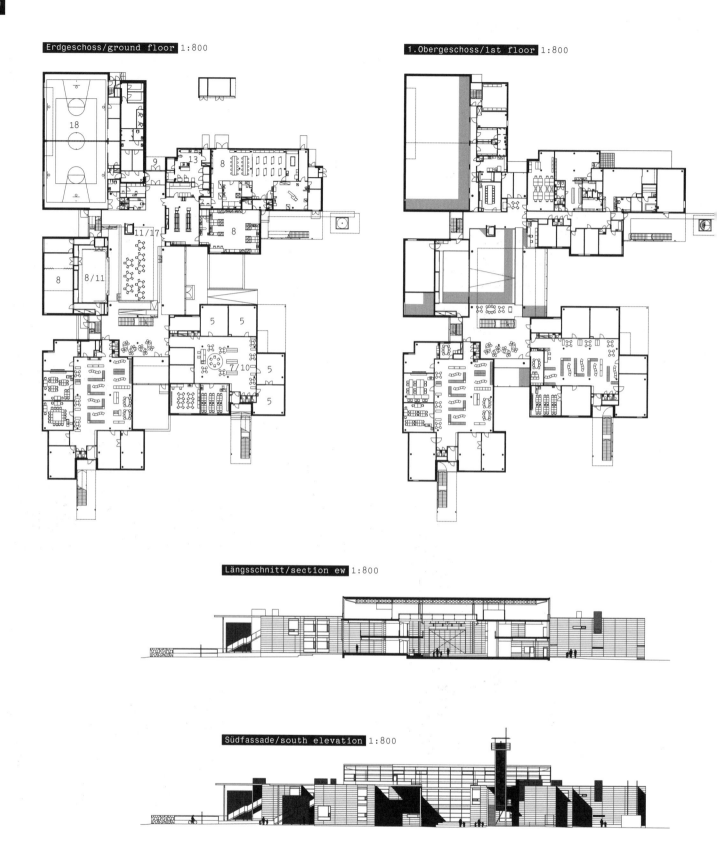

`Erdgeschoss/ground floor` 1:800

`1.Obergeschoss/1st floor` 1:800

`Längsschnitt/section ew` 1:800

`Südfassade/south elevation` 1:800

Theaterbühne zur Halle hin geöffnet werden. Zu dieser orientieren sich auch die zweigeschossige Mediothek, die Schulverwaltung, die Lehrerbereiche und die Spezial-Unterrichtsräume im dritten Geschoss. Die drei je zweigeschossigen Unterrichtseinheiten sind über die zentrale Halle, aber auch über einen gedeckten Treppenaufgang, der als zusätzlicher Fluchtweg geplant wurde, direkt von aussen erschlossen. Die Klassenzimmer organisieren sich als Cluster rund um einen zentralen Aktionsraum. So entstehen überschaubare, in sich geschlossene Gemeinschaften. Glaswände sorgen für einen intensiven Kontakt zwischen den Klassen.

create a stage. Facing towards the hall are the two-storey media library, the school management offices, the teachers' areas, and the special teaching rooms on the third floor. The three classroom units, which occupy two storeys each, are accessed via the central hall as well as via the covered outside stairs, which also serve as an additional escape route. The classrooms are arranged as clusters around the central activities room, creating manageable communities inside the school. Glass walls foster contact between the classes.

2.Obergeschoss/2nd floor 1:800

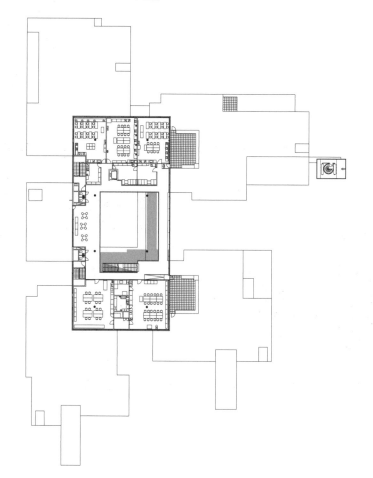

1:5000

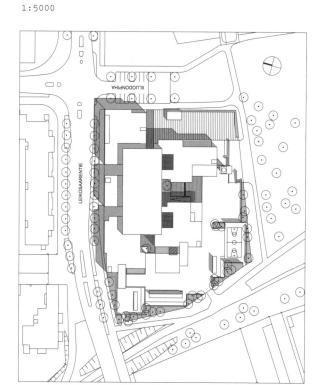

Querschnitt/section ns 1:800

Aurinkolahti
Sekundarschule/secondary school
Architektur/architecture Jeskanen-Repo-Teränne Arkkitehdit Oy & Arkkitehtitoimisto Leena Yli-Lonttinen
Landschaftsplanung/landscape architecture Jan Personen (preliminary phase), Satu Niemelä (construction phase)
Wettbewerb/competition 1998
Bauzeit/construction period 2001–2002
SchülerInnen/students 540 (Alter/age 9–15)
Klassen/classes 22 + 3 Kleinklassen
Spezialangebote/special features Kantine/canteen
Geschossfläche/total floor area 6'370 m²
Geschossfläche pro SchülerIn/floor area per student 12 m²
Nutzfläche/net area 4'245 m²
Gebäudevolumen/volume 30'400 m³
Anlagekosten (inkl. MWSt.)/overall costs incl. VAT 13'400'000 EUR
Gebäudekosten (inkl. MWSt.)/net construction costs incl. VAT 9'600'000 EUR
Anlagekosten/m² GF/cost of building/m² floor area 2'104 EUR/m²
Anlagekosten/m³ GV/cost of building/m³ volume 441 EUR/m³
Energiekennzahl Wärme/specific energy consumption 36.1 kWh/m²a
Anmerkung/remark Technologieunterricht und Kunsthandwerk als Spezialfächer/technology and arts and crafts as special subjects

Z

Klassenzimmer/classroom

Eingangsbereich/entrance

Hahnenkammschule
**Hahnenkamm Special School**
Alzenau, Deutschland/Germany
(se) arch, Stephan Eberding, Stefanie Eberding, Stuttgart

Text: Daniel Kurz, Photo: Wolfram Janzer, Oliver Schuster

## Drei Flügel

Die Kleinstadt Alzenau in Franken ist Standort einer
heilpädagogischen Sonderschule, die vom Landkreis Aschaffenburg betrieben wird. Anstelle der bestehenden «Hahnenkammschule» war auf demselben Grundstück ein Neubau zu errichten.
Der bescheidene Massstab und die sorgfältig durchdachte
Konzeption dieser Schulanlage erinnern an führende Schulbauten
der fünfziger Jahre. Der zweigeschossige Neubau fügt sich
mit seinen drei Flügeln in das Hanggrundstück ein. Der Y-
förmige Grundriss nutzt das Gelände optimal aus und erlaubt
es, alle Klassenräume konsequent nach Südwesten oder Südosten
zu orientieren. Da die meisten Kinder mit Bussen zur Schule
kommen, ist der Zugang als Vorfahrt konzipiert. Eine zwei-

## Three Wings

The small town of Alzenau in the region of Franken is
the home of a remedial school run by the rural district
of Aschaffenburg. A new building was planned for erection
on the site of the Hahnenkamm School. The new school's
modest scale and its well thought-through planning concept
recall the architecture of leading schools of the 1950s.
The three-wing two-storey new building is perfectly adapted
to the sloping site. Its Y-shaped ground plan optimally
exploits the site, making it possible to face all the
classrooms southwest or southeast. Since most of the children travel to school by bus, the entrance is designed
as a drive. On arrival, the children enter a central, open,
two-storey hall from where they can reach all the rooms
via stairs and short corridors. This hall serves for the

Klassenzimmer/classroom

Westflügel von Süden/west wing from the south

Klassenzimmer mit Oberlicht/
classroom with skylight

Aktionshalle, Eingangsbereich/entrance hall, entrance

geschossige offene Halle empfängt die Schüler und Schülerinnen. Von diesem zentralen Ort aus sind alle Räume über Treppen und kurze Korridore erreichbar. Die Halle ist als Veranstaltungssaal nutzbar und kann mit dem Musiksaal zusammengeschlossen werden. Der Südflügel beherbergt mit acht Klassenräumen die Grundschule. Im Westflügel befinden sich Mehrzweckraum und Werkklassen, in seinem Obergeschoss ist die Hauptschule untergebracht. Zwei Klassen verfügen jeweils über einen Gruppenraum, die Endklassen können mit Vorhängen geteilt werden, um sozial auffällige Kinder einzeln oder in kleineren Gruppen getrennt von der Klasse zu betreuen. Im

staging of all kinds of events and can be combined with the music room. The south wing accommodates the eight primaryschool classrooms. The west wing contains workshops, a multifunctional room and, on the storey above, the secondary school. Two classes share one group room. The classrooms for the older children can be partitioned by curtains to let the staff attend to children with behavioural problems individually or in small groups. The north-eastern wing contains the teachers' rooms as well as additional classrooms designed for flexible use, such

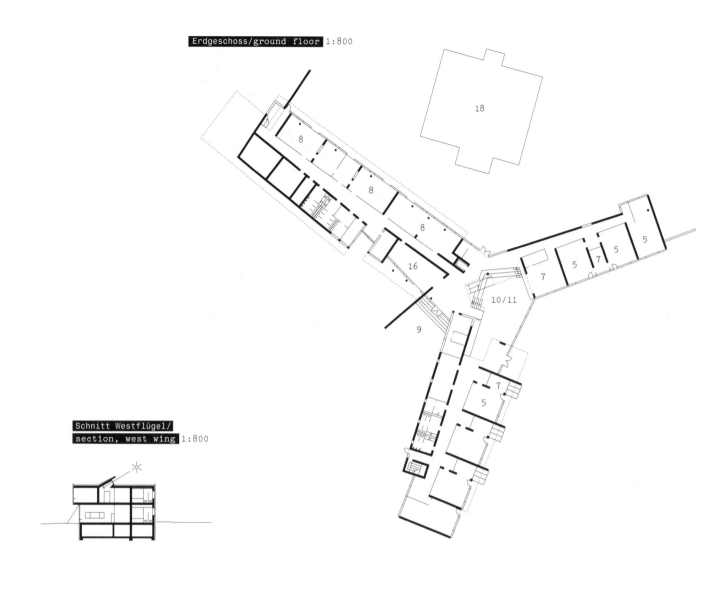

Schnitt Westflügel/ section, west wing 1:800

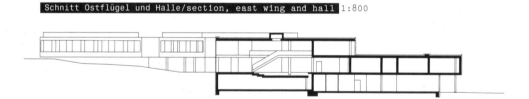

Schnitt Ostflügel und Halle/section, east wing and hall 1:800

nordöstlichen Flügel liegen das Lehrerzimmer sowie zusätzliche Klassenräume zur flexiblen Nutzung, in denen besonders verhaltensauffällige Kinder unterrichtet werden können. Jeder Gebäudeflügel hat eine andere Farbkombination mit jeweils eigener Grundfarbe erhalten; die kleinen Vorräume der Klassen sind ebenfalls durch eine besondere Farbgebung gekennzeichnet. Natürliche, in den Klassen zweiseitige Belichtung und die verwendeten hellen, freundlichen Farben sollen ebenso wie die kontrollierte Lüftung die Lern- und Konzentrationsfähigkeit der Schüler fördern und bei der Orientierung helfen. Die Schulumgebung ermöglicht den Unterricht im Freien und ergänzt das Raumangebot durch unterschiedlich gestimmte Erlebnis- und Aufenthaltsräume in freier Natur.

as teaching children with striking behavioural disorders. Each wing has a distinct colour scheme based on a primary colour. The small anterooms to the classrooms are also distinguishable by their colour schemes. Natural light enters the classrooms from both sides. The light, friendly colours and the regulated ventilation improve the children's learning ability and powers of concentration and also facilitate orientation. The surroundings are conducive to outdoor activities, thus extending the space available for teaching and offering the children direct experience of nature in different settings.

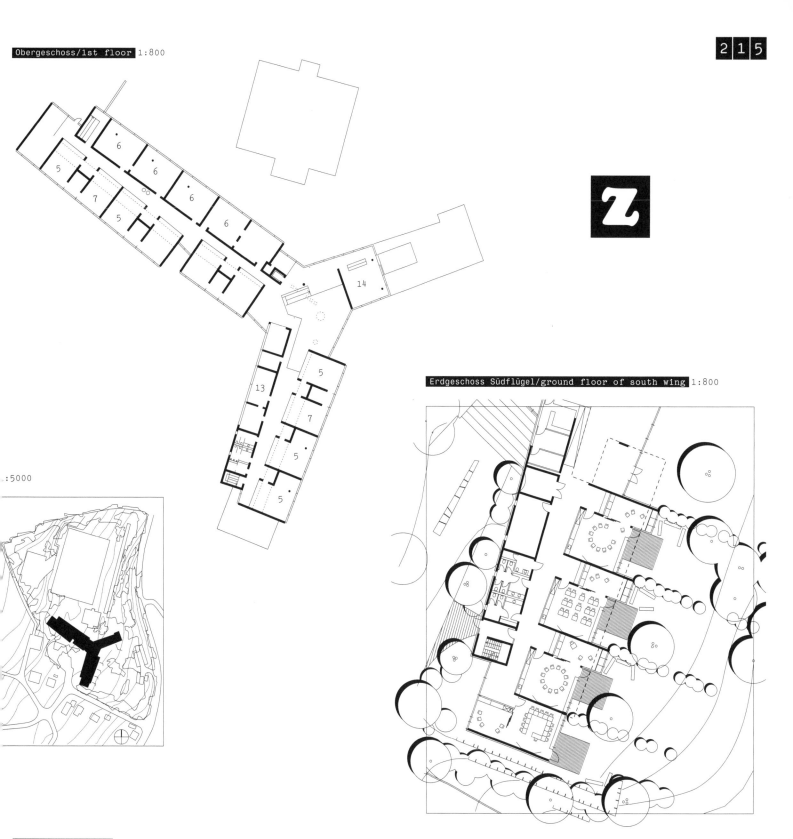

**Z**

Erdgeschoss Südflügel/ground floor of south wing 1:800

:5000

## Hahnenkammschule

Lern-Förderschule, Grund- und Hauptschule/remedial school, junior and secondary school
Architektur/architecture (se) arch, Stephan Eberding, Stefanie Eberding, Stuttgart
Landschaftsplanung/landscape architecture (se) arch mit welsner, welsner, Nürtingen
Wettbewerb/competition 1997
Bauzeit/construction period 2000–2003
SchülerInnen/students 270 (Alter/age 6–16)
Klassen/classes 18
Spezialangebote/special features spezielle Lernförderung, kleine Klassen (12–18 Schüler)/special tutoring, small classes (12–18 pupils)
Geschossfläche/total floor area 4'444 m²
Geschossfläche pro SchülerIn/floor area per student 16 m²
Nutzfläche/net area 2'600 m²
Gebäudevolumen/volume 21'516 m³
Anlagekosten (inkl. MWSt.)/overall costs incl. VAT 10'500'000 EUR
Gebäudekosten (inkl. MWSt.)/net construction costs incl. VAT 5'500'000 EUR
Anlagekosten/m² GF/cost of building/m² floor area 2'363 EUR/m²
Anlagekosten/m³ GV/cost of building/m³ volume 488 EUR/m³

31 Projekte, weitere Informationen
31 Projects, Further Information

**a**
Schulanlage Im Birch/Im Birch School
Margrit Rainer-Strasse 5, 8050 Zürich
Bauherrschaft/client: Stadt Zürich
Architektur/architecture: Peter Märkli, Architekt Zürich, mit Gody Kühnis, Trübbach, pm_info@bluewin.ch
Mitarbeit/responsible collaborators: Christof Ansorge, Jakob Frischknecht
Bauleitung/site management: Bauengineering AG, St. Gallen (Totalunternehmung)
Statik/structural engineering: Bänziger + Bacchetta + Fehlmann, Zürich
Kunst am Bau/art: Hans Josephsohn
Kosten Schulhausumgebung/costs of site environment: 4'761'000 CHF
Stichtag Baukostenindex/reference date of construction costs: 1.4.2003
Anteil Mehrwertsteuer/value added tax: 7.1%
Energiebezugsfläche (EBF)/energy reference area (floorspace): 27'015m$^2$
Heizwärmebedarf/heating energy demand: 28.6 kWh/m$^2$a
Energieträger/energy source: Fernwärme/district heating
Nachhaltigkeitsmassnahmen/special sustainability measures: Kontrollierte Lüftung, Recyclingbeton,
Solarstromanlage (Contracting)/controlled ventilation, recycled concrete, solar-energy plant
Auszeichnung, Standard/energy standard classification: Minergie
Literatur/publications: WERK 1−2, 2003

**æ**
Schulanlage Leutschenbach/Leutschenbach School
Andreasstrasse/Saatlenfussweg, 8050 Zürich
Bauherrschaft/client: Stadt Zürich
Architektur/architecture: Christian Kerez, Architekt ETH SIA, Zürich, mail@kerez.ch
Mitarbeit/responsible: Michael Eidenbenz, Steffen Lemmerzahl
Bauleitung/site management: BGS Architekten, Rapperswil
Statik/structural engineering: Dr. Joseph Schwartz, Oberägeri, Dobler,Schällibaum & Partner, Greifensee
Kosten Schulhausumgebung/costs of site environment: 4'900'000 CHF
Stichtag Baukostenindex/reference date of construction costs: 1.12.2003
Anteil Mehrwertsteuer/value added tax: 7.6%
Energiebezugsfläche (EBF)/energy reference area (floorspace): 14'363m$^2$
Heizwärmebedarf/heating energy demand: 21.7 kWh/m$^2$a
Energieträger/energy source: Fernwärme/district heating
Nachhaltigkeitsmassnahmen/special sustainability measures: Kontrollierte Lüftung/controlled ventilation
Auszeichnung, Standard/energy standard classification: Minergie

**b**
Oberstufenschulhaus Albisriederplatz/Albisriederplatz Secondary School
Badenerstrasse 388, 8004 Zürich
Bauherrschaft/client: Stadt Zürich
Architektur/architecture: bbesw architekten eth htl, Zürich, kontakt@bbesw-architekten.ch
Mitarbeit/responsible: Lorenz Bettler, Johannes Wick, Roger Eifler
Bauleitung/site management: BGS Architekten GmbH, Rapperswil
Statik/structural engineering: Aerni + Aerni AG, Zürich
Kosten Schulhausumgebung/costs of site environment: 1'175'000 CHF
Stichtag Baukostenindex/reference date of construction costs: 1.4.2004
Anteil Mehrwertsteuer/value added tax: 7.6%
Energiebezugsfläche (EBF)/energy reference area (floorspace): 7'671m$^2$
Heizwärmebedarf/heating energy demand: 33.1 kWh/m$^2$a
Energieträger/energy source: Abgasrekuperation Exhaust/fumes heat recovery
Nachhaltigkeitsmassnahmen/special sustainability measures: Kontrollierte Lüftung/controlled ventilation
Auszeichnung, Standard/energy standard classification: Minergie

**c**
Heilpädagogische Schule Allenmoos II/Allenmoos II Special School
Bei Schürbungert 25, 8057 Zürich
Bauherrschaft/client: Stadt Zürich
Architektur/architecture: Scheitlin − Syfrig + Partner Architekten AG Luzern, m.meyer@scheitlin-syfrig.ch
Mitarbeit/responsible: Andi Scheitlin, François Guillermain, Mathis Meyer
Bauleitung/site management: Kunz Architekten, Sursee
Statik/structural engineering: Desserich + Partner AG, Luzern
Kosten Schulhausumgebung/costs of site environment: 1'502'000 CHF
Stichtag Baukostenindex/reference date of construction costs: 1.4.2001
Anteil Mehrwertsteuer/value added tax: 7.6%
Energiebezugsfläche (EBF)/energy reference area (floorspace): 6'368m$^2$
Heizwärmebedarf/heating energy demand: 32.2 kWh/m$^2$a
Energieträger/energy source: Fernwärme/district heating
Nachhaltigkeitsmassnahmen/special sustainability measures: Kontrollierte Lüftung/controlled ventilation
Auszeichnung, Standard/energy standard classification: Minergie

**ç** Schulanlage Falletsche/Falletsche School
Rebenstrasse 67, 8041 Zürich
Bauherrschaft/client: Stadt Zürich
Architektur/architecture: Rolf Mühlethaler, Architekt BSA SIA, Bern, architekt@rolf-muehlethaler.ch
Mitarbeit/responsible: Beat Jaeggli, Philipp Urech
Bauleitung/site management: Rolf Mühlethaler, Bern
Statik/structural engineering: Stocker & Partner, Bern/Zürich
Kosten Schulhausumgebung/costs of site environment: 1'264'000 CHF
Stichtag Baukostenindex/reference date of construction costs: 1.4.2003
Anteil Mehrwertsteuer/value added tax: 7.6%
Energiebezugsfläche (EBF)/energy reference area (floorspace): 9'956 m$^2$
Heizwärmebedarf/heating energy demand: 29.2 kWh/m$^2$a
Energieträger/energy source: Erdsonden/ground-coupled heat pipe
Nachhaltigkeitsmassnahmen/special sustainability measures: Kontrollierte Lüftung/controlled ventilation
Auszeichnung, Standard/energy standard classification: Minergie

**d** Quartierschule Scherr/Scherr Neighbourhood School
Stapferstr. 54, 8006 Zürich
Bauherrschaft/client: Stadt Zürich
Architektur/architecture: Patrick Gmür Architekten AG, Zürich, info.gmuer@bluewin.ch
Mitarbeit/responsible: Fränzi Plüss, M. Geschwentner, M. Milosavljevic, A. Hahn, M. Strüby, A. Epper,
B. Ruppeiner, A. Boggia, K. Albiez, D. de Stoppani, M. Mambourg
Bauleitung/site management: GMS Partner AG, Zürich-Flughafen
Statik/structural engineering: Aerni + Aerni AG, Zürich
Kunst am Bau/art: Peter Roesch, Luzern
Kosten Schulhausumgebung/costs of site environment: 812'000 CHF
Stichtag Baukostenindex/reference date of construction costs: 1.4.1998
Anteil Mehrwertsteuer/value added tax: 7.6%
Energiebezugsfläche (EBF)/energy reference area (floorspace): 2'796 m$^2$
Heizwärmebedarf/heating energy demand: 41.9 kWh/m$^2$a
Energieträger/energy source: Gas/gas
Literatur/publications: Kunstbulletin 6, 2003; AIT, 5, 2003; Archithese 5, 2003;
WERK 11, 2003; Eine Kinderstadt, Luzern 2004
Auszeichnungen/awards Auszeichnung guter Bauten im Kanton Zürich 2003

**e** Schulanlage Luchswiesen/Luchswiesen Primary School
Glattwiesenstrasse 86, 8051 Zürich
Bauherrschaft/client: Stadt Zürich
Architektur/architecture: Covas Hunkeler Wyss Architekten ETH, Zürich, covas_wyss@rchitekten.ch
Mitarbeit/responsible: C. Covas, P. Hunkeler, B. Hurschler, D. Wyss
Bauleitung/site management: Bosshard + Partner Baurealisation AG, Zürich
Kosten Schulhausumgebung/costs of site environment: 1'943'000 CHF
Stichtag Baukostenindex/reference date of construction costs: 1.4.2003
Anteil Mehrwertsteuer/value added tax: 7.6%
Energiebezugsfläche (EBF)/energy reference area (floorspace): 4'752 m$^2$
Heizwärmebedarf/heating energy demand: 29.1 kWh/m$^2$a
Energieträger/energy source: Fernwärme/district heating
Nachhaltigkeitsmassnahmen/special sustainability measures: Kontrollierte Lüftung exkl. Tageshort/
controlled ventilation except day-care centre
Auszeichnung, Standard/energy standard classification: Minergie

**f** Schulanlage Bachtobel/Bachtobel School
Bachtobelstrasse 105, 8045 Zürich
Bauherrschaft/client: Stadt Zürich
Architektur/architecture: Marco Graber, Thomas Pulver Architekten ETH BSA SIA, Bern/Zürich, arch@graberpulver.ch
Mitarbeit/responsible: Marcel Weiler, Susana Elias
Bauleitung/site management: Bosshard + Partner Baurealisation AG, Zürich
Statik/structural engineering: Marchand & Partner AG, Bern
Kunst am Bau/art: Istvan Balogh, Zürich
Kosten Schulhausumgebung/costs of site environment: 1'429'000 CHF
Stichtag Baukostenindex/reference date of construction costs: 1.4.2000
Anteil Mehrwertsteuer/value added tax: 7.6%
Energiebezugsfläche (EBF)/energy reference area (floorspace): 3213 m$^2$
Heizwärmebedarf/heating energy demand: 38.9 kWh/m$^2$a
Energieträger/energy source: Gas/gas
Nachhaltigkeitsmassnahmen/special sustainability measures: Kontrollierte Lüftung/controlled ventilation
Literatur/publications: architectura, Heft 16, 4/5 03; arkitektur 2, 2003;
AW 193, March 2003; tec 2125, 1999; WERK 7/8, 1999; WERK 11, 2002

**g** Schulanlage Lachenzelg/Lachenzelg School
Imbisbühlstrasse 80, 8049 Zürich
Bauherrschaft/client: Stadt Zürich
Architektur/architecture: ADP Architekten AG, Zürich Beat Jordi Caspar Angst, adp@adp-architekten.ch
Mitarbeit/responsible: Ivana Bertolo, Axel Nerz, Andrea Lenggenhager, René Lechleiter
Bauleitung/site management: Allreal Generalunternehmung, Zürich
Statik/structural engineering: Makiol und Wiederkehr, Beinwil am See
Kunst am Bau/art: Kerim Seiler, Zürich
Kosten Schulhausumgebung/costs of site environment: 500'000 CHF
Stichtag Baukostenindex/reference date of construction costs: 1.4.2000
Anteil Mehrwertsteuer/value added tax: 7.6%
Energiebezugsfläche (EBF)/energy reference area (floorspace): 1'547 m²
Heizwärmebedarf/heating energy demand: 53.6 kWh/m²a
Energieträger/energy source: Gas/gas

**h** Schulanlage Kügeliloo/Kügeliloo School
Maienstrasse 7–11, 8050 Zürich
Bauherrschaft/client: Stadt Zürich
Architektur/architecture: Fosco Fosco-Oppenheim Vogt Architekten Zürich, info@ffv.ch
Mitarbeit/responsible: Klaus Vogt, Benno Fosco, Jacqueline Fosco-Oppenheim, Dani Bischof, Philippe Monod, Gregor Katz
Bauleitung/site management: Fosco Fosco-Oppenheim Vogt. Dani Bischof
Kunst am Bau/art: Daniel Schibli, Andres Lutz + Anders Guggisberg
Kosten Schulhausumgebung/costs of site environment: 296'717 CHF
Stichtag Baukostenindex/reference date of construction costs: 1.4.2001
Anteil Mehrwertsteuer/value added tax: 7.0%
Energiebezugsfläche (EBF)/energy reference area (floorspace): 2'630 m²
Heizwärmebedarf/heating energy demand: 45.3 kWh/m²a
Energieträger/energy source: Erdsonde/ground-coupled heat pipe
Nachhaltigkeitsmassnahmen/special sustainability measures:
Kontrollierte Lüftung, Solarstromanlage (Contracting)/controlled ventilation, solar-heat plant
Auszeichnung, Standard/energy standard classification: Minergie

**i** Schulhaus Mattenhof/Mattenhof School
Dübendorfstrasse 300, 8051 Zürich
Bauherrschaft/client: Stadt Zürich
Architektur/architecture: B.E.R.G. Architekten GmbH, Zürich, info@bergarchitekten.ch
Mitarbeit/responsible: Sibylle Bucher, Christoph Elsener, Michel Rappaport, Volker Lubnow, Mila Milosavljevic
Bauleitung/site management: Arthur Schlatter Bauleitungen, Wernetshausen
Statik/structural engineering: DSP Ingenieure und Planer AG, Greifensee
Kosten Schulhausumgebung/costs of site environment: 780'000 CHF
Stichtag Baukostenindex/reference date of construction costs: 1.1.2001
Anteil Mehrwertsteuer/value added tax: 7.6%
Energiebezugsfläche (EBF)/energy reference area (floorspace): 2'437 m²
Heizwärmebedarf/heating energy demand: 26.7 kWh/m²a
Energieträger/energy source: Gas/gas
Nachhaltigkeitsmassnahmen/special sustainability measures: Kontrollierte Lüftung/controlled ventilation
Auszeichnung, Standard/energy standard classification: Minergie
Literatur/publications: WERK 3, 2004

**j** Gesamtschule In der Höh/In der Höh Comprehensive School
In der Höh 9, 8604 Volketswil
Bauherrschaft/client: Gemeinde Volketswil
Architektur/architecture: Gafner & Horisberger Architekten GmbH, Zürich, arch@gafnerhorisberger.ch
Mitarbeit/responsible: Reto Gafner, Detlef Horisberger, Lars Kundert (Projektleitung), Christian Meier, Vincent Traber
Bauleitung/site management: Bosshard + Partner Baurealisation AG, Zürich
Kosten Schulhausumgebung/costs of site environment: 835'000 CHF
Stichtag Baukostenindex/reference date of construction costs: 1.4.2001
Anteil Mehrwertsteuer/value added tax: 7.6%
Energiebezugsfläche (EBF)/energy reference area (floorspace): 4'228 m²
Energieträger/energy source: Gas/gas
Nachhaltigkeitsmassnahmen/special sustainability measures: Kontrollierte Lüftung/controlled ventilation
Auszeichnung, Standard/energy standard classification: Minergie
Literatur/publications: WERK 3, 2004

**k** Zurich International School/Zurich International School
Steinacherstrasse 140, 8820 Wädenswil
Bauherrschaft/client: International School, Wädenswil
Architektur/architecture: Galli & Rudolf Architekten ETH SIA, Zürich, galli.rudolf@noa.ch
Mitarbeit/responsible: Martin F. Gehring (Projektleitung), Antonia Brand, Reto Stalder, Michael Bucher
Bauleitung/site management: BGS Architekten, Rapperswil
Statik/structural engineering: Max Meyerhans AG, Wollerau
Kosten Schulhausumgebung/costs of site environment: 1'601'000 CHF
Stichtag Baukostenindex/reference date of construction costs: 1.5.2002
Anteil Mehrwertsteuer/value added tax: 7.6%
Energiebezugsfläche (EBF)/energy reference area (floorspace): 8'850 m²
Heizwärmebedarf/heating energy demand: 41.9 kWh/m²a
Energieträger/energy source: Gas/gas
Literatur/publications: WERK 1–2, 2003

**1** Primarschulhaus Linden/Linden Primary School
Lindenstrasse 21, 8155 Niederhasli
Bauherrschaft/client: Gemeinde Niederhasli
Architektur/architecture: Bünzli & Courvoisier Architekten ETH SIA, Zürich, mail@bcarch.ch
Mitarbeit/responsible: Dario Mirra
Bauleitung/site management: Bosshard + Partner Baurealisation AG, Zürich
Statik/structural engineering: Aerni + Aerni, Zürich
Kosten Schulhausumgebung/costs of site environment: 1'145'000 CHF
Stichtag Baukostenindex/reference date of construction costs: 1.4.2002
Anteil Mehrwertsteuer/value added tax: 7.0%
Energiebezugsfläche (EBF)/energy reference area (floorspace): 3'580 m$^2$
Heizwärmebedarf/heating energy demand: 47.8 kWh/m$^2$a
Energieträger/energy source: Holz/wood
Nachhaltigkeitsmassnahmen/special sustainability measures: Kontrollierte Lüftung/controlled ventilation
Auszeichnung, Standard/energy standard classification: SIA 380/1
Literatur/publications: WERK 3, 2004

**m** Oberstufenzentrum Thurzelg/Thurzelg Secondary School
Chäsiwis, 9245 Oberbüren
Bauherrschaft/client: Gemeinde Oberbüren-Niederwil-Niederbüren
Architektur/architecture: Staufer & Hasler Architekten BSA SIA, Frauenfeld und Zürich, info@staufer-hasler.ch
Mitarbeit/responsible: R. Bernath, A. Bühler, E. Häberlin
Bauleitung/site management: Bauengingeneering, St. Gallen (örtliche Bauleitung)
Statik/structural engineering: Wagner & Brühwiler Gossau, SJB, Herisau
Kosten Schulhausumgebung/costs of site environment: 2'117'000 CHF
Stichtag Baukostenindex/reference date of construction costs: 1.4.2000
Anteil Mehrwertsteuer/value added tax: 7.6%
Energiebezugsfläche (EBF)/energy reference area (floorspace): 11'016 m$^2$
Heizwärmebedarf/heating energy demand: 48.6 kWh/m$^2$a
Energieträger/energy source: Gas/gas
Nachhaltigkeitsmassnahmen/special sustainability measures: Teilweise kontrollierte Lüftung/
partial controlled ventilation
Literatur/publications: WERK 1–2, 2003

**n** Volta-Schulhaus/Volta School
Wasserstrasse 40, 4056 Basel
Bauherrschaft/client: Kanton Basel-Stadt
Architektur/architecture: Miller & Maranta Architekten ETH BSA SIA, Basel, info@millermaranta.ch
Mitarbeit/responsible: O. Brügger, P. Baumberger, M. Meier, M. Hug
Bauleitung/site management: Miller & Maranta, Basel
Statik/structural engineering: Conzett Bronzini Gartmann AG, Chur
Kunst am Bau/art: Erik Steinbrecher, Berlin
Kosten Schulhausumgebung/costs of site environment: 1'195'000 CHF
Stichtag Baukostenindex/reference date of construction costs: 1.4.2000
Anteil Mehrwertsteuer/value added tax: 7.0%
Energiebezugsfläche (EBF)/energy reference area (floorspace): 6'651 m$^2$
Energieträger/energy source: Fernwärme/district heating
Nachhaltigkeitsmassnahmen/special sustainability measures: Teilweise kontrollierte Lüftung/
partial controlled ventilation
Literatur/publications: FACES 49, 2001; WERK 3, 2001; Architektur für Basel 1990–2000; DETAIL 3, 2003

**ñ** Umnutzung Turnhalle, Schulanlage Bündtli/Conversion of a Gymnasium, Buendtli School
Bündtliweg 3, 7304 Maienfeld
Bauherrschaft/client: Kreisschule Fläsch, Jenins, 7304 Maienfeld
Architektur/architecture: Pablo Horváth Architekt SIA SWB, Chur, pablo.horvath@bluewin.ch
Mitarbeit/responsible: A. Offergeld, M. Holzwarth
Bauleitung/site management: Reto Bernhard, Möhr & Partner, Maienfeld
Statik/structural engineering: Bänziger, Köppel, Brändli und Partner, Chur
Kosten Schulhausumgebung/costs of site environment: 206'842 CHF
Stichtag Baukostenindex/reference date of construction costs: 30.10.2003
Anteil Mehrwertsteuer/value added tax: 7.6%
Energiebezugsfläche (EBF)/energy reference area (floorspace): 2'626 m$^2$
Heizwärmebedarf/heating energy demand: 65.0 kWh/m$^2$a
Energieträger/energy source: Holzschnitzel/wood chips
Literatur/publications: tec 21 35, 2003

**o** Gesamtschule Flims/Flims Comprehensive School
Via Punt Crap 2, 7017 Flims
Bauherrschaft/client: Gemeinde Flims
Architektur/architecture: Philipp Wieting, Martin Blättler — Werknetz Architektur Zürich, philipp.wieting@werknetz.ch
Mitarbeit/responsible: Philipp Wieting, Martin Blättler, Sebastian Geiger, Gianpiero Sibau
Bauleitung/site management: Mobag AG, Chur
Statik/structural engineering: Jürg Buchli, Dipl. Ing. ETH SIA, Haldenstein
Kunst am Bau/art: Anna-Rita Stoffel, Chur und Zürich
Kosten Schulhausumgebung/costs of site environment: 1'139'914 CHF
Stichtag Baukostenindex/reference date of construction costs: 5.9.2003
Anteil Mehrwertsteuer/value added tax: 7.6%
Energiebezugsfläche (EBF)/energy reference area (floorspace): 6'825m$^2$
Heizwärmebedarf/heating energy demand: 52.5 kWh/m$^2$a
Energieträger/energy source: Luft-Wärmepumpe/air-to-air heat pump
Literatur/publications: Archithese 06, 2003

**œ** Schulanlage Herti/Herti School
St.-Johannes-Strasse 36, 6300 Zug
Bauherrschaft/client: Stadt Zug
Architektur/architecture: Enzmann + Fischer AG Architekt/innen BSA SIA Zürich, enzmannfischer@smile.ch
Mitarbeit/responsible: E. Enzmann, P. Fischer, A. Zimmermann
Bauleitung/site management: Ghisleni, Zug
Kosten Schulhausumgebung/costs of site environment: 1'900'000 CHF
Stichtag Baukostenindex/reference date of construction costs: 1.4.2003
Anteil Mehrwertsteuer/value added tax: 7.6%
Literatur/publications: WERK 1—2, 2003

**p** Primarschule Riedmatt/Riedmatt Primary School
Riedmatt 41, 6300 Zug
Bauherrschaft/client: Stadt Zug
Architektur/architecture: Reinhard Nägele und Adrian Twerenbold, Dipl. Architekten ETH SIA, Zürich,
arch.twerenbold@dplanet.ch
Bauleitung/site management: Reinhard Nägele und Adrian Twerenbold, Zürich
Statik/structural engineering: Berchtold und Eicher, Zug
Kunst am/Bau art: Nina Stähli, Cham
Kosten Schulhausumgebung/costs of site environment: 615'000 CHF
Stichtag Baukostenindex/reference date of construction costs: 1.4.2000
Anteil Mehrwertsteuer/value added tax: 7.6%
Energiebezugsfläche (EBF)/energy reference area (floorspace): 6029 (5231)m$^2$
Heizwärmebedarf/heating energy demand: 46.7 kWh/m$^2$a
Energieträger/energy source: Gas, Sonne/gas, sun
Nachhaltigkeitsmassnahmen/special sustainability measures:
Solaranlage für Warmwasser (18m$^2$ Kollektoren), Versickerungsanlage/
solar-heat plant for warming water, rainwater drainage

**q** Centre scolaire des Ouches/Les Ouches School
Rue Camille-Martin, Quartier des Ouches, 1203 Genève
Bauherrschaft/client: Ville de Genève/city of Geneva
Architektur/architecture: Andréa Bassi, Architecte EAUG/FAS/SIA; Genève, a.bassi@andrea-bassi.ch
Mitarbeit/responsible: Cédric Ilegems, Christiane de Roten, Kristina Sylla
Bauleitung/site management: Roberto Carella, Genève
Statik/structural engineering: Amsler & Bombeli, Genève
Kosten Schulhausumgebung/costs of site environment: 1'330'000 CHF
Stichtag Baukostenindex/reference date of construction costs: 27.6.2002
Anteil Mehrwertsteuer/value added tax: 7.6%
Energiebezugsfläche (EBF)/energy reference area (floorspace): 9'382m$^2$
Energieträger/energy source: Gas/gas
Nachhaltigkeitsmassnahmen/special sustainability measures:
Kontrollierte Lüftung Korridore/controlled ventilation corridors
Literatur/publications: A. Bassi, Figures, Luzern 2004

**r** Evangelische Gesamtschule EGG/EGG Evangelical Comprehensive School
Laarstrasse 41, D-45889 Gelsenkirchen-Bismarck
Bauherrschaft/client: Landeskirche von Nordrhein Westfalen
Architektur/architecture: Plus+ Bauplanung GmbH, Peter Hübner Neckartenzlingen; info@plus-bauplanung.de
Mitarbeit/responsible: P. Hübner, C.Forster, K. Eggler, O. Hübner, T. Strähle, A. Shirota,
F. Hübner, B. Hübner, U. Engelhardt, M. Gulde, C. Perkuhn
Bauleitung/site management: M. Müller, M. Busch, S. Nix-Pauleit
Statik/structural engineering: Weischede, Herrmann und Partner GmbH
Anteil Mehrwertsteuer/value added tax: 16%
Energiebezugsfläche (EBF)/energy reference area (floorspace): 16'500m$^2$
Energieträger/energy source: Fernwärme/district heating
Nachhaltigkeitsmassnahmen/special sustainability measures: Natürliches Ventilationssystem/natural air ventilation
Auszeichnung, Standard/energy standard classification: Niedrigenergie
Literatur/publications: Lifelong learning/AR 2001; Intelligente Architektur 2001;
Schulen der Zukunft, Heidelberg 2002; Die Zeit 26 2003

**s** Primarschule De Eilanden/De Eilanden Primary School
Grote Bickersstraat 102, Amsterdam
Bauherrschaft/client: City of Amsterdam
Architektur/architecture: Architectuurstudio Herman Hertzberger Amsterdam; office@hertzberger.nl
Mitarbeit/responsible: Herman Hertzberger, Heleen Reedijk, Geert Mol, Sonja Spruit, Roos Eichhorn,
Margreet van der Woude, Henk de Weijer, Cor Kruter
Bauleitung/site management: De Principaal
Statik/structural engineering: Constructiebureau Tentij
Kunst am Bau/art: Akelei Hertzberger
Anteil Mehrwertsteuer/value added tax: 19%
Energiebezugsfläche (EBF)/energy reference area (floorspace): 1300m$^2$
Energieträger/energy source: Gas/gas
Literatur/publications: Herman Hertzberger, Articulations, Munich 2002; Area 9/10 2003

**t** Kindercluster Voorn/Voorn Children's Cluster
Akkrumerlaan 101, Leidsche Rijn, Utrecht
Bauherrschaft/client: City of Utrecht
Architektur/architecture: Frencken Scholl Architecten Maastricht; frenckenscholl.architecten@inter.nl.net
Mitarbeit/responsible: Huub Frencken, Katleen Vanagt
Bauleitung/site management: Free Lentz, Fred Lentz
Statik/structural engineering: Adviesbureau Brekelmans
Kunst am Bau/art: Marin Kasimir
Kosten Schulhausumgebung/costs of site environment: 152'685 EUR
Stichtag Baukostenindex/reference date of construction costs: 1.11.2001
Anteil Mehrwertsteuer/value added tax: 19%
Energiebezugsfläche (EBF)/energy reference area (floorspace): 6'305m$^2$
Energieträger/energy source: Fernwärme (Erdwärme)/district heating
Nachhaltigkeitsmassnahmen/special sustainability measures: Kontrollierte Lüftung/controlled ventilation
Auszeichnung/awards: Dutch Ministry of Education Innovation Prize 1998
Literatur/publications: Gebouwen met een ziel, Amsterdam/Antwerpen 2003;
Novem, Energieprestaties vormgegeven, Waddinxveen 2000

**u** Sekundarschule Heimdalsgade/Heimdalsgade Secondary School
Heimdalsgade 29–33, DK-220 Copenhagen
Bauherrschaft/client: City of Copenhagen
Architektur/architecture: Kant Architekter A/S, Copenhagen; klaus.holm@kant.dk
Mitarbeit/responsible: Klaus Holm Jensen Niels Ole Sørensen Michael Royal Petersen, Charlotte Nielsen
Bauleitung/site management: Ason A/S og Karl A Hansen
Statik/structural engineering: RIA, Rådgivende Ingeniører og arkitektkant
Stichtag Baukostenindex/reference date of construction costs: 01.01.2000
Anteil Mehrwertsteuer/value added tax: 25%
Literatur/publications: ARKITEKTUR DK April 2003

**û** Hellerup Primarschule/Hellerup Primary School
Gammel Wartovvej 32, DK-2900 Hellerup
Bauherrschaft/client: Municipality of Gentofte
Architektur/architecture: Arkitema, Arhus; khl@arkitema.dk
Mitarbeit/responsible: P. Fischer, L. Gronlund, L. Kvist, P. Lindberg, U. Dybro, S. Gothelf, M. Herrebek, P. Jensen,
M. Lyshoj, M. Martinusen, J. Lind, P. Uglvig
Bauleitung/site management: NCC Danmark A/S
Statik/structural engineering: Søren Jensen
Stichtag Baukostenindex/reference date of construction costs: 1.4.2002
Anteil Mehrwertsteuer/value added tax: 25%
Energiebezugsfläche (EBF)/energy reference area (floorspace): 8'000m$^2$
Energieträger/energy source: Fernwärme/district heating
Nachhaltigkeitsmassnahmen/special sustainability measures: Natürliches Ventilationssystem/natural air ventilation
Literatur/publications: ARKITEKTUR DK, April 2003

**v** Bakkeløkka Sekundarschule/Bakkeløkka Secondary School
Skogasvn. 26, Fagerstrand
Bauherrschaft/client: Municipality of Nesodden
Architektur/architecture: NAV A.S. Arkitekter, Oslo; per@nav.no
Verantwortlich/responsible: Per Arne Bjørnstad
Statik/structural engineering: Dr.techn Olav Olsen AS
Kunst am Bau/art: V. Bjerkeseth Andresen, Kai Hjelseth, Jon Gundersen
Kosten Schulhausumgebung/costs of site environment: 1'200'000 EUR
Stichtag Baukostenindex/reference date of construction costs: 1.1.2003
Anteil Mehrwertsteuer/value added tax: 24%
Energiebezugsfläche (EBF)/energy reference area (floorspace): 5'900m$^2$
Energieträger/energy source: Öl, elektrisch/oil, electricity
Nachhaltigkeitsmassnahmen/special sustainability measures: Kontrollierte Lüftung/controlled ventilation
Auszeichnung/awards: Norsk Form Innovation Prize 2003
Literatur/publications: BYGGEKUNST 6, 2003

**w**
Öko-Hauptschule Mäder/Mäder Eco-School
Schulstrasse 7, A-6841 Mäder
Bauherrschaft/client: Gemeinde Mäder
Architektur/architecture: Baumschlager & Eberle Lochau; office@baumschlager-eberle.com
Mitarbeit/responsible: Rainer Huchler (Projektleitung)
Statik/structural engineering: Rüsch, Diem + Partner, Dornbirn
Haustechnik/energy engineering: GMI Gasser & Messner Ingenieure, Dornbirn
Stichtag Baukostenindex/reference date of construction costs: 18.5.1998
Anteil Mehrwertsteuer/value added tax: 20%
Energieträger/energy source: Biomasse/biomass
Nachhaltigkeitsmassnahmen/special sustainability measures: Kontrollierte Lüftung/controlled ventilation
Auszeichnung, Standard/energy standard classification: Niedrigenergie/eco-school
Literatur/publications: Architektur Szene Österreich, Salzburg 1999;
L'architecture écologique, Le Moniteur 2001; Atlas Gebäudegrundrisse-Lehre, München 2002

**x**
Karviaistie Schule/Karviaistie Special School
Karviaistie 1, Malmi, 00099 Helsinki
Bauherrschaft/client: City of Helsinki
Architektur/architecture: Kirsti Sivén & Asko Takala Arkkitehdit Oy, Helsinki; kirsti.siven@arksi.fi
Mitarbeit/responsible: Kirsti Sivén, Asko Takala, Liisa Neiramo, Erja Luhtala/Sisustusark.tsto Antti Paatero Oy
Bauleitung/site management: Pasi Romppainen, City of Helsinki, Public Works Department
Statik/structural engineerin:g Insinööritoimisto Pertti Ranta Oy, Helsinki
Kunst am Bau/art: Tarja Pitkänen-Walters, Helsinki
Stichtag Baukostenindex/reference date of construction costs: 1.1.2000
Anteil Mehrwertsteuer/value added tax: 22%
Energiebezugsfläche (EBF)/energy reference area (floorspace): 2'124m$^2$
Energieträger/energy source: Fernwärme (Gas)/district heating (gas)
Nachhaltigkeitsmassnahmen/special sustainability measures: Kontrollierte Lüftung/controlled ventilatio
Literatur/publications: PUU 4, 2001

**y**
Aurinkolahti Gesamtschule/Aurinkolahti Comprehensive School
Leikoosaarentie 17, Vuosaari, Helsinki
Bauherrschaft/client: City of Helsinki
Architektur/architecture: Jeskanen-Repo-Teränne Arkkitehdit Oy & Arkkitehtitoimisto Leena Yli-Lonttinen
leena.yli-lonttinen@arkyl.com
Mitarbeit/responsible: T. Jeskanen, T. Repo, R. Teränne, L. Yli-Lonttinen, arkkidetehdit/architects SAFA,
Interior design: Pasi Hämäläinen, Martti Lukander
Bauleitung/site management: Main contractor: Seicon Oy
Statik/structural engineering: Insinööritoimisto Oy Matti Ollila & Co / Kari Lemettinen
Kunst am Bau/art: Veikko Björk, Tülay Schakir
Stichtag Baukostenindex/reference date of construction costs: 27.6.2002
Anteil Mehrwertsteuer/value added tax: 22%
Energiebezugsfläche (EBF)/energy reference area (floorspace): 6'370m$^2$
Energieträger/energy source: Fernwärme/district heating
Nachhaltigkeitsmassnahmen/special sustainability measures: Kontrollierte Lüftung/controlled ventilation
Literatur/publications: Arkkitehti 5, 2002, Teräsrakenne 3, 2002, Architektur+Wettbewerbe 193, 2002

**z**
Hahnenkammschule/Hahnenkamm Special School
Schwedenstrasse 2, D-63755 Alzenau
Bauherrschaft/client: Landkreis Aschaffenburg
Architektur/architecture: (se) arch, Stephan Eberding, Stefanie Eberding, Stuttgart; S.E.ARCH@t-online.de
Mitarbeit/responsible: Stephan Eberding, Stefanie Eberding, Janno Himpel, Cornelia Sailer
Bauleitung/site management: (se)arch mit Ritter + Bauer, Aschaffenburg
Statik/structural engineering: Pfefferkorn+Partner, Stuttgart
Kosten Schulhausumgebung/costs of site environment: 1'960'000 EUr
Stichtag Baukostenindex/reference date of construction costs: KV 1999/1.8.2003
Anteil Mehrwertsteuer/value added tax: 16%
Energiebezugsfläche (EBF)/energy reference area (floorspace): 3'958m$^2$
Energieträger/energy source: Biomasse/biomass
Nachhaltigkeitsmassnahmen/special sustainability measures: Korridorbereich wird mit vorgewärmter
Frischluft versorgt/corridor is supplied with pre heated fresh air
Auszeichnung, Standard/energy standard classification: Wärmeschutzverordnung/heat insulation ordinance

Autoren/Authors

**Karin Dangel**
(1961) lic. phil., Kunsthistorikerin.
Leiterin Inventarisation, Denkmalpflege, Amt für
Städtebau der Stadt Zürich.
(1961) Art historian, head of inventory section,
office for the preservation of historic buildings,
City of Zurich Urban Planning Department.

**Prof. Peter Eberhard**
(1943) Architekt ETH/SIA. Leiter Departement Lehrberufe
für Gestaltung und Kunst, Hochschule für Gestaltung
und Kunst Zürich.
(1943) Architect ETH/SIA, head of department of the teaching professions on art and design at the University of
Applied Sciences and Arts Zurich.

**Peter Ess**
(1945) Architekt FH/SIA. Direktor des Amts für
Hochbauten der Stadt Zürich. Verantwortlich für
gegenwärtig 18 Schulbauprojekte.
(1945) Architect FH/SIA, director of the City of
Zurich Building Department. Currently responsible for
18 school construction projects.

**Elisabeth Gaus**
(1952), Dozentin für Gestaltung und Kunst,
Pädagogische Hochschule Zürich.
(1952), Lecturer on Art and Design at the University of
Applied Sciences Zurich, School of Education.

**Prof. Dr. Hans-Jürg Keller**
(1955) Leiter Departement Primarstufe an der
Pädagogischen Hochschule Zürich.
(1955) Head of department for primary teaching at
the University of Applied Sciences Zurich,
School of Education.

**Daniel Kurz**
(1957) lic. phil. Historiker und Publizist,
Amt für Hochbauten der Stadt Zürich.
(1957) Historian and publicist, City of Zurich
Building Department.

**Urs Meier**
(1953) Lehrer, Pädagoge, Dozent für Pädagogik,
Hochschule für Gestaltung und Kunst Zürich.
(1953) Teacher, Lecturer on education at the
University of Applied Sciences and Arts Zurich.

**Martin Schneider**
(1962) Architekt ETH/SIA, Mitarbeiter am ETH
Wohnforum, Eidgenössische Technische Hochschule Zürich.
(1962) Architect ETH/SIA, member of staff at the ETH
Wohnforum, Swiss Federal Institute of Technology, Zurich.

**Alan Wakefield**
(1970) Architekt ETH/SIA, Projektleiter, Amt für
Hochbauten der Stadt Zürich.
(1970) Architect ETH/SIA, project manager,
City of Zurich Building Department.

Ausgewählte Literatur/Select Bibliography

Geschichte (Schweiz)/history (Switzerland)

Henry Baudin, Les constructions scolaires en Suisse, Geneva 1907.

Werner Moser, Wilhelm Gonzenbach, Willi Schohaus,
Das Kind und sein Schulhaus, Zurich 1932.

Alfred Roth, Das Neue Schulhaus, Zurich 1950.

Heinrich Schneider, Schulhausbau aus der
Sicht des Lehrers, Winterthur 1969.

Michael Luley, Eine kleine Geschichte des deutschen
Schulbaus, Frankfurt a.M. 2000.

Schule/school

Thomas Ziehe, Zeitvergleiche. Jugend in kulturellen
Modernisierungen, Weinheim, 1996.

Per Dalin, Schule auf dem Weg ins 21. Jahrhundert. Neuwied 1997.

Uri Peter Trier, Was bringt unsere Bildung? Zum Abschluss
des Nationalen Forschungsprogramms Wirksamkeit unserer Bildungs-
systeme, Chur 1999.

Hermann Giesecke, Was Lehrer leisten, Porträt eines schwierigen
Berufs, Weinheim 2001.

Manuel Castells, Das Informationszeitalter (3 Bände/vols.),
Opladen, 2001–2003.

Peter Gasser, Neue Lernkultur. Eine integrative
Didaktik, Aarau 2002.

Jürgen Oelkers, Schulrefom und Schulkritik, Würzburg 2002.

Ernst Buschor, Heinz Gilomen, Huguette McCluskey, PISA 2000.
Synthese und Empfehlungen. Bildungsmonitoring Schweiz, Bundesamt
für Statistik, Schweizerische Konferenz der kantonalen Erzie-
hungsdirektoren, Bern 2003.

Martin Stauffer, Entwicklungen im Bildungsbereich. IDES-Trend-
bericht, Stand 2002. Information Dokumentation Erziehung Schweiz.
EDK, Schweizerische Konferenz der kantonalen Erziehungs-
direktoren, Bern 2003.

Architektur/architecture

Mark Dudek, Architecture of Schools.
The new Learning Environments, Oxford 2000.

Roy Strickland, Designing a City of Learning,
Paterson, New Jersey 2001.

Sharon Haar, Schools for Cities:
Urban Strategies, New York 2002.

Eleanor Curtis, School Builders, Chichester 2003.

Nikolaus Hellmayr, Wien, Schulbau. Der Stand der Dinge,
Hg. Magistrat der Stadt Wien, Wien 2003.

Schulen in Deutschland, Neubau und Revitalisierung,
Hg. Wüstenrot-Stiftung, Stuttgart 2004.

Zeitschriften/magazines

Baumeister 4, 1997, Nichts dazugelernt?
Schulbauten der neunziger Jahre.

ARK/Arkkitehti 4, 2001, Kouluja/Schools.

Architektur + Wettbewerbe 193, 2003, Ganztagsschulen.

Detail/Konzept 3, 2003, Schulbau/School Buildings.

Arkitektur DK 2, 2003, Folkeskoler/Public Schools.

Byggekunst 6, 2003.

werk/bauen+wohnen 1–2, 2003, Schulhäuser/Schools.

werk/bauen+wohnen 3, 2004, Schulen etc./Schools.